LUFTWAFFE The Allied Intelligence Files

LUFTWAFFE The Allied Intelligence Files

Christopher Staerck
and Paul Sinnott

Potomac Books, Inc.
Washington, D.C.

Library of Congress Cataloging-in-Publication Data

Staerck, Chris.
    Luftwaffe : the allied intelligence files / Christopher Staerck and Paul
Sinnott.—1st ed. p. cm.
    Includes bibliographical references and index.
    ISBN 1-57488-387-9 (cloth : alk. paper)
    1. Airplanes, Military—Germany.   2. World War, 1939–1945—Military
intelligence—Great Britain.   3. World War, 1939–1945—Military
intelligence—United States.   I. Sinnott, Paul.   II. Title.

    UG1245-G4 S74   2002
    940.54'4943—dc21

                                                            2002018418
    ISBN 1-57488-537-5 (paper)

Printed in the United States of America on acid-free paper that meets the
American National Standards Institute Z39–48 Standard.

Potomac Books, Inc.
22841 Quicksilver Drive
Dulles, Virginia 20166

10 9 8 7 6 5 4 3 2 1

Contents

Preface

The idea for this book arose when the authors stumbled across several files stuffed full of photographs of Luftwaffe aircraft in the archives of the Public Record Office. The photographs were arranged by manufacturer but with no other information to explain their history or reason for having been originally collected by the British Air Ministry.

Further investigation in the archives revealed the purpose of collecting these pictures: it was part of a little-known but significant contribution to the Allied war effort. A small but clearly dedicated team of Royal Air Force officers, later to be joined by their USAAF colleagues, had been building up a dossier on each German aircraft in operation and in development. It was hoped that by understanding their enemy's aircraft, Allied aircrew would know how best to tackle their opponents and hopefully not be surprised by new equipment or tactics.

For all the major and some of the more interesting minor types of Luftwaffe aircraft we have provided a summarized history of the intelligence data on the plane. The idea is to put you, the reader, in the position of an Allied intelligence officer during the war. You receive various fragments of information from a diverse group of sources on a German aircraft, possibly a type that has not been encountered before. You may not even be sure exactly which type of aircraft the information is referring to or its correct designation. Some sources, such as enemy prisoner of war accounts, perhaps shouldn't be fully trusted. But it is your responsibility to piece together the size, shape, and capabilities of the aircraft concerned.

These brief intelligence reports are edited down from large files on each aircraft; for some of the more common types, there are several bulging folders stuffed with reports, diagrams, technical drawings, and photos. Within the scope of this book it is only possible to very briefly cover the main revelations about each aircraft and some of the fascinating nuggets of information contained in the files. Indeed for some of the types it would be possible to produce a whole book on the intelligence record. You may find the intelligence history contains what we now know to be mistakes. Where these are obvious the authors have pointed them out in square brackets in the text.

The "War Record" section on each type of aircraft is present to provide the actual story, with the benefit of hindsight, of how the aircraft initially was created and how it performed in the war. This the reader can compare with what Air Intelligence (AI) knew at the time. In general, and particularly for the second half of the war, what AI knew was impressive. Indeed, it was very rare for a new Luftwaffe aircraft to enter service without the Allies already knowing a good deal about it and having a reasonably clear picture of its capabilities. This book should stand as a record of the achievement of those intelligence officers who, though employed in a less glamorous role than their aircrew comrades, produced sterling work and contributed to the victory in the air war.

This book concentrates on the operational and tactical aspects of Luftwaffe aircraft. The reason for this is twofold. First, the intelligence files, although they contain a wealth of technical data, do not add to the considerable sum of knowledge that has been built up in this field. Other works have drawn from the manufacturers' files and those of the designers of the aircraft themselves; obviously this information will be more accurate and comprehensive than what could be gathered by the Allies during the war. Second, the authors also feel that the technical history of World War II aircraft has been exhaustively covered already in published books and that there is little point in repeating it here.

The introduction and sections on Dornier, Heinkel, and Junkers aircraft were written by Christopher Staerck, the other aircraft by Paul Sinnott. The authors would like to thank the following people for their help and encouragement in putting this book together and getting it published: Paul Johnson, Brian Carter, Hugh Alexander, Anne Kilminster, Don McKeon, Roy Conyers Nesbit, Georges Van Acker, Kate Flaherty and Simon Kooter, John Staerck, Dominic Staerck, and Chris Hills.

Introduction

Before the outbreak of war with Germany, British Intelligence (badly understaffed and underfunded) could not provide accurate analysis or detail about the Luftwaffe. It was this arm of the German military machine—with the perceived threat of its ability to rain explosives and gas on London—that most scared British prime minister Neville Chamberlain and influenced his policy of "appeasement" toward the Nazi leader, Adolf Hitler. However, after 1 September 1939 Air Intelligence expanded and developed swiftly, pulling in resources and data from any and every avenue open to it, especially after American entry into the war against Germany on 12 December 1941 and the initiation of the Combined Bomber Offensive. A comprehensive picture of every Luftwaffe aircraft was built, including many of those that reached only the prototype stage.

The Directorate of Air Intelligence was responsible for the organization and coordination of all types of air intelligence—military, political, and civil—at home and abroad, liaison with air attachés and missions, and questions of security and censorship. It gathered data in the form of reports and photographs of enemy aircraft and airfields; details of engines, armaments, fuel systems, and other technical data; as well as records of enemy air operations. The files, now held in the archives at the Public Record Office (the UK national archive) in London, provide the only authoritative guide to Allied Intelligence's wartime knowledge of the German air arm.

Many books on the Luftwaffe are written with the benefit of hindsight. This book differs; it aims to utilize a unique source of intelligence by putting the reader back into the Air Ministry at the time. It will tell the story of each aircraft as it unfolded, but purely in terms of the data that was achievable to Allied intelligence at the time.

Prewar British Air Intelligence

None of the German armed services was of greater concern to the British government than the air force. At the start of Nazi rule, Germany was banned from ownership of an air force under the terms dictated at Versailles. The Weimar governments had commenced some clandestine rearmament, but by 1933 the Luftwaffe existed chiefly on paper, with only a small cadre of experienced aircrew and a few planes, built under contract overseas. No one in Britain expected this situation to persist under the Nazis. The Air Ministry's long-range predictions of Luftwaffe strength played a major role in the changing picture in Whitehall of German airpower. The poor quality of these predictions before September 1936 represents a significant and important failure in the work of Air Intelligence.[1] However, the German aircraft industry was the object of intense study by the Industrial Intelligence Center (IIC) and the Air Ministry, which collaborated in producing twelve reports upon it between March 1934 and July 1939.[2]

Intelligence is an activity that has to perform three functions: information has to be acquired, it has to be analyzed and interpreted, and it has to be put into the hands of those who use it. In Britain, at the outbreak of the war, the organizations that carried out these functions were disorganized both internally and in terms of coordination of work. There was no efficient system.[3] An additional obstacle to the achievement of better intelligence assessments between 1933 and 1936 was the depth of bitterness and mistrust between the Foreign Office and the Air Ministry. The Air Ministry took umbrage at Foreign Office criticism and intrusion on what it viewed as its domain—the interpretation of data on the Luftwaffe.[4]

The most extensive system for acquiring information was an overt one—British overseas diplomatic missions and the stream of messages, dispatches, telegrams, and letters they sent to the Foreign Office.[5] Visits by observers to German factories are recorded as having been a major source of intelligence, as were the reports of the "energetic" air attaché in Berlin, who used his own plane to observe factories and German air force installations from the air.[6] The principal sources of information used by overseas Foreign Office personnel to keep London informed of political, military, and economic developments were the press and other public media. These reports were not regarded as "intelligence," a term restricted to information obtained from secret sources—that is, material supplied by overseas representatives of SIS, the Secret Intelligence Service, controlled by MI6.

The Secret Intelligence Service

The diplomatic missions, like the press, radio, and other open sources, were alive with conflicting rumors and warnings. Consequently the SIS was driven to devote its limited resources to collecting political intelligence in an attempt to reduce the confusion inherent in such a chaotic system.[7] Short of officers and staff, the SIS placed the burden and responsibility for developing its network of agents within Nazi Germany upon the SIS stations in Warsaw, Prague, Bern, Paris, Copenhagen, and The Hague. By 1936, these had become the intelligence-collection front line. However, as the 1930s progressed, London realized that it was receiving insufficient factual information from its hard-worked section heads. Too much of what flowed in was merely political gossip. More technical data was required, as were economic statistics and greater detail on military installations.[8] In the absence of any input from signals intelligence (sigint), it was difficult to distinguish what was reliable from what was dubious in the SIS's own reports. As well as casting doubt on the credibility of its agents, this preoccupation led to complaints that the SIS was failing to meet the need for factual intelligence about foreign military capabilities, equipment, preparations, and movements, and that what little it was providing was inferior even to that provided by the attachés.[9]

By the beginning of 1938 the War Office was regularly complaining that the SIS was failing to meet its increasingly urgent need for factual information about the German military. In the same year, the Air Ministry was denouncing MI6 and SIS reports of this nature as 80 percent unreliable.[10] However, the permanent undersecretary of state at the Foreign Office, Sir Alexander Cadogan, issued a minute in defense of MI6. Later, in a letter to Sir Nevile Henderson, the British ambassador to Berlin, he said, "Moreover, it is true to say that the recent scares have not originated principally with the SIS agents in Germany, but have come to us from other sources."[11]

Not all the news regarding MI6 and the SIS was gloomy. One development that reflected a changing emphasis in the British intelligence community was the introduction of an air section within MI6. Located at Broadway Buildings, directly behind and linked to MI6 headquarters, which were at 21 Queen Anne's Gate, it was headed by Wing Commander Frederick Winterbotham, Royal Flying Corps/Royal Air Force.[12] Recommended for the job personally by the Director of Air Intelligence, Charles Blount, and his deputy, Air Commodore Archibald Boyle, Winterbotham was head of the AI1(c) branch of the Directorate of Air Intelligence, which was de facto the air intelligence section of MI6.[13]

Once in the post, he began analyzing and assessing Soviet air strength. However, finding that all Soviet technical assistance came from Germany, he switched his focus to the Reich. Winterbotham could extract very little intelligence on the Luftwaffe from the SIS station heads in Berlin, Frankfurt, Hamburg, Cologne, or Munich, because the Abwehr (military intelligence) and the Gestapo (secret police) were too active and too efficient. In fact, he had little opportunity to obtain accurate reports on the Luftwaffe other than from his one main source, Baron William de Ropp, an agent in the employ of SIS.

De Ropp was the Berlin representative of the Bristol Aircraft Company, a position that opened many doors for him, including that of Alfred Rosenberg, Chief Nazi Philosopher and head of the party's foreign policy office—the Aussen-Politisches Amt der NSDAP. A Baltic émigré aristocrat, De Ropp lived with his English wife in Berlin, where he was nurtured by Winterbotham over a period of three years. His standing among leading Nazis helped facilitate a visit by Winterbotham to Germany in 1934, an early coup for the MI6 officer. While in Germany he obtained a significant amount of useful data on the growth of the Luftwaffe, including types, engines, numbers, and other technical information on the various machines being constructed by Junkers, Heinkel, and Messerschmitt. For example, Winterbotham became aware of the problems facing the Ju 87 Stuka in dive-bombing and warned the RAF. However, it remained skeptical as to his assessment, because little confirming data was available from other sources.

As the interwar crisis deepened, other avenues and sources of information became open to the British. A good case in point is the story of Paul Thummel. He was a high-ranking Abwehr officer who initially furnished first-class political and military intelligence on Germany, including information about the equipment of the Luftwaffe, to the Czechoslovak government in Prague. After the outbreak of war in September 1939, he supplied MI6 with the same information; it was forwarded by the London-based Czech government-in-exile for the first two years of the war.[14]

The prewar problem facing MI6 and its network of SIS agents was one of resources and funding, a problem that was exacerbated during the Rhineland crisis in 1936. When Hitler ordered the Wehrmacht to reoccupy the Rhineland, a blatant contravention of the 1919 Versailles treaty, SIS's principal source of information was its Paris station. This station, in turn, relied heavily upon collaboration with the two French intelligence organizations, the Deuxième Bureau, headed by General Gauche, and Colonel Rivet's Service de Renseignments.

Photographic Reconnaissance

One positive result of this collaboration was the joint Anglo-French establishment of an aerial reconnaissance program. In 1938 MI6 made an invaluable contribution to the future increase of factual intelligence on the Luftwaffe by helping to develop aerial photographic reconnaissance (PR). Instrumental in getting funds allocated to the project was Freddie Winterbotham. Prewar clandestine flights over Germany were made under the cover of the Aeronautical Sales and Research Corporation, a Paris-based civilian firm. Operating from a French airfield and supplied through the SIS with aircraft and cameras, in March 1939 the "company" became operational. Its head, Australian Sidney Cotton, aided by Canadian Robert Niven, put Leica cameras into a pair of Lockheed 12A aircraft and proceeded to over fly Germany.

As a result the Anglo-French intelligence communities gleaned much valuable data on German aircraft numbers and locations. By the outbreak of war, when the Air Ministry took over his firm, Cotton had photographed much of Germany and the Mediterranean. The Air Ministry's Air Intelligence Branch was able to produce a sound appreciation of the Luftwaffe order of battle, thanks to the work of Winterbotham's Cotton/Niven team and also the at-times-perilous work undertaken by the air attaché in Berlin, Group Capt. John Vachell, in aerial reconnaissance work.[15] PR rapidly developed during the war—by the summer of 1940 it had overcome the consequences of prewar neglect—and was to become the second most important source of intelligence for the Allies, second only to sigint. It is worth noting that the RAF objected to this unorthodox approach and that it was not until the war had started that the RAF's Photographic Reconnaissance Unit (a PRU wing) was created.

The Air Ministry

Changes and developments were also under way at the bureaucratic level in the Air Ministry. From 1935 the status and the establishment of the intelligence staff, particularly the German Section, were steadily improved. As well as creating the post of deputy director of intelligence, the Air Ministry authorized a modest increase in the staff and effort devoted to Germany. Until 1935 the intelligence component of the Directorate of Operations and Intelligence—the central authority responsible, on the one hand, for advising the Air Staff on all information about foreign air forces and, on the other hand, for providing the air commands with the intelligence they needed for plans and operations—had consisted of only ten staff officers since 1918.

Nevertheless, the Air Ministry, like the War Office, was not an executive command. Consequently, it was equally, if not more, important that steps were taken from 1936 to form intelligence staffs at the headquarters and lower levels in the operational commands of the Metropolitan Air Force—Fighter Command, Bomber Command, and Coastal Command. It is somewhat ironic that intelligence staffs at these levels already existed in the overseas commands. Now they were created for the first time in the United Kingdom, and their function was to filter and disseminate intelligence prepared elsewhere down to the squadrons, as well as to pass information obtained by the squadrons upward for analysis and interpretation.

Additionally, in 1938 the Air Ministry took the further step of arranging that in the event of war all immediately exploitable intelligence would be passed directly from the main RAF interception station at Cheadle to the operational command concerned. In practical terms, this meant all that could be derived from low-grade Luftwaffe tactical wireless traffic, especially the prolific air-to-ground communications of its bomber and long-range reconnaissance units. It should be noted that the scheme did not become fully operational immediately on the outbreak of war. It was thought necessary that the Air Intelligence Branch at the Air Ministry, which also received this wireless intelligence and mated it with information from other sources, should play a part in its interpretation. By the time intensive German air operations against Britain began, however, most teething troubles had been overcome.[16]

Also in 1935, the Air Ministry established the Committee for the Scientific Survey of Air Defense (CSSAD), under the chairmanship of Sir Henry Tizard. In 1939, under recommendation of Sir Henry, and in consultation with the SIS and the DDI, the Air Ministry appointed a "scientific officer" to the staff of the director of scientific research. Funding for the position was not made available until late 1939, and the post was not filled until a few days after war began. Its first incumbent, responsible for liaison with the Air Intelligence Branch "as a preliminary measure towards improving the co-operation between scientists and the intelligence organization," was Professor R. V. Jones.[17] The Tizard Committee, sponsoring the development of radar, had wondered whether if Britain had it, Germany might as well. MI6's inquiries revealed that the British intelligence service had virtually no knowledge of German scientific and technical developments. It must be remembered that pre-1939 MI6 had not only been underfunded and understaffed but had been focused primarily on gathering political, economic, and order-of-battle intelligence.[18]

At the Tizard Committee's recommendation, MI6 accepted the appointment of a scientist to oversee the arrangements for gaining scientific intelligence data on Germany. However, the Whitehall mandarins in the treasury refused to grant the money to cover the appointee's salary—yet another classic symptom of British prewar malaise. The post was not actually inaugurated until 1 September 1939, the day the Germans invaded Poland. Once in place, Professor Jones's job was to anticipate the German applications of science to warfare so that the British (then later the Anglo-Americans) could counter these applications before they gave the enemy a decisive edge. His first recommendation was the creation of scientific sections within the directorates of military, air, and naval intelligence, as well as MI6—which covered the Government Code and Cipher School (GC & CS) at Bletchley Park.[19]

None of the major powers had an organization in place to monitor, evaluate, and disseminate scientific intelligence until the British established one in 1939, as a direct result of the threat that the Luftwaffe was believed to represent. The dramatic increase in the applications of science to the conduct of modern warfare throughout the interwar years made it inevitable that intelligence relating to this field would sooner or later become as significant as traditional forms of military intelligence data. More significantly for the British, it took the Air Staff fully three years to recognize that the Luftwaffe was the brainchild of the Nazi system, a product of Hitler and Göring's desire to build the biggest air force possible in the shortest possible time. In 1934 Luftwaffe front-line strength stood at 228 aircraft, but by the outbreak of war in September 1939 it was 3,541.

It should be pointed out in defense of Air Intelligence that it had perceived that German front-line strength would be 3,700 aircraft by the end of 1939. This degree of accuracy was too little, too late; it was painfully obvious that even despite the post-Munich fighter-production program Britain had lost the 1930s air arms race.[20] Air parity had been the first victim. Early RAF rearmament programs were directed toward the achievement of long-term numerical equality with the Luftwaffe, but that goal eluded the air force. The German military occupation of Austria in March 1938 prompted the government to abandon all fiscal restrictions to air rearmament; in April 1938, it approved the production of 12,000 aircraft over two years.[21] The Munich crisis pushed Britain and Germany to the brink of war, heightened fears that there was a significant air gap and that if Britain were to be at war in the not too distant future she would be ill prepared to meet the Luftwaffe onslaught.[22] The problem was exacerbated by faulty intelligence predictions that by and large underestimated the rate of Luftwaffe expansion.[23]

Wartime

With the outbreak of war contact with the Luftwaffe increased, as did the amount and variety of intelligence available. At the same time, the existing intelligence organizations benefited from an increase in resources, especially in the size and quality of staff. Additionally, organizations were created to gather intelligence from new "wartime only" sources. For example the Political Warfare Executive (PWE) was set up to scrutinize enemy and foreign press, radio, and propaganda.

Another "wartime only" establishment was the Combined Services Detailed Interrogation Centre (CSDIC), set up to interrogate prisoners of war. It proved useful in gleaning technical data from Luftwaffe ground and flying personnel. The first German airmen to fall into British hands were imprisoned in the Tower of London, where there was a reception and interrogation center; early in 1940 they were moved to Trent Park, in north London. Interrogators were sent to interview prisoners as soon as possible after capture, the first interview often taking place in a police station. Those believed to have valuable information were sent to Trent Park, where skilled interrogators, receiving at first nothing more from the prisoners than name, rank, and serial number, made crude threats and then placed them in solitary confinement. If this did not loosen the tongue, a prisoner would be placed in cells with other airmen (and sometimes an émigré stooge), where hidden microphones both inside and outside the cell would often pick up valuable information. This would help later interrogators, who could display an intimate knowledge of a prisoner, his comrades, and his unit.[24] RAF technical interrogation of Luftwaffe POWs was conducted by AI1(k), a subsection of the Air Intelligence directorate. For example, during the Battle of Britain, AI1(k) reports extensively circulated within the Air Ministry and to the commands (Fighter, Bomber, Coastal) as well as to the intelligence directorates of the Admiralty and the War Office. In total about 40 copies would be distributed, the idea being to disseminate technical data to the fighting commands.

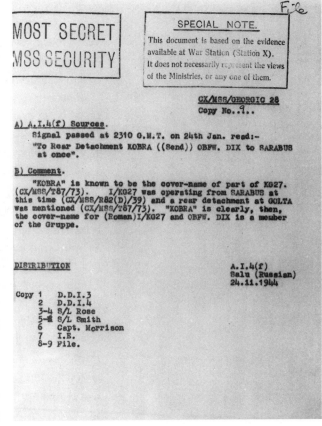

Bletchley Park was given the wartime cover name of "Station X"

However, two of the already existing sources of intelligence particularly came of age during the war: German sigint at Bletchley Park, and photo-reconnaissance. Still under MI6 control, GC & CS at Bletchley Park was to hold most promise for Air intelligence. With the help of the French Deuxième Bureau, the SIS Paris station evacuated the Polish cryptographic service to Britain along with its much-prized Enigma code machine. With this specimen, by January 1940 GC & CS achieved a notable success in breaking the German Enigma keys.[25] It established early on that each of the German services used different keys for its Enigma machines. The code breakers at GC & CS provided information about German strategy, operations, and *Gruppen* locations but could furnish very little in terms of technical data about individual Luftwaffe aircraft types. This was so because the Germans did not use encrypted communications to transfer data of this nature.

Photo-reconnaissance was one of the outstanding successes of intelligence gathering during the war. Originally using twin-engine Bristol Blenheims of Bomber

The process of wartime photographic interpretation

Command, PR sorties suffered disproportionately high casualties, a factor that was remedied by mid-November 1939. Two modified Spitfires were allocated to the special SIS Flight—at the outbreak of war taken over by the RAF and renamed the Photographic Development Unit (PDU). Active operations began immediately over the Siegfried Line from bases in Belgium.

The ever-active, ever-inventive Sidney Cotton was, according to R. V. Jones, better at operating cameras and aircraft than were the regular RAF airmen. RAF cameras suffered from condensation on the lenses and other components as a result of flying at 30,000 feet. Cotton was able to rectify those faults. He was also aware of the need for speed and was successful in getting an additional 30 mph from each aircraft by stripping it of protruding items (such as gun barrels) and applying a smooth gloss finish to the outer surface. Before long Cotton had acquired two Spitfire I fighters, which he proceeded to modify to suit his needs. First, he improved their speed from 360 to 396 mph, second, he "persuaded" RAF technicians at RAE (Royal Aircraft Establishment) Farnborough to install two twenty-inch focal length cameras to replace the previous single eight-inch F24 camera.[26]

The initial Spitfire I's assigned to PR work were originally known as the Special Survey Flight, later as 212 Squadron.[27] Deficiencies in operational limits restricted coverage until April 1940, when a longer-range Spitfire became available. Difficulties were also overcome in photographic interpretation, thus enabling useful intelligence to be derived from the pictures taken. It was not until July 1940 that the Air Ministry set up the Photographic Interpretation Unit (PIU) of the PDU to interpret photographs for the army and the navy, not just the RAF.

Until sigint and PR began to yield results of operational value, the service intelligence branches were dependent upon the SIS, British diplomatic missions, neutral attachés in Germany, German press and radio, and whatever the French were prepared to provide. Additionally, the British military mission in Poland submitted accurate reports on the nature of the Polish campaign, highlighting especially the close cooperation of air units with the army. During the "phoney war" period, Air intelligence was able to locate and identify a large number of Luftwaffe formations via the sigint coming from GC & CS. At the same time, the SIS helped military intelligence to build up its knowledge of the German order of battle for the forthcoming war in the West.

The American Intelligence Establishment

If the situation was some way short of perfect for the British during the early years of the war, it was not much better for the Americans. At the start of World War II, the U.S. Army Air Corps had no coherent philosophy or doctrine on intelligence. In 1938 the War Department printed Field Manual 30-5, *Military Intelligence, Combat Intelligence,* which remained the cornerstone of U.S. thinking in this field. Effectively, the principles of military intelligence would develop as the conflict evolved. FM 30-5 espoused greater emphasis on command decisions and the role of intelligence in their formulation, urging intelligence officers to base their evaluations upon an enemy's combat forces and intentions, where known.

Prior to U.S. entry into the war, the chief source of military intelligence on European countries was from the reports regularly sent to Washington by U.S.

military attachés stationed in overseas capitals. This was a seriously flawed system. As Dwight D. Eisenhower pointed out, few of these attachés knew the basic principles of intelligence work. In fact the reports sent by Maj. Truman Smith from Germany in the 1930s were deliberately alarmist about the strength of the Luftwaffe—especially regarding the order of battle of the *Kampfgeschwader*. It was not until fall 1939 that the Assistant Chief of Staff, Intelligence created a separate air section in the War Department's Military Intelligence Division with the duty of coordinating all U.S. air intelligence activities. It was this department's responsibility to acquire aviation-related data and write technical air intelligence reports.[28]

However, the picture was not all gloomy. In the late 1930s the U.S. Army's Signal Intelligence Service broke the Japanese diplomatic "Magic" code and built "Purple" machines for the decoding process. At the same time, with significant Polish help, the British GC & CS at Bletchley Park unlocked the secrets of the Luftwaffe's Enigma code. In the closely guarded dimension of signals intelligence, Anglo-American cooperation was discussed at top government levels in April 1940.

In the resulting spirit of cooperation, by August 1940 the British government officially welcomed U.S. military observers to the combat zones. American service personnel rushed to Britain to witness firsthand the prevailing conditions; by April 1941 a U.S. Army Special Observers Group had opened in London. In June 1941 the British Security Co-ordination Office was established in New York. That summer Maj. Haywood Hansell was posted to Britain, where he sought target information from the RAF intelligence establishment. His British hosts did not let him down. Although he felt the U.S. Army Air Forces (USAAF) as the Army Air Corps was renamed that year, was better informed about petroleum, synthetic chemicals, and electric power, the RAF was far more knowledgeable about the Luftwaffe and German transportation. Hansell returned to the United States with almost a ton of classified intelligence data, most of it in target folders. This British-supplied information formed the core data for the USAAF's Air War Plans Division Number 1 document.[29]

Despite these efforts, when America entered the Second World War, U.S. Army intelligence was insufficiently prepared. In September 1941 the Office of Assistant Chief of Air Staff Intelligence (AC/AS A-2) numbered just twelve officers and nine civilians. By 1 June 1945, it was to reach 550 military and 420 civilian personnel, a fair indication of the rapid expansion in this field.

USAAF Daylight Raids

In January 1942, the USAAF established a bomber command in the United Kingdom under the command of Brig. Gen. Ira C. Eaker. Within his entourage were two intelligence officers, Maj. Harris Hull and Capt. Carl Norcross, tasked with establishing the first intelligence section specifically aimed

These Ultra decrypts were shown to Churchill on a daily basis. "C" is Sir Stewart Menzies, the head of MI6 and overseer of the Government Code and Cypher School at Bletchley Park. This decrypt was given to Churchill the day before the "Palm Sunday Massacre"—see Ju 52.

at catering to the needs of daylight precision bombing. The RAF served as a role model, although serious differences were apparent. Although much information was gleaned from the experiences of the RAF's Bomber Command, Hull and Norcross had to take into consideration factors that were uncommon in night area-bombing operations. For instance, staff were needed to assess the observations of the B-17 crews and their reports concerning the tactics employed by the Luftwaffe's fighter units, as well as other evaluations of the enemy and his capabilities.

On 24 June 1942, Gen. Carl Spaatz arrived in England as head of the USAAF's Eighth Air Force. With him he brought Col. George C. McDonald, who almost immediately opened an Eighth Air Force A-2 liaison office in the Air Ministry. The U.S. officers assigned there not only provided normal liaison but worked in tandem with their British hosts in collecting, collating, and evaluating intelligence. Except for crew reports, certain aspects of PIU interpretation, and technical intelligence, the U.S. strategic air forces in the United Kingdom remained largely dependent upon British intelligence sources. For example the British "Y" teams bore the burden of radio-signal decryption and analysis, while Ultra intelligence from Bletchley Park was closely guarded, each field command having a special liaison unit attached with the responsibility of revealing "special intelligence" to a select few officers. For example, by early 1943 Ultra and PR enabled the Allied air forces to enforce a debilitating blockade of supply to the Axis forces in Libya and Tunisia. On 18 April 1943, Ultra alerted the Allies that there was going

 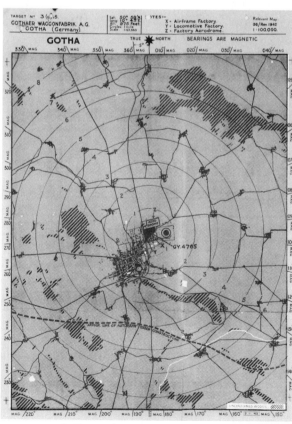

From aerial photographs such as this (left), target maps (right) were created. The airfield, clearly discernible on the photograph, can also be made out on the much larger target map.

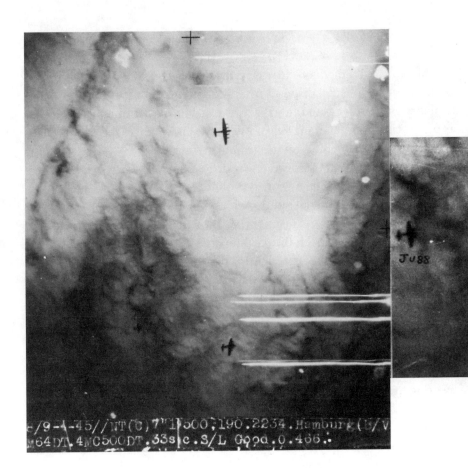

-/9-4-45//MT(C)7"1.500,190.2234.Hamburg(S/V
.64DT.4xC500DT.33sec.S/L Good.0.466.

Sometimes aircrew would capture German planes on camera. This image is unique. It is the only time a German night fighter was captured on film trailing a bomber it was about to attack. The RAF bomber that took the photograph from above had just released its payload, triggering the flash camera system, but what an image it captured!

to be an air convoy of about 100 Junkers Ju 52s attempting to break the blockade. In the ensuing aerial melee over half the Luftwaffe's transports were destroyed, in what subsequently became known as the "Palm Sunday Massacre."

Ultra and low-grade sigint was vital for the knowledge it provided on the strength, disposition, composition, production, wastage, and serviceability of the Luftwaffe. It was this element of the Reich's armed services that remained the major American strategic air target until the implementation of the Transportation Plan in April 1944 during the buildup to Operation Overlord.[30] In April 1943 Whitehall's order-of-battle intelligence showed that Luftwaffe fighter strength was 44 percent higher than in December 1941. In June 1943, low-grade sigint showed that many fighter squadrons in France and Belgium were transferring to Germany, and by July that the Luftwaffe's top priority was to defeat the USAAF's daylight deep-penetration raids over the Reich. By this time frontline fighter strength had also risen to 1,800 single-engine machines, from 1,250 in December 1942.[31] Using operational intelligence from Enigma, AI calculated that 60 percent of the Luftwaffe's fighter strength had been recalled to defend the Reich, at the expense of other fronts. It estimated 780 single-engine and 740 twin-engine fighters, when actual strength was 964 single-engine and 682 twin-engine aircraft. Further evidence that the Luftwaffe's top priority was defeating the USAAF daylight raids was revealed by Enigma and German fighter radio telephone traffic during September 1943. These sources indicated that the Luftwaffe was diverting twin-engine fighters to day fighting and equipping them with a variation of the army's 21 cm mortar, a weapon that proved deadly against the packed formations of B-17s and B-24s.[32]

The Luftwaffe Enigma code was an invaluable source of information on German order of battle, dispositions, production, wastage, casualties, serviceability and reserves. Additionally it revealed much useful information on airfields, depots, and training fields—all just as important to the USAAF in its attacks on German fighters on the ground.[33]

In January 1944, the U.S. Strategic Air Force (USSTAF) was established in Britain, with Spaatz in command. Although he wanted close integration between intelligence and operations, which would permit air combat intelligence to be more effective, during spring 1944 USSTAF continued to get the bulk of its intelligence from the Air Ministry. Ultra and Y sigint continued to supply valuable means of determining Luftwaffe air order of battle, and sigint enabled the A-2 to establish the serviceability, fighting value, and projected capabilities of the Luftwaffe. The information-sharing partnership with the British was formalized on 24 February 1944. Under the terms of this agreement, each partner recognized the other's area of expertise. Responsibility for all aviation-related intelligence on Germany would be centered in London, around the existing Air Ministry organization, with U.S. personnel augmenting the arrangement. Washington would reciprocate by taking the lead role in developing intelligence on the Japanese.

Tactical information was largely still derived from the hard won experiences of the air crews flying into the defensive German maelstrom over the Reich. Effectively, the Americans took the best the British had to offer and produced the balance of the required data themselves. For example, by mid-February 1944, Enigma showed that U.S. P-51D Mustang long-range fighters were altering the course of the air war. Outmatched by the American fighters, Luftwaffe twin-engine fighters were being escorted by Bf 109s and Fw 190s, which themselves were no match for the superior P-51Ds. Consequently, German losses were so severe that the U.S. bomber streams were deliberately directed at Berlin, overflying known belts of heavy fighters with the aim of forcing the Luftwaffe into the air where it could be destroyed in detail.[34]

As a result of wartime experience, air intelligence gathering and assessment came of age. Colonel McDonald bluntly observed that "Air Intelligence throughout the war . . . was at once an operating agency, a training school and a proving ground—it had to be, for intelligence had to produce—if one method didn't work, another was tried, and still another if necessary, in order that requirements would be fulfilled."[35]

RAF Night Bombing

The story of the RAF night offensive is an altogether different one. It was extremely costly in men and material, owing largely to the efficiency of the German defenses, a subject on which intelligence could provide little data for Bomber Command. For example Enigma yielded little information on Luftwaffe night fighters. The case of Nachtjagdgeschwader 1 (NJG1) is quite pertinent. Ultra decrypts identified it only in August 1940; in late 1941, AI discovered it had its own Enigma key, "Cockroach," which GC & CS broke in February 1942. It was not until mid-1942 that AI had any understanding of the German night-fighter and radar systems. During the spring, significant data on German radar was forthcoming from Luftwaffe Enigma codes, the SIS, PRU, and the CIU, which enabled AI to start establishing the constituent elements of the night-fighter system and its control mechanism.[36]

Thus, during mid-1942 AI began to understand the nature and buildup of the German radar and night-fighter aircraft systems, but it was not until 1943 that this had any influence on the introduction of Allied technical countermeasures. Nor did it contribute heavily to more effective bombing policies. By the end of 1942, the characteristics of German ground radar systems were well understood. However, collecting intelligence on the Luftwaffe's night-fighter force presented problems for AI. Despite the steady accumulation of information from contact reports since June 1940, when Bomber Command began sorties into Germany, a complete picture of the Luftwaffe's capabilities was not gained until about September 1942.

It must be said that the Germans themselves kept upgrading and expanding this force as the war progressed, which only added complications to the work of Air intelligence. As a result GC & CS Enigma sources were able to provide virtually no useful information on the equipment, tactics, deployment, or expansion of the enemy's organization. Other sources had to be used; SIS briefed its agents especially in how to report on radar and night-fighter matters. But by the start of 1943, a combination of technical and order of battle intelligence enabled AI to understand completely not only the German defense system but also the evolution of the night-fighter organization and how it functioned. AI realized that the radius of operation of the radar-controlled night-fighters, initially twenty-five miles, was now about forty miles. GCI (ground-controlled interception) radar illuminated the bombers and then vectored the aircraft to the target.[37]

As the Germans retreated, they had to leave behind much of their materiel. As the Allies overran former enemy airfields, technical crew pored over abandoned aircraft for the slightest piece of useful data.

Therefore, beginning in March 1943, Bomber Command commenced the Battle of the Ruhr. Over a five-month period Bomber Command flew 15,504 sorties and dropped 42,349 tons of bombs but lost 718 aircraft, prompting a strategic rethink. This was in due part to refined German tactics of which the RAF was unaware, and to a reinforcement of the twin-engine fighter defenses from 349 aircraft in January to 478 by July. It was not until August 1944, after completion of the Overlord support operations that Bomber Command resumed large-scale night bombing sorties against German cities. (They quickly established air superiority, because enemy defenses were by then collapsing due to the shortages of fuel, losses of trained pilots, and the seizure of the ground radar stations by the advancing Allied armies.)

The Combined Bomber Offensive

Although the RAF was free to pursue city bombardment, oil was defined as a panacea target. An 11 July decrypt (XL 1671) revealed that Göring had banned all nonessential flying on account of the fuel shortage problem. On 7 August, Japanese diplomatic decrypts testified to the shortages of fuel when the head of the naval mission declared to Tokyo, "Oil is Germany's problem."[38] The Joint Intelligence Committee (in JIC[44] 407) declared on 16 September that the Combined Intelligence Committee believed the shortage of fuel would stop Germany from any revival of Luftwaffe activity.[39] Again the Berlin Japanese naval mission provided valuable data when a 13 September 1944 intercept revealed that although fighter and rocket aircraft production was improving, the fuel shortage would prevent the Luftwaffe from displaying the show of strength necessary to regain control of the air.

Improvement wasn't all one-way, for in November 1944 the Luftwaffe's day-fighter arm recovered to an extent that affected the conduct of USSTAF operations. Encounters with jet and rocket-propelled fighters began to increase, and fighter production was up. In October 1944 AI believed that numbers of available fighters had risen to 1,330 from 690 the previous month and that sorties of up to 700 aircraft were not out of the question. Spaatz accordingly directed bomber operations against fighter production plants and airfields as well as oil installations.

The Luftwaffe

The Germans, fully aware of the ultimate consequences for the Reich should the decline not be arrested, devoted more energy and resources to their new aircraft types. However, for the Allies, as the war progressed, so too the sources and volume of intelligence on German aircraft types increased. Information came from attachés, POWs, SIS agents, neutral observers, PR, captured documents, postal censorship, and patent specifications. Early in the war section AI1(g) within the Air Ministry collated data on all the aircraft wrecks in Allied territory and disseminated pamphlets of its findings to the frontline squadrons. It paid little to no attention to the other sources, upon which it was later to rely. At the beginning of 1942, when AI1(g) was renamed AI2(g), the technical section of AI became a fully-fledged research section, under the aegis of the Director of Intelligence (Operations). As the war progressed, AI2(g) increasingly assumed responsibility for assessment of all sources of intelligence on enemy aircraft developments. It provided evidence to the Air Staff and various Whitehall departments, depending on the perceived nature of the threat and whether it was from new types of aircraft, new air engines, new weapons, radar, or other myriad equipment.[40]

During the first half of 1942, Enigma, low-grade sigint, and in particular Japanese diplomatic signals began to be sent to AI2(g), but these sources did not reveal information on new types until early 1944. PR was valuable because it detected new aircraft types, but only after they were built and at their test airfields. From mid-1943, more reliable data came from POW and agents and captured documents. SIS agents in particular proved valuable sources at this stage of the war. One of the most unusual sources of technical intelligence on the Luftwaffe was the Royal Aircraft Establishment (RAE). The RAE's Farnborough Experimental Flying department accumulated its own Luftwaffe as the war progressed. Mock dogfights over Farnham Common and Frensham Ponds in Surrey (southern England) became commonplace and enabled Allied fighter pilots to evaluate the performance of enemy machines, notably the vaunted Fw 190, in combat conditions.

When war broke out, little technical knowledge of the Luftwaffe's aircraft existed. As the early air battles were mainly over Allied territory, a steady supply of wrecks was made available that yielded data on equipment and components from gun-mountings, gearboxes, exhaust systems, radio equipment, engines, propellers, reconnaissance cameras, magnetos, and self-sealing fuel tanks. However, this information could not provide evaluations of enemy aircraft performance; complete machines were needed for this. Of the hundreds of Luftwaffe aircraft that RAE handled, many genuinely landed in error, "but others, still officially described as having arrived that way, were the result of defections and deals arranged by Intelligence."[41]

Professor R. V. Jones remembers being telephoned on the morning of 10 May 1943 by Jack Easton, one of the directors of Air Intelligence, to state that a Ju 88C-6 night-fighter had landed at Dyce, near Aberdeen in Scotland. Interestingly, the crew had radioed their base in Norway to say they were on fire and were ditching. Liferafts spotted by the German rescue services provided convincing evidence that this was the case. However, the Ju 88 landed under Spitfire escort! Professor Jones went to Scotland immediately to inspect the enemy aircraft, and within five days its valuable, brand-new FuG 202 Lichtenstein BC radar equipment was being evaluated at RAE under the supervision of the MI6 scientific intelligence officer.[42]

Before German aircraft were passed to the RAF's Enemy Aircraft Flight at Duxford, where they were demonstrated to the Observer Corps, antiaircraft personnel, ground crew, and pilots, initial evaluation work was shared between Farnborough and Boscombe Down. It was typical of Allied inventiveness that as maintenance proved problematic, the RAE developed its own POW camp of technicians disaffected with the Nazis. These men were only

L. Dv. T. 2088 A-5/Fl
Exerzier-Karte

Ju 88 A-5
Exerzier-Karte

Ausgabe Dezember 1942

Der Reichsminister der Luftfahrt
und Oberbefehlshaber der Luftwaffe   Berlin, 31. Dezember 1942
Chef des Ausbildungswesens

Hiermit genehmige ich die L. Dv. T. 2088 A—5/Fl Exerzier-Karte „Ju 88 A—5 Exerzier-Karte, Ausgabe Dezember 1942." Sie tritt mit dem Tage der Herausgabe in Kraft.

I.A.
Kreipe

Diese Karte gilt als Verbrauchsmaterial!

AI made much use of captured enemy maintenance manuals.

An Si 204 of the RAE's "Farnborough Luftwaffe"

too keen to exchange the boredom of regular camp life for a quasi-free lifestyle at Farnborough, once they realized Germany would not win the war.

For an understanding of the work undertaken by the RAE, some examples of specific aircraft need highlighting. The first is a sad tale. On 9 February 1940 an He 111H-3 of 5./K.G.26 was shot down by Spitfires while on anti-shipping duty. It crash-landed on moorland at North Berwick Law and was flown to RAE Farnborough and then passed on to Duxford. Unfortunately, on a demonstration flight for U.S. airmen in November 1943, it crashed after taking measures to avoid a head-on collision with a captured Ju 88A. The RAF pilots of both machines were trying to land on the same runway but from different directions. Tragically, six out of the Heinkel's ten American passengers were killed. Perhaps the RAE's biggest prize was Oberleutnant Arnim Faber's Fw 190, from III/J.G.2, which he mistakenly landed at RAF Penbury in broad daylight on 23 June after chasing raiding Spitfires back from the raid on his airfield at Morlaix in Brittany. The most formidable of Germany's fighter aircraft, its constant success against the Spitfire V had created a mood of despondency among Fighter Command's pilots. Fortunately, tests with this Fw 190 against the soon-to-be-introduced Spitfire IX restored pilot morale.[43]

Although the RAE provided useful evaluations on the performance characteristics of individual Luftwaffe aircraft types, it could say nothing on operations or tactics. As regards intelligence on Luftwaffe operations within Western Europe, until D-day this was derived chiefly from low-grade sigint, PR, and POW interrogations, backed up by MI6 reports and whatever was available from Enigma. British intelligence authorities, having already built up a considerable fund of knowledge on these matters, continued to increase their familiarity with the overall state of the Luftwaffe and with its strength, deployment, and order of battle on every front. For example, in early April 1942 sigint provided information that *Kampfgeschwader* strength in the West was to be increased, with II/K.G. 100 and IV/K.G. 40 ordered to Holland. Even though the 1942 German bomber offensive against the UK failed—primarily due to Luftwaffe limitations—it did succeed in keeping 1,400 fighters in Britain when they were desperately needed in other theaters. In its defense, AI soon deduced that the enemy's biggest "show" would be no more than 150 aircraft, with the predominant force size averaging eighty bombers.[44]

Perhaps the single most rewarding source on German aircraft development was Hiroshi Oshima. He continually proved to be a most valuable, if somewhat unwitting, source, purely in terms of what and whom he saw and heard. He was the Japanese ambassador in Berlin, and as such he had access to some of the Reich's most senior political and military leaders. He reported regularly to his superiors at the Japanese foreign ministry in encoded transmissions. Little did he know that the cipher he was employing had long been compromised by Allied decryption teams using Magic. Magic, like Ultra, supplied the Allies with a unique insight regarding intelligence about Germany's intentions, armaments and economic problems.

> Of all the technical information which Magic produced from the signals of the Japanese Embassy in Berlin, perhaps none was more valuable than data concerning a weapon whose potentialities the Germans developed more effectively than the Allies. This was the jet-propelled aircraft, which, when it was first employed operationally by the Luftwaffe, looked as though it might provide the enemy with an advantage in the skies as significant as the Americans' upgrading of the Mustang into a long-range fighter capable of escorting bombers to the far side of Germany. The Japanese were avid for information about jet propulsion. In consequence, the Berlin Embassy filed many reports which, as translated in the Magic intercepts, often have the same authority and exact description as a purloined blueprint might have provided.[45]

Ronald Lewin, author of *The Other Ultra*, takes the case of the Arado Ar 234 jet bomber, which, along with the Me 262, was probably the most efficient jet type produced and delivered for service with the Luftwaffe. In 1944 over 527 were delivered. The Allies knew virtually everything about it. A 31 October 1944 Magic decrypt from the Berlin embassy naval attaché supplied the Ar 234's dimensions, its maximum speed at varying altitudes, the reduction in speed caused by different bomb payloads, the rate of climb, the optimum ceiling range and cruising range, the landing speed, the characteristics of its automatic pilot, and details of the Luftwaffe units that specialized in operating the Arado. He argues, legitimately, that Magic, Ultra, and systematic sifting of deciphered low-grade Luftwaffe sigint resulted in the creation of an almost encyclopedic awareness of what the Germans were doing with their jet programs.[46]

Intelligence of this caliber was to pay huge dividends to the Allies until the close of the war in the air. At the end of February 1945, the Allies became increasingly anxious about the Heinkel He 162 and the Messerschmitt Me 262, as well as about mounting references in sigint to the overall expansion of the jet production program. For example, regarding monthly production figures, AI compared the Japanese estimates with its own. In Me 262 production AI estimated 150–200, which compared to the Japanese figure of 500. In fact it was actually 296, although the Germans had planned to produce

450 in February 1945. About the same time, there was a marked increase in jet aircraft activity, which continued throughout March 1945.

Jet fighter opposition marginally increased against Allied bomber raids toward the end of February. On 2 March a combined force of fifty Me 163 and Me 262 fighters attacked USAAF bombers operating against oil targets. On 15 March, twenty-four U.S. bombers were shot down, predominantly by a force of thirty-six jets that attacked with new tactics. This trend was enough to suggest to the Allies that the possibility existed for a new phase in the air war owing to the new jets. In the middle of March, sigint discovered that the Germans were trying to expand the jet fighter arm rapidly, calling for pilots from night-fighter, day-fighter, and jet ground-attack units, and even personnel from the V-1 launcher crews.[47] The token jet force soon disintegrated as the Allied ground forces overran its airfields and their production plants.[48]

Notes

1. Wesley Wark, *The Ultimate Enemy* (London: Cornell University Press, 1985), 35–79.
2. Public Record Office, Kew [hereafter PRO], CAB 4/22 and CAB 4/30.
3. F. H. Hinsley, *British Intelligence in the Second World War,* abridged ed. (London: 1993), Her Majesty's Stationery Office [hereafter HMSO], 3.
4. Wark, *The Ultimate Enemy,* 35–79.
5. F. H. Hinsley, *British Intelligence in the Second World War: Its Influence on Strategy and Operations* (London: HMSO, 1979), vol. 1, 45.
6. Hinsley, vol. 1, 61.
7. Hinsley, abridged ed., 11.
8. Nigel West, *MI6: British Secret Intelligence Service Operations, 1909–1945* (London: Weidenfeld and Nicolson, 1986), 45.
9. Hinsley, abridged ed., 11.
10. Hinsley, vol. 1, 55–56.
11. PRO, FO 800/270, 39/9.
12. West, *MI6,* 46–49.
13. R. V. Jones, *Most Secret War: British Scientific Intelligence 1939–1945* (London: Hodder and Stoughton, 1978).
14. Hinsley, vol. 1, 58.
15. West, *MI6,* 67.
16. Hinsley, abridged ed., 14–15.
17. R. V. Jones, "Scientific Intelligence of the Royal Air Force in the Second World War," in *The Conduct of the Air War in the Second World War: An International Comparison,* ed. Horst Boog (Berg, Oxford, 1992), 580.
18. Jones, "Scientific Intelligence," 580–81.
19. Jones, "Scientific Intelligence," 581.
20. Wark, *The Ultimate Enemy,* 35–79.
21. PRO, CAB 23/94.
22. Wesley, Wark, "The Air Defense Gap: British Air Doctrine and Intelligence Warnings in the 1930s," in *The Conduct of the Air War in the Second World War: An International Comparison,* ed. Horst Boog (Berg: Oxford, 1992), 521.
23. Wark, "Air Defense Gap," 516.
24. E. R. Hooton, *Eagle in Flames. The Fall of the Luftwaffe* (London: Arms and Armour Press, 1997), 30.

25. West, *M.I.6.*, 67.

26. R. V. Jones, *Most Secret War,* 179–81.

27. Roy Conyers Nesbitt, *The RAF in Camera,* vol. 2, *1939–1945* (London: Sutton and PRO, 1996), 7.

28. R. F. Futrell, "US Army Air Forces Intelligence in the Second World War," in *The Conduct of the Air War in the Second World War: An International Comparison,* ed. Horst Boog (Berg: Oxford, 1992), 531.

29. Futrell, "US Army Air Forces," 532–33.

30. Futrell, "US Army Air Forces," 539–40.

31. F. H. Hinsley, *British Intelligence in the Second World War: Its Influence on Strategy and Operations* (London: HMSO, 1984), vol. 2, 517–20.

32. Hinsley, abridged ed., 403–4.

33. Ronald Lewin, *The Other Ultra* (London: Hutchinson, 1982).

34. Hinsley, vol. 1, 317–18.

35. Futrell, "US Army Air Forces," 530–31.

36. Hinsley, vol. 2, 250–51.

37. Hinsley, abridged ed., 170.

38. F. H. Hinsley, *British Intelligence in the Second World War: Its Influence on Strategy and Operations* (London: HMSO, 1988), vol. 3, 511.

39. Hinsley, vol. 3, 513.

40. Hinsley, vol. 3, 329–30.

41. Reginald Turnill and Arthur Reed, *Farnborough: The Story of RAE* (Robert Hale: London, 1980), 85.

42. Jones, "Scientific Intelligence," 417, and Turnhill and Reed, *Farnborough,* 87.

43. Turnhill and Reed, *Farnborough,* 86–87.

44. PRO, ADM 223/93, and Hinsley, vol. 2, 235–39.

45. Lewin, *The Other Ultra,* 237.

46. Lewin, *The Other Ultra.*

47. PRO HW 1/3108.

48. Hinsley, vol. 3, 617–19.

ONE FIGHTERS

Arado Ar 240/440

Rare photograph of Arado Ar 240 in flight. Three photographs of the aircraft were captured during the Allied invasion of Sicily in August 1943. [AIR 40/121]

War and Intelligence History

The Arado Ar 240 was designed as a "heavy fighter-bomber" and first flew in May 1940. It was an aerodynamically adept aircraft with excellent performance. Two entered service during 1941, flying reconnaissance missions over England, successfully avoiding interception due to their speed. However, the aircraft was dogged by instability problems and was rejected for mass production in favor of the Me 210—somewhat ironically, considering that plane's own aerodynamic problems. The Ar 440 *schnellbomber* (fast bomber), a development of the Ar 240, showed promising test results but was rejected in the 1944 production program in favor of Dornier's revolutionary Do 335 "push-pull" aircraft. Allied air intelligence commented in August 1944, "Thank the German Air Force for not having accepted this plane."

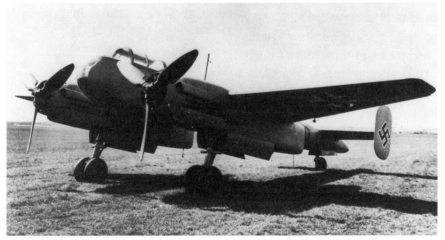

The V3 prototype of the Arado 240. This prototype was developed for dive-bombing and reconnaissance, first flying in late summer 1940. It lacked the propeller bosses added to later versions. [AIR 40/121]

Data File

(ARADO AR 440A-0) DIMENSIONS

Wingspan	54 ft. 5 in.
Length	39 ft. 9 in.
Height	15 ft. 3 in.
Max. Speed	466 mph
Range	1,248 miles
Engines	2 × Daimler Benz DB 603 G
Armament	2 × MK 108 cannon, 2 × MG 151/20, 2 × MG 131, 1 × MG 151/20
Bomb load	1,000 kg
Crew	2

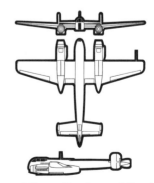

AI issued these drawings of the Arado 240 in November 1943. [AIR 40/120]

Focke-Wulf Fw 187 Falke (Falcon)

A pilot is strapped into his Fw 187. The aircraft's cockpit was so narrow that as can be seen here, some of the instruments were placed on the inside of the engine cowling. [AIR 40/187]

War Record

The Fw 187 first flew in spring 1937, having been designed without an RLM specification. Despite its superior performance in comparison to the Bf 110, it was not selected for production for the heavy fighter role, partly because it was too short to accommodate rear armament. Its cabin was so small that some instruments were placed outside the cockpit.

A few *"falke"* were unofficially deployed in Norway with 13/ZG 77 with successful results; Bf 110 aircrew preferred them. The aircraft was also used by the Focke-Wulf Company to defend its Bremen plant from Allied bombers. A few of the aircraft were painted in false Luftwaffe markings to fool Allied air intelligence into thinking they were in service.

Intelligence History

September 1940. Article appears in the Swedish press about a fighter being built at Focke-Wulf's Bremen plant. Built to same specification as Bf 110 but with reportedly superior performance, it was very maneuverable, fast, and possessed extraordinary firepower.

4 January 1941. Air attaché Belgrade reports Fw 187 has excellent aerodynamic form, is the fastest *zerstörer* in use at the front, possesses flying and fighting qualities supposedly better than Bf 110.

Data File

(FW 187 A-0) DIMENSIONS

Wingspan	50 ft. 2½ in.
Length	36 ft. 5½ in.
Height	21 ft. 7 in.
Max. Speed	326 mph
Ceiling	32,800 ft.
Engines	2 × 730 bhp Jumo 210
Armament	4 × MG 17, 2 × MG FF cannon
Crew	1

An Fw 187 warms up its engines. The fighter possessed better performance than its two main contemporaries from Messerschmitt, the Bf 109 and 110, but despite this, it never received any production orders from the RLM. [AIR 40/187]

1941. POW source declares the Fw 187 probably better than Bf 110 but came out too late to compete with it; Luftwaffe standardization resulted in its not going to operational units.

13 July 1941. From U.S. naval attaché, Vichy France—French journal described Fw 187 as successor to Bf 110.

12 August 1943. AI report: about twelve manufactured, then series discontinued. ADI (K) report, five aircraft assembled at Neuenland during 1942 then production stopped; believed to be due to difficulty in getting engines.

Side view of an Fw 187. The lack of markings suggests it had only recently left the production line. [AIR 40/124]

Focke-Wulf Fw 190

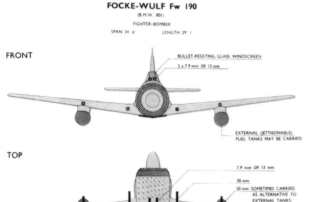

FOCKE-WULF Fw 190
(B.M.W. 801)
FIGHTER-BOMBER
SPAN 34' 6"   LENGTH 29' 1"

FRONT

BULLET-RESISTING GLASS WINDSCREEN
2 x 7.9 mm OR 13 mm

EXTERNAL (JETTISONABLE)
FUEL TANKS MAY BE CARRIED

A vulnerability and armament diagram of an Fw 190 produced by AI in 1944. It features a BMW 801 engine, which also powered the earlier versions of the Focke-Wulf fighter. [AIR 40/5]

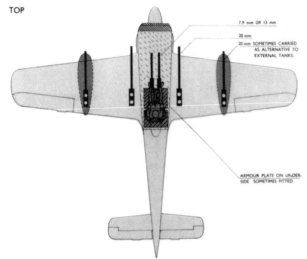

TOP

7.9 mm OR 13 mm
20 mm
20 mm SOMETIMES CARRIED AS ALTERNATIVE TO EXTERNAL TANKS.

ARMOUR PLATE ON UNDER-SIDE SOMETIMES FITTED

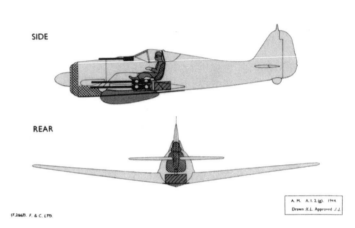

SIDE

REAR

A.M. A.I.2.(g). 1944
Drawn :K.L. Approved :J.J.

War Record

As early as 1937 the RLM issued a requirement for a replacement for the Bf 109 as the Luftwaffe's main fighter. Consequently, Kurt Tank, Focke-Wulf's designer, produced one of the truly great aircraft in aviation history.

When it first entered service over France in August 1941, the RAF could not believe its pilots' reports that the new Spitfire Mark V was being outclassed. The only shortcoming of the Fw 190 A-1 was its relatively light armament, four 7.9 mm machine guns. In speed and all other major factors, the Fw 190 outperformed all Allied fighters when it was introduced. Luftwaffe pilots aptly dubbed their new machine with the nickname *Würger* (Butcher Bird).

The Fw 190's first major operation came when it was employed to give fighter cover to the "Channel dash" made by the battlecruisers *Scharnhorst* and *Gneisenau* and the heavy cruiser *Prinz Eugen* from Brest on 12 February 1942. The Fw 190s decimated the hopelessly outdated Swordfish biplane torpedo bombers sent by the British to intercept the warships.

The next major encounter with the RAF came during the Dieppe raid. Following the capture of an intact Fw 190, the RAF analyzed the plane and hurriedly pushed the Spitfire Mark IX into service to counter it. The British and Canadians were surprised on 19 August 1942 when Fw 190 A-3/111 fighter-bombers flew in below the RAF fighter cover to sink two ships involved in

Data File

(FW 190D-9) DIMENSIONS

Wingspan	34 ft. 5½ in.
Length	33 ft. 5½ in.
Height	11 ft.
Max. Speed	426 mph
Ceiling	39,370 ft.
Range	519 miles
Engine	1 × 1,776 bhp Jumo 213A-1
Armament	2 × 0.51 in MG 131 2 × 20 mm MG 151 cannon 1 × 500 kg bomb
Crew	1

the Dieppe raid. In aerial combat Fw 190s accounted for ninety-seven of the 106 RAF losses that day.

In late 1942 and early 1943, Fw 190s were used in a series of "tip and run" raids on Southern England. Schnellkampfgeschwader 10 used Fw 190s in low-level pinpoint attacks; their Fw 190 A-3 and A-4 Jabos (*Jagdbomberstaffeln*) inflicted serious damage on several industrial targets. The RAF was forced to divert over twelve squadrons to counter these raiders, although antiaircraft fire caused most Luftwaffe casualties.

Surprisingly, the Fw 190 was introduced on the Eastern Front only in September 1942. Mostly used in the ground-attack role, heavily laden with bombs and cannon, the Fw 190s would often be escorted by Bf 109Gs. Fw 190s were heavily involved in the struggle for Sicily in August 1943. Although still more than a match for any Allied fighter, they suffered heavy losses due to the overwhelming weight of numbers of Allied aircraft that continually attacked German airfields.

However, by mid-1943 the growing scale of American daylight raids on Germany led to several *Gruppen* withdrawing from Russia and Italy to defend the Fatherland. At the end of August Fw 190s and Bf 109s shot down sixty and damaged a further 100 American heavy bombers raiding Regensberg and Schweinfurt.

Meanwhile the night-fighter wings NJG 1 and NJG 2 had started experimenting with the Fw 190. The plane was adopted in the *Wilde Sau* role; this involved solitary aircraft searching for bombers independently of the radar-detection system, which at the time was suffering heavily from RAF countermeasures. During August and September 1943, Fw 190 and Bf 109 Wild Boars of JG 300 accounted for 150 RAF heavy bombers. Although continu-

An Fw 190 displaying USAAF markings and a distinctive skull with eagle's wings insignia below the cockpit. [AIR 40/124]

The original V1 prototype of the Fw 190, which first flew on 1 June 1939, bearing civil markings. Unlike the production version it featured a ducted spinner. [AIR 40/124]

ing in this role until the end of the war, the relatively small number of planes available, typically twenty to thirty on any one night, limited the potential effect of this tactic.

During late 1943, heavily armed and armored Fw 190 A8/R-7s entered the battle against the USAAF. Göring personally ordered the formation of Stürmstaffel I, a unit made up of volunteers and pilots undergoing disciplinary action. The unit flew specially armored Fw 190 A6s. Before commencing each mission, pilots signed a declaration stating they would not return to base unless they had destroyed at least one enemy bomber—if all else failed, by ramming the opponent. More successful was JG 3, led by a Major Moritz, which employed more conventional tactics. On 7 July 1944, JG 3 shot down thirty-two American heavy bombers, for the loss of only two aircraft.

Following D-day in June 1944, the Luftwaffe rushed Fw 190s to northern France, mainly to be employed in the ground-attack role. Allied fighters still had great difficulty in shooting down Fw 190s, especially when they used their nitrous-oxide power boosts to outrun the hunters. However, Allied antiaircraft fire soon whittled down their numbers, the units being eventually withdrawn to Germany.

In fall 1944, the last significant Fw 190 variant was introduced. The D-9 is generally recognized as the best German piston-engine fighter of the Second World War. Its speed and maneuverability, coupled with a heavy cannon armament, enabled the Fw 190D to dogfight Allied fighters adequately and shoot down bombers.

Over two hundred Fw 190s took part in the last great offensive operation carried out by the Luftwaffe. On 1 January 1945, over eight hundred German aircraft launched Operation *Bodenplatte,* attacking Allied aircraft on the

A *Jabo* version of the Fw 190 with two 50 kg bombs under each wing. [AIR 40/124]

ground, but the loss of 214 experienced fighter pilots in the offensive was one the Luftwaffe could ill afford. Over eight hundred Fw 190s were being produced each month up till the end of the war, but by then the great scarcity of experienced aircrew and aviation fuel meant they could do little more than dent the Allies' air superiority on all fronts.

The Fw 190 was one major aircraft that largely took AI by surprise. Although aware of the type before it entered service, because of its similar appearance to the far inferior French Bloch 152 and American Vultee Vanguard 48A, AI had not rated it as a particular threat. Adolf Galland stated that if priority in production had been switched to Fw 190 earlier, he could have matched the Allies in the battle for air superiority in the West by the end of 1943.

Intelligence History

3 December 1940. Informant reports an Oberleutnant of JG27 claiming to have seen the new Fw 190 in flight achieving 375 mph.

10 April 1941. Informant tells AI the "[Fw] 190 proved a disappointment to the Germans," lacking speed and firepower. It was designed primarily as a bomber escort; hence the large fuel tanks.

23 November 1941. Report from 401 Squadron, Royal Canadian Air Force, of combat with Fw 190s. The Canadian pilots report the aircraft to have good maneuverability. They describe it as being similar in appearance to the Curtis Mohawk but much faster, apparently going into a "rocket climb."

16 June 1942. POW interrogation reveals Fw 190 being tested as a "Jabo" (ground attack aircraft); it was thought to be more suitable for this role than the Bf 109, due to its more robust airframe.

23 June 1942. Fw 190A2 lands at RAF Pemberley in South Wales. The pilot had been involved in combat over the Devon coast and made a navigational

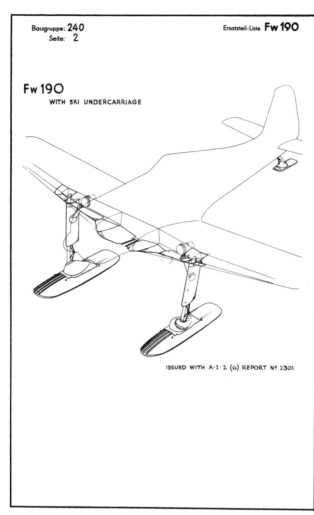

Baugruppe: 240
Seite: 2

Ersatzteil-Liste **Fw 190**

Fw 190
WITH SKI UNDERCARRIAGE

ISSUED WITH A·I·2 (G) REPORT Nº 2301

From the "Special List" of drawings, an Fw 190 design sporting skis [AIR 40/151]

error, believing he had reached France. The captured aircraft was examined and test flown at the RAE Farnborough, reaching a speed of 390 mph. The test pilot found it pleasant to fly, with light controls and possessing excellent aerobatic qualities, even at high speeds.

November 1942. Captured document reveals Luftwaffe factory submission to RLM summarizing possible future developments of the type. It stated that the armament would be increased to incorporate 30 mm cannon on the fighter version. Second, the ground-attack version would have extensive armor protection added to it. The Daimler-Benz 603 engine was also to be used, which would produce superior performance to the BMW 801; it would also feature a 30 mm cannon firing through the propeller hub. [These points probably refer to the B and C versions of the Fw 190, which did not progress past the prototype stage.]

20 January 1943. RLM technical instructions for Fw 190 are captured in the Middle East.

22 February 1943. Combat report from B-17 bomber crew. They had been damaged by flak and were returning to base over the French coast at 9,000 feet. Two Fw 190s dived to 150 feet above them and released cluster bombs that produced fifty to seventy scattered red and yellow bursts. This "aerial bombing" tactic was corroborated by a POW interrogation. The prisoner stated this aerial bombing was achieved by one aircraft flying alongside the bomber formation at the same altitude. The pilot would relay his position to the Fw 190s flying above, which could then correctly set the fuses on their bombs.

28 February 1943. Soviets report that increasing numbers of Fw 190s are being encountered in the air battle over Leningrad. Their tactics differed from Bf 109s in that they liked to attack head-on. The Russians believed this was because the Fw 190 possessed greater armor protection for the pilot and engine than did the Messerschmitt.

29 May 1943. First report of the Fw 109 D, featuring increased wing area and slots, being ready to enter operational service.

31 May 1943. At the request of the USAAF, AI issues a report on endurance of Fw 190 when attacking formations of B-17s. The report assumes that the Luftwaffe aircraft would be able to land at a base fairly near the combat, not necessarily the one it had taken off from. On this basis it was calculated that Fw 190s taking off from a twenty-five-mile radius of the bombers would have forty-two minutes combat time; those 150 miles away would have twenty minutes. The use of two external drop tanks would allow aircraft from up to 320 miles away to attack the bombers.

23 June 1943. POW reports the BMW 801–powered Fw 190 being withdrawn from the Western Front due to poor performance at high altitude. He claimed they were being converted to tank-busters for the Eastern Front, by fitting 37 mm cannon under the fuselages.

17 July 1943. Eighth Air Force Bomber Command reports recurrent sightings of Fw 190s using long-barreled rocket tubes. The rockets were being fired at up to 1,000 yards range, producing a twelve-foot-long muzzle flash. The projectile was judged to be almost fifty inches long, with a diameter of 8.27 inches and a high-explosive warhead of seventy to eighty pounds. In German reports the term *Gluehbruechen* (literally "glow bridge") was associated with the weapon. The tubes were approximately five feet long and probably are carried on bomb or drop-tank racks. It was estimated that carrying the weapon would reduce the plane's maximum speed to 365 mph.

1 September 1943. RAF Fighter Command reports pilots seeing Fw 190s emitting white smoke, apparently from an engine boost, which dramatically increased their speed.

16 September 1943. Report from 384th Group U.S. Eighth Air Force from a mission to Nantes: eight Fw 190s were seen to form up eight hundred yards behind the bomber formation in line abreast. Each was carrying three rockets, which they proceeded to fire one at a time, with short pauses between firings. They then peeled off singly to attack with machine guns and cannon.

1 October 1943. Training instruction sheets for pilots are captured in Sicily. These showed Fw 190 pilots how to attack ships. They had been issued by I/KSG3 dive-bombing school at Cognac as part of a two-month operational training course.

This Fw 190A-3 came into Allied hands on 23 June 1942. It had taken off from Morlaix in Brittany, France piloted by *Oberleutnant* Armin Faber of 7/JG 2 for a mission over Southwestern England. After dogfighting with Spitfires over the Devon coast, the pilot flew a reciprocal course in error and mistook the RAF airfield at Pemberley, South Wales for a friendly base. The captured aircraft was given the RAF designation MP 499 and was tested in mock combat with Spitfires. [AIR 41/49]

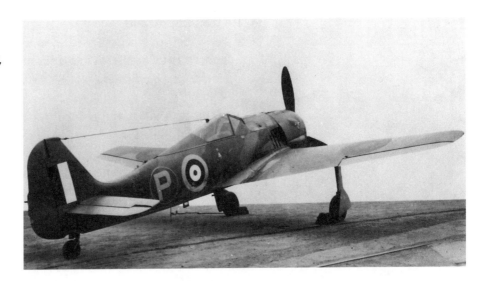

11 December 1943. Report from USAAF bomber crews from raid on Emden: they had been attacked by "wire-bombs." These weapons consisted of six-hundred-foot cables with twenty pound charges on the end of them. One B-17 had been hit by one of these, trailed from an Fw 190 flying above it. The wire had cut into the Fortress's nose, injuring the bombardier and navigator. The wire then swung up under the plane, and the charge detonated, blowing the exit door off. The bomber managed to make it back to base with one hundred feet of German wire still entangled around it.

12 June 1944. British diplomatic mission at Bern reports an Fw 190 has been equipped with two 75 mm radio-directed projectiles.

30 August 1944. Luftwaffe ferry pilot deserts and lands brand-new Fw 190A-8 in a field near Birchington. The cockpit features a new button labeled "Engine Performance Boost," and there is an additional twenty-five-gallon fuel tank fitted.

13 November 1944. A POW reveals experiments with upward-firing rocket mortars. One version saw twenty 0.8-in rocket tubes being aligned in two rows behind the cockpit. The tubes were angled upward and backward at seventy-four degrees. Each contained a four-inch-long projectile. The rockets had three fins, which unfolded on exiting the tubes. The firing was to be controlled by a *Magisches Auge* (Magic Eye), consisting of a three-inch diameter eye comprising four reduction lenses and a photo-electric cell. When the cell was activated by an image passing over it, a solenoid was energized to complete a circuit connected to the rocket tubes, firing the missiles. This weapon was tested in an experiment where an Fw 190 flew under an old He 177. The Heinkel bomber's pilot bailed out, and the weapon was fired, shooting it down. The "Magic Eye" would only work at a 180-foot range, so the fighter would have to fly directly below the bomber to trigger its rockets. Unsurprisingly, the prisoner felt the weapon would be extremely dangerous to use in combat. Another experiment featured fitting a rearward-firing 20 mm cannon. This would allow the aircraft to fire a "Parthian shot" as it pulled away from enemy aircraft.

1 January 1945. Several Fw 190s are shot down in Belgium during Ardennes offensive, first confirmation of Fw 190D-9 entering service.

19 January 1945. Captured Luftwaffe document shows plans for fitting Fw 190 with skis.

15 April 1945. Specimen found in factory featuring a new design for the tail end of the fuselage, to be constructed of wood.

21 May 1945. In a postwar interview with Allied intelligence officers, the designer of the Fw 190, Kurt Tank, claims to have flown one at 602 mph while diving from 33,000 feet.

Focke-Wulf Ta 152

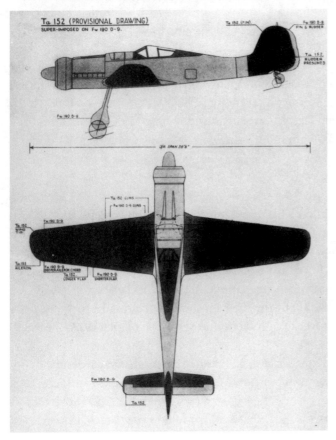

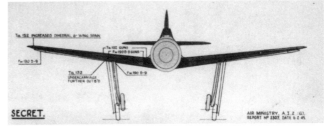

Initial sketches of the Ta 152 produced by AI on 6 February 1945 [AIR 40/209]

War Record

The Ta 152 was essentially a high-altitude version of the Fw 190D. The Ta 152 featured a lengthened fuselage and larger tail surface area. The first proto-type appeared in fall 1944. Erprobungskommando 152, at the Rechlin test center, carried out service trials. The first operational task allotted to the Ta 152 was to defend bases used by Me 262s, the jets being particularly vul-nerable just after takeoff and prior to landing. Several units received small numbers of the aircraft, most notably JG 301. On one notable occasion the Ta 152's designer, Kurt Tank, was flying a Ta 152H from Langenhagen to the Focke-Wulf plant at Cottbus when he was attacked by several USAAF P-51 Mustangs. Tank quickly operated his plane's MW-50 injection control and left the Americans behind. With its top speed of over 470 mph, and maneuver-ability akin to the Fw 190, the Ta 152 was one of the best piston-engine fight-ers ever developed. But for the familiar problems—lack of aviation fuel and experienced pilots—it could have posed great problems for the Allies had it entered service in significant numbers.

Intelligence History

31 January 1945. Officials from French SNASCO aviation company are inter-viewed. They had been commissioned to work on the wing and tail unit

Data File

(TA 152H-1) DIMENSIONS

Wingspan	47 ft. 6¾ in.
Length	35 ft. 5½ in.
Height	13 ft. 1½ in.
Max. Speed	472 mph
Ceiling	48,560 ft.
Range	745 miles
Engine	1 × 1,750 hp Jumo 213E-1
Armament	1 × Mark 108 30 mm, 2 × Mark 151/20 cannon
Crew	1

design for the Ta 152. The director of the Bordeaux office claims the plane was to be a night-fighter. The Paris branch asserts (correctly) that the aircraft was a development of the Fw 190D-1 and intended as a high-altitude fighter. German documents captured at SNASCO offices mentioned B, C, E, and H subtypes of the Ta 152.

11 May 1945. USAAF intelligence officers inspect an undamaged Ta 152H-1 at the Mittel Deutsche Metalwerke plant at Erfurt North aerodrome. The test pilot and flight engineer are interviewed. The pilot claims he had flown the aircraft up to 50,000 feet, its critical altitude being 32,000 feet. He states it could reach 315 mph with full throttle open at critical altitude.

Postwar

During his interrogation with Allied intelligence, Adolf Galland spoke glowingly of the potential of the Ta 152. It had been referred to as "the fighter for fighting fighters" and was to have been used exclusively against Allied escort fighters. Galland believed it to be the best fighter in the world, possessing greater maneuverability than any opponent. III/JG 301 had begun conversion training to the Ta 152 at Husum, just south of the Danish border, in March 1945. It was to take over the protection of synthetic oil plants from Me 163 units.

Milch planned to start series production in September 1944, despite opposition from Messerschmitt, but Allied air raids and pressure within the Rüstungsstab to maintain production figures prevented this. Then Soviet forces overran the factories due to start assembly in the winter of 1944–1945.

Kurt Tank, the designer of the Ta 152, when interviewed, claimed to have evaded six Mustangs while flying a Ta 152, by virtue of its superior speed. He revealed that a planned version of the aircraft featuring a Jumo 222 engine would have reached 500 mph.

Ta 152 C-0, seen here in winter camouflage and with the bad weather *Rüstätze* package, which included blind landing equipment and an autopilot [AIR 40/124]

Focke-Wulf Ta 154

Initial Air Intelligence sketch of the Ta 154 produced on 23 March 1945, drawn by H. Redmill [AIR 20/963]

War Record

The Ta 154 was intended as the Luftwaffe's response to the British Mosquito, the "Wooden Wonder." It was to be used as a night-fighter to combat RAF Bomber Command's ever-increasing assault on German cities. Ironically, it was an RAF night raid that effectively sabotaged the aircraft's chances of success. The all-wood airframe used Tego-Film adhesive to hold it together. A British raid on Wuppertal destroyed the Goldmann factory that produced this special glue. An inferior cold adhesive had to be used instead. This led to some of the production versions breaking up in mid-air, as the glue was incapable of withstanding the stresses produced in flight. The inability of Focke-Wulf to find an adequate adhesive prevented completion of a Luftwaffe order for 250 planes, and the type from entering service. Six of the completed aircraft were modified to form the bottom half of Mistel composite aircraft.

Intelligence History

29 July 1943. Letter to a German soldier is captured at Cosimo, Sicily. The female writer was a worker at a Focke-Wulf factory. She wrote, "Yesterday the first Ta 154 has come off the production lines. This machine is even more compact in construction than the Fw 190 and it is to be used as a one-seat fighter-bomber. They say the machine is to be used in the attack against Britain. More I cannot and must not say."

4 November 1943. French source reports Focke-Wulf completed plans for a new night-fighter, said to be faster than Fw 190.

Data File

DIMENSIONS (Ta 154)

Wingspan	52 ft. 6 in.
Length	41 ft. 2¾ in.
Height	11 ft. 9¾ in.
Max. Speed	404 mph
Ceiling	35,760 ft.
Range	1,156 miles
Engine	2 × Jumo 211N
Armament	2 × Mark 108, 2 × MG 151
Crew	2

The wreckage of a crashed Ta 154. Its belly landing on 30 April 1945 was witnessed by a Yugoslavian worker, later interviewed by AI. [AIR 40/210]

20 December 1943. Initial AI report shows the Allies were aware of Germans trying to imitate the Mosquito. Few technical details of the Ta 154 were known, but it was thought to be capable of 400 mph.

May 1944. An informant at the Veltrup factory in France reports six prototype steering columns for the Ta 154 being produced, which was followed by an order for 1,500 more.

June 1944. Production reported stopped due to inability to find appropriate adhesive. There was talk of producing an all-metal version of the aircraft, but the design was abandoned.

23 March 1945. Captured documents and PR suggest limited operational activity. Possibly being used as night-fighter.

The initial V1 prototype of the Ta 154 that made its maiden flight on 1 July 1943 at Langenhagen, later reaching a speed of 435 mph [AIR 40/124]

Heinkel He 100/112/113

War Record

The Luftwaffe rejected the Heinkel He 113 before the war began. However, in the spring of 1940, nine He 100s were employed in an elaborate intelligence hoax to deceive British intelligence into believing that the Germans had a new fighter in service. It succeeded, as during the Battle of Britain many RAF pilots reported combats with, and sightings of, the He 113. The British based their belief largely on POW interrogations and propaganda photographs. False unit markings, victory bars, and squadron formation appearances in the pictures, taken from magazines printed in occupied France, served to reinforce the belief.

Intelligence History

31 May 1940. He 113 is alleged to be in combat for the first time with the RAF over Dunkirk. A 213 Squadron Hurricane pilot claims to have shot one down.

10 June 1940. Fighter Command alerts RAF pilots about recognition difficulties associated with He 113. A case of mistaken identity due to its similarity in appearance with the Spitfire caused one pilot in combat to dive toward a "friendly" formation of 20 He 113s.

17 June 1940. POW interrogation reports that He 113 is in fact the He 100, developed by updating the He 112. This aircraft had been produced for export, with some completed models being ready to go to Russia. It is possi-

Data File

DIMENSIONS

Wingspan	31 ft. 4 in.
Length	27 ft. 3 in.
Height	8 ft. 4 in.
Max. Speed	406–437 mph
Engine	1 × DB 603
Armament	1 × 20 mm cannon, 2 × 13 mm machine guns
Crew	1

ble that some of these aircraft have formed a squadron for the defense of the Heinkel factory airfield at Marienehe. POW does not believe that the Luftwaffe employs large numbers.

30 June 1940. Air attaché Bern confirms the He 113 is a series production model of the He 112U prototype and that "it is a low-wing cantilever monoplane of all metal construction with a monocoque fuselage."

7 July 1940. Air attaché Bern reports rumor in Swiss aeronautical press that large numbers of German fighter units have been equipped with the He 113.

24 July 1940. As the Battle of Britain begins in earnest, a POW states under interrogation that He 113s are based in Holland and Norway, but definitely not in France.

1 August 1940. *Volkischer Beobachter* reports that the He 113 is the latest German night-fighter aircraft.

3 August 1940. RAF publication *The Aeroplane* states that three He 113s "have been shot down over this country during the past week."

27 August 1940. A POW of 6/JG 51 says that He 113 is not very satisfactory to fly and would probably not be widely adopted by the Luftwaffe. Source cannot confirm any details, as his information is based on hearsay.

4 January 1941. Air attaché Belgrade sends report based on "certain confidential information" that He 113 may be an elaborate German hoax in order to give the enemy the impression that the Luftwaffe possesses such a powerful fighter.

23 January 1941. AI produces first summary of He 113 based on all intelligence accumulated. It states that the aircraft can be employed in either a fighter or high-speed reconnaissance role. Additionally night-fighting equipment can be fitted. Although it is known that the Luftwaffe was using a few, AI believes that the Soviet Union is predominantly producing the He 113, under license.

20 June 1941. Berlin correspondent of *Giornale d'Italia* reports the He 113 has been "distinguishing itself amongst German fighters" and thus has been in series construction for several months.

30 December 1942. French intelligence reports that He 112/113 is being tested as a torpedo-bomber and is already employed as a night-fighter over Belgium, Holland, and the Rhineland. He 112Us built in 1939 were sold to Hungary, except a few left at the Rostock-Marienehe Heinkel factory airfield for tests.

28 June 1943. Lt. S. A. Peck of 432 Squadron positively identifies as

In AI Report 5823 (17 June 1940), a German POW stated that these photographs were taken for the benefit of the neutral press. They were issued for propaganda purposes to make possible customers believe that the He 113 was in regular use by the Luftwaffe as a frontline fighter aircraft. After examining these photographs the prisoner maintained that it was in fact the He 100. There had been talk of numbering the He 100, which was a development of the He 112, as the He 113. However, since the number 13 was unlucky, the prisoner said, this had been dropped. About 100 He 113s were built, with several squadrons being sold to Russia, Bulgaria, and Rumania. The He 113s excellent maneuverability made it potentially a good ground-attack aircraft. However, its broad undercarriage made it especially suitable for night flying. For this reason those few Luftwaffe flights equipped with the He 113, based around Kiel and in Norway, were allocated this role. [both AIR 40/237]

He 113 fighters that attacked his bomber formation on a raid over St. Nazaire. The gunners did not open fire until he ordered them to do so, as they mistook the enemy aircraft for RAF Spitfires. The Germans pressed home their attack on the bomber formation, diving in from twelve o'clock high.

Heinkel He 162 Salamander

This is the first image of the He 162, taken on 6 December 1944 by PR. The subsequent AI interpretation report (L.273) stated that the light-colored aircraft "may possibly be jet-propelled, but there is at present no conclusive evidence of this. Activity at SCHWECHAT, which for the past few months has been gradually increasing, appeared to be at a fairly high level on 6.12.44, and large numbers of personnel and vehicles were seen in movement near all the factory buildings." [Air 40/164]

War Record

By late 1944 Germany's desperate military situation, coupled with the need to reduce the impact of Anglo-American bombing on industrial output, led to a concentration on fighter production within the German aircraft industry. Consequently, the RLM issued a demand for a cheap and expendable jet fighter capable of a top speed of 750 km/h, armed with two 30 mm cannon, to be ready for production by 1 January 1945.

The RLM envisaged initial production of a thousand aircraft per month rising to a peak of four thousand. The aircraft was to be manufactured at Heinkel's Rostock-Marienehe factory, the Junkers Bernburg plant, and the Mittelwerke GmbH works at Nordhausen. To speed up production the RLM extensively subcontracted component manufacture and, where possible, used underground factories. The pilots were to come from the Hitler Youth.

Such a requirement and time frame for the design, testing, and production was unheard of. Yet Heinkel managed to meet the requirements and built the He 162 Salamander, or Volksjager (People's Fighter). The design was completed nine days after the RLM issued the specification and was approved by 30 October. The first prototype was flown on 6 December, when chief test pilot Flugkapitan Peter reached a top speed of 840 km/h during a twenty-minute trial. Peter lost his life four days later when the He 162 he was flying crashed during a high-speed, low-level pass over the Vienna-

Data File

DIMENSIONS

Wingspan	23 ft. 7½ in.
Length	29 ft. 8¼ in.
Height	8 ft. 4½ in.
Max. speed	522 mph
Ceiling	39,500 ft.
Range	410 miles
Engines	1 × BMW 003A-1 turbojet
Armament	2 × 20 mm cannon
Crew	1

Schwechat airfield, in front of an assembled host of political and military dignitaries.

Other than replacing the 30 mm cannon with 20 mm-caliber weapons, Heinkel kept to the original directive, and He 162 production models appeared during the first week of January 1945—a remarkable achievement, even by today's standards.

The initial jets were delivered to Erprobungskommando 162 based at Rechlin for operational trials and service evaluations. By February 1945 1/JG 1 began training on the He 162, swiftly followed by 2/JG 1 on 3 May 1945 at the Leck airfield in Schleswig-Holstein. On 4 May 1945 both *Staffel* were amalgamated into one composite *Gruppe* of about fifty jets. However, the *Gruppe* did not have enough fuel to fly its complement of jets. By the time the war ended three hundred He 162s had been built with a further eight hundred in varying stages of construction.

This is the set of images, included in AI2(g) Report 2335 of 21 April 1945, that was found by an American enlisted soldier among the debris at Weimar airfield. In the report, Wing Commander Proctor stated, "From these it is evident that the aircraft is powered with the new Heinkel-Hirth turbo-jet unit, now known to be designated as 109.11." [Air 40/2022]

Intelligence History

6 December 1944. PR sweep over the Heinkel factor airfield at Schwechat near Vienna reveals "an unidentified aircraft with a span of only about 25 ft., and in some ways resembling a small edition of the He 280." AI designates it Schwechat 25.

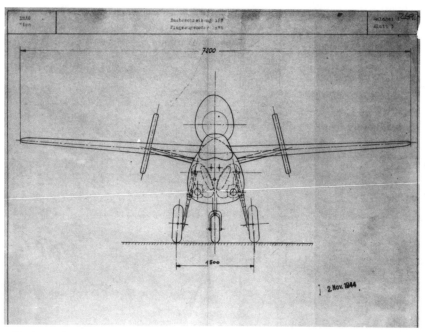

Allied produced technical drawings of the He 162 that accompanied AI Report A-686/RAF, dated 11 May 1945 [Air 40/2022]

29 December 1944. AI Interpretation Report L.273 on the 6 December PR sweep estimates the Schwechat 25 to be a midwing or low-wing monoplane of unusually low span-length ratio, with "almost certainly" a tricycle undercarriage.

24 March 1945. Wing Commander Proctor of AI2(g) writes Report 2326 about the Me 162 Volksjager, in which he says "a new and exceptionally interesting type of jet-propelled single-seat fighter is scheduled soon to play its part in the defense of the Reich." The report adds, "It is estimated that the 162 will have a maximum speed of about 500 mph at 20,000 ft."

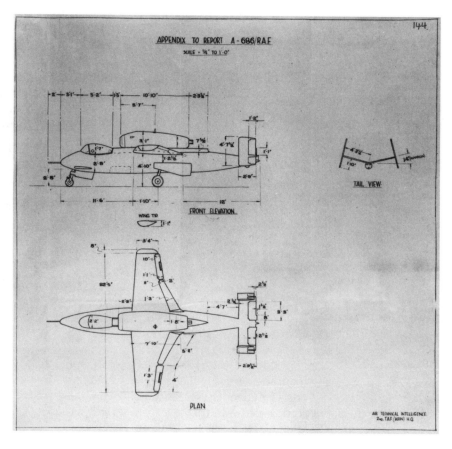

Heinkel operated a large underground assembly plant for He 162 production. It was eventually overrun by U.S. ground forces. [Air 40/2022]

After British ground forces captured the He 162 airfield at Leck, RAE personnel conducted several tests and evaluations before the jet fighter was "ferried" to Farnborough in England. This photograph is of the He 162 landing at Leck on 2 June 1945 in the test conducted to establish its ferry range. [Air 40/2022]

5 April 1945. AI Interpretation Report L.294 asserts there is little doubt that the Schwechat 25 "is the new German single-jet fighter, the Volksjager." The aircraft had by this time only been seen on five occasions at Schwechat, and AI still lacked good-quality photographs.

17 April 1945. U.S. Colonel Springer at HQ (Twelfth Army Group) issues first prints of the He 162 at ground level after several are captured from an officer's mess at Weimar.

21 April 1945. Wing Commander Proctor at AI2(g) receives the images of the He 162 Volksjager from Colonel Springer. The subsequent AI report (2335) asserts that the narrow-track tricycle undercarriage, which retracts into the fuselage, "suggests Ar 234 influence." The report also regards the configuration of the tail plane as "remarkable."

1 May 1945. AI2(g) Report 2340 on the He 162 is issued. The report is centered around a document arrived from Germany "issued by the Heinkel Works at Vienna." The report reveals an intriguing feature—"the special seat-type parachute" (an ejection seat).

In the trials conducted at Leck, the RAE staff were ably assisted by a German pilot (left) and engineer (right) who had worked extensively on the He 162. Commenting on the "ejecting pilots seat" the pilot said "It had been tried many times and always worked." The RAE examination found the cockpit controls were rugged and the oxygen tank insufficient. [Air 40/2022]

Heinkel He 219

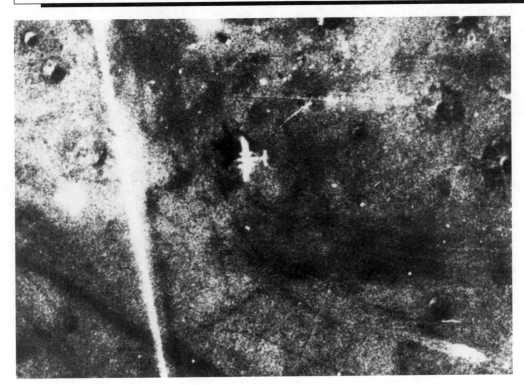

The "Schwechat 70" He 219 variant first spotted at Schwechat on 1 November 1944. From this photograph AI was able to determine that this version had an increased wingspan of seventy feet. [Air 40/111]

War Record

The Heinkel He 219 night-fighter (informally called the Uhu, or Owl) could have been one of the best aircraft in the Luftwaffe but was not extensively developed. Unfortunately for the Luftwaffe, it never received the attention it deserved, largely because Generalfeldmarschall Milch (Luftwaffe General Inspector) favored the Ju 388J. Additionally, the RLM was wary of the project from its inception.

The He 219 incorporated a number of novel features; for example, it was the world's first operational aircraft equipped with ejection seats. The He 219 was manufactured at Rostock, Vienna-Schwechat, and Mielec and Buczin in Poland.

In April 1943, a few He 219s flew in operations with I/NJG 11, based at Venlo in Holland. On 11 June 1943, Maj. Werner Streib shot down five Lancaster bombers in one sortie. In fact, the first six operational sorties flown by I/NJG 11 resulted in twenty enemy aircraft shot down, including six Mosquitoes. Although production was canceled in May 1944 due to the emergency fighter-construction program, deliveries were made to some units.

Despite the worsening fuel situation facing Germany, He 219s formed a significant part of the attacking force in Operation Gisella, the last great success of the Luftwaffe's night-fighter force. On the night of 4/5 March 1945, over a hundred Ju 88 and He 219 night-fighters took off in pursuit of 450 Lancasters, Halifaxes, and Mosquitos that had raided Ladbergen and Kamen in western Germany. In a perfectly executed plan, the German force trailed the bombers home and then strafed and bombed twenty-seven of Bomber Com-

Data File

DIMENSIONS

Wingspan	60 ft. 8¼ in.
Length	50 ft. 11¾ in.
Height	13 ft. 5½ in.
Max. speed	416 mph
Ceiling	40,025 ft.
Range	1,243 miles
Engine	2 × DB 603G
Armament	6 × 30 mm,
	2 × 20 mm cannon
Crew	2

mand's airfields. Additionally, twenty bombers engaged on training flights were shot down, for a loss of just three to six German planes.

Intelligence History

14 April 1943. A PR mission over the Schwechat Heinkel factory airfield photographs the He 219 for the first time, alerting AI to its existence.

3 October 1943. AI learns from a "most secret, not to be quoted" source that the He 219 is armed with 4 × 20 mm cannon and 4 × 13 mm machine guns, is powered by two DB603 engines, has a two-man crew, and excellent visibility as a night-fighter.

28 March 1944. Air attaché Stockholm files dispatch Ger. 70/44. He reports that the aircraft will soon be in its production phase and has been designed as twin-engine night-fighter, with radial engines driving four-bladed propellers. He believes that only German service personnel are working on the project and that series manufacture is being carried out at the Schwechat factory.

17 April 1944. Air attaché Stockholm reports the He 219 has a "remarkably steep" rate of climb from takeoff and that four or five are being constructed. The information is from a "source" at the Rostock-Marienehe airfield.

20 April 1944. PR missions over Schwechat reveal an increase in He 219 activity. A sweep conducted 3 April 1944 reveals sixteen at the airfield, the most seen at one time.

19 June 1944. Under interrogation, a POW discloses that he worked on the He 219 at the Rostock factory in July 1943. Output amounted to only two aircraft per week, mainly due to a lack of skilled labor. Completed machines were test flown by the factory's chief test pilot, Herr Schaab, and three other civil-

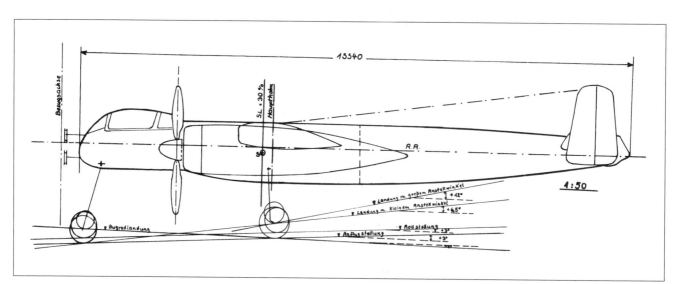

Captured German technical drawings of the He 219, dated 22 June 1944 [Air 40/111]

AI2(g) Report 2266 dated 27 September 1944 included this general-arrangement drawing. It was prepared from all the available information possessed about the external appearance of the He 219 night-fighter and was circulated among Allied air crews. [Air 40/111]

ian pilots. They were then handed over to a Luftwaffe contingent, consisting of a major, three lieutenants, and twenty other ranks, for ferrying to military airfields.

27 August 1944. AI Report SRA5595 declares that the He 219 long-range night-fighter is "filled with the latest inventions" and refers to the pilot being catapulted out of the aircraft, complete with his seat.

27 November 1944. AI Report 639/44 states the Heinkel Schwechat factory near Vienna was put out of commission by the heavy bombing raid on 26 June 1944.

7 January 1945. AI Report SRA5706 states He 219 requires an exceptionally long runway for takeoff.

22 February 1945. AI interrogation of POW reveals insights into the He 219 program. The prisoner, a former technician drafted into the army in mid-1944, claims that experimental work on the He 219 was originally undertaken at Schwechat in late 1942. Series production began in early 1944, and forty aircraft of the "08" type were constructed, accepted by the Luftwaffe, and placed in service. Weekly output at Schwechat never exceeded three aircraft, and production halted in June 1944 after the heavy bombing raids, after which manufacture was shifted to Rostock-Marienehe.

1 March 1945. AI learns that alterations to the cockpit of the He 219 held back full-scale series production throughout 1943.

21 March 1945. An 85 Squadron Mosquito XXX from RAF Swannington on high-altitude bomber escort to Bohlen engages and shoots down an He 219 night-fighter. The pilot, Flight Lieutenant Chapman, reported that after closing to within 1,000 feet he "visually identified a twin-engine A/C [aircraft] with rocket apparatus slung under the fuselage—He 219. Considerable quantities of flames and sparks were flying back preventing me from identifying the tail unit, so I decided to open fire at that range." The He 219 was shot down, exploding "on the ground with a tremendous glare."

The He 219 in the markings of the RAE "Farnborough Luftwaffe"
[Air 40/126]

Messerschmitt Bf 109

A Spitfire Mk.1 flown by Squadron Leader Henry Sawyer of 65 Squadron, RAF, on 24 July 1940, shot down this Bf 109E-1 of Stab III/JG26. This picture shows two RAF personnel examining the fuselage access panel. The pilot, *Oberleutnant* Werner Bartels, crash-landed the aircraft near Margate, in south-eastern England; he was wounded and taken prisoner. He had been escorting Do 17s on a raid on shipping in the Thames Estuary. [AIR 40/127]

War Record

The Messerschmitt Bf 109 stands as one of the truly great aircraft in aviation history. Over thirty-five thousand Bf 109s were produced, from the first early prototype in 1935 to the last one, manufactured in Spain, in 1956. Ironically both the first and last produced were powered by British-made Rolls Royce engines. The Bf 109 fought from the first to the last day of the Second World War in Europe and claimed more "kills" than any other aircraft in history.

The aircraft started life as one of the candidates to win the October 1935 German air ministry specification for a monoplane fighter to replace the Heinkel He 51 biplane. At the time, Messerschmitt were a relatively minor company with no track record in military aircraft, and it was not given much chance against its vaunted rivals, such as Heinkel. However, Willi Messerschmitt had other ideas. The legendary aircraft designer and entrepreneur came up with a plane that combined speed, acceleration, maneuverability, and a high rate of climb and dive in a way that was years ahead of its time. Aside from its exceptional performance, the Bf 109 was relatively cheap and easy to produce, a crucial factor in wartime.

The first operational Bf 109D-1s were delivered to the elite JG 132 Richthofen Geschwader in 1937. The plane first saw combat with the Condor Legion in the Spanish Civil War. Bf 109s quickly gained air superiority for the Falangist forces; the Soviet-built Loyalist fighters proved no match for

Data File

(BF 109 G-6) DIMENSIONS

Wingspan	32 ft. 6½ in.
Length	29 ft. 7 in.
Height	8 ft. 6 in.
Max. Speed	385 mph
Ceiling	37,895 ft.
Range	373 miles
Engines	1 × 1,475 hp DB 605 AM
Armament	1 × Mark 108, 2 × MG131
Crew	1

them in combat. Legendary Bf 109 aces like Werner Mölders gained their first victories during this conflict.

By the start of World War II, the Bf 109E "Emil" had largely replaced earlier variants in frontline Luftwaffe units. During the Polish campaign of 1939, Bf 109s easily outclassed the Polish air force's biplane fighters. The plane's first victory over an RAF aircraft came when JG 77 pilot Unteroffizer Alfred Held shot down a Wellington bomber on the second day of the war.

Luftwaffe successes continued in the Norwegian campaign and the blitzkrieg advance through Holland, France, and Belgium during May and June 1940. The battle in the skies over Dunkirk saw the first encounter between the Bf 109 and Supermarine Spitfire, the only contemporary aircraft that could match it. The duels between Messerschmitt 109s and Spitfires became the stuff of legend. There is still controversy over which was the superior fighter. Both were developed in series of modifications throughout the war. Their duel continued into the late 1940s, when Egyptian Spitfires fought Czech-built Israeli Bf 109s over Palestine.

The Battle of Britain saw the Luftwaffe's first major defeat of the war. In straight dogfights the Bf 109Es at least matched their RAF adversaries. The German aircraft possessed one distinct advantage, a fuel-injection system that allowed it to break off a combat if in trouble and outclimb its opponent. In early skirmishes the German airmen's greater experience told. Many had fought in Spain, Poland, and the battle for France. Their tactics involved the employment of a *schwarm*—a loose formation of four aircraft spread out like the fingers of a hand. The RAF initially countered this with strictly regimented

A two-seater training version, the Bf 109G-12 was converted from a Bf 109 G-5 airframe. [AIR 40/127]

This Bf 109G-6/U2, piloted by Lt. Horst Prenzel, landed by mistake at RAF Manston on 21 July 1944. It was test-flown at RAE and used in mock combats with Mustangs and Spitfires. It crashed during takeoff in November 1944 and was written off. [AIR 40/192]

V formations. The *schwarm* allowed fighters to cover each other far more effectively and relieved pilots of the effort of maintaining strict formation. However, the British pilots quickly began to copy their opponents' tactics, and the Germans' disadvantages became clearer. The Messerschmitt's greatest handicap was its short range. This allowed for only twenty minutes' combat time on missions over southern England. In addition, Bf 109s had to protect the vulnerable Luftwaffe bombers. Ace and fighter leader Adolf Galland likened the situation to "a dog on a chain trying to catch flies." The Luftwaffe's intended long-range bomber-escort fighter, the Bf 110, proved inadequate against RAF Hurricanes and Spitfires and, ironically, needed the protection of Bf 109s itself. Unable to sustain its losses, the Luftwaffe switched to night bombing of Britain.

During 1941 the Bf 109F "Franz" came into service. It is regarded as the best version of the fighter, with a powerful combination of performance and armament. The Balkan and Russian campaigns of 1941 saw the Bf 109 dominating the skies once more. In North Africa, Bf 109Fs of JG 27 were more than a match for RAF P-40 Kittyhawks and Hurricane Mark IIs.

The story of the Messerschmitt 109 would not be complete without mention of two legendary aces. Eric "Bubi" Hartmann's record of 352 kills remains a world record, likely never to be matched. Hartmann achieved this feat exclusively in the Bf 109 on the Eastern Front. The red heart he sported on the nose of his aircraft became an emblem of fear for Soviet pilots; indeed, he was forced to remove the heart, as his opponents would flee to avoid combat when they saw it. His style was based on his supreme skill as an airman. He would fly very close to his victims before opening fire, swerving away at the last moment. He crash-landed several times, but always due to his plane's being damaged by debris from exploding victims rather than from Soviet bullets. Hartmann survived the war and 10 years as a prisoner in the Soviet Union.

Gun camera shot of a damaged Bf 109 in flight. Smoke can be seen coming out of the port wing and fuselage, and the drop tank appears to have been hit. [AIR 40/127]

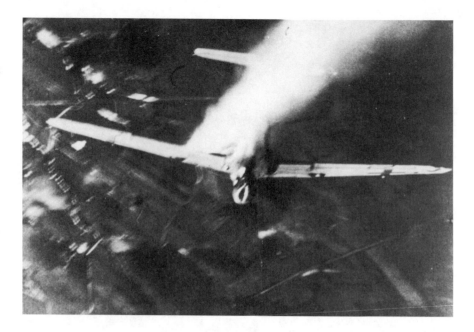

Hans-Joachim Marseilles's style of dogfighting contrasted sharply with that of Hartmann's. He relied on his supreme skill as a marksman for his kills. Marseilles possessed uncanny ability in the three-dimensional deflection shooting that was key to a fighter pilot's success. He would often return from missions with only half his cannon shells spent, despite having shot down several Allied aircraft. On one day Marseilles shot down no less than seventeen enemy fighters. His total of 158 kills does not put him near the top of the German aces' scoring charts; however, when it is considered that almost all his victories were against modern RAF fighters, not the more vulnerable bombers or obsolete enemy aircraft on the Eastern Front, and that they were achieved in less than two years, Marseilles has to be recognized as one of the great aces. He was killed in an accident in September 1942 when bailing out after engine failure. Hundreds of German and Italian troops and aviators attended his funeral.

When the USAAF's Eighth Air Force began daylight raids over the Reich, Bf 109s were deployed in a different role. The heavy armor and armament of the American B-17 and B-24 heavy bombers led to the introduction of the Bf 109G, possessing a more powerful engine and extra cannon armament. The weight of these additions somewhat hampered the performance of the aircraft; the Bf 109's airframe was small and designed for maneuverability. But the aircraft could still hold its own against new generations of Allied fighters when in the hands of experience pilots. The Bf 109G, the most numerous of the Bf 109 types, would often fly as cover for more heavily armed Fw 190s, which would attack the bombers.

Bf 109s were also employed as *wilde-sau* against the RAF's night offensive (see Fw 190 for tactics). The aircraft achieved some success in this role, but the relatively small numbers deployed could only dent Bomber Command's onslaught on German cities.

Along with the more common variants and roles of the Bf 109, there were some more outlandish variants of the aircraft. The Bf 109T was developed for the never-completed aircraft carrier *Graf Zeppelin*. The Bf 109H was a high-altitude version with a pressurized cockpit. Late in the war Bf 109s were deployed as one half of *Mistel* composite aircraft (see *Mistel*). Another tactic was to drop 550-pound bombs from above enemy bomber formations. One lucky direct hit destroyed three B-17s.

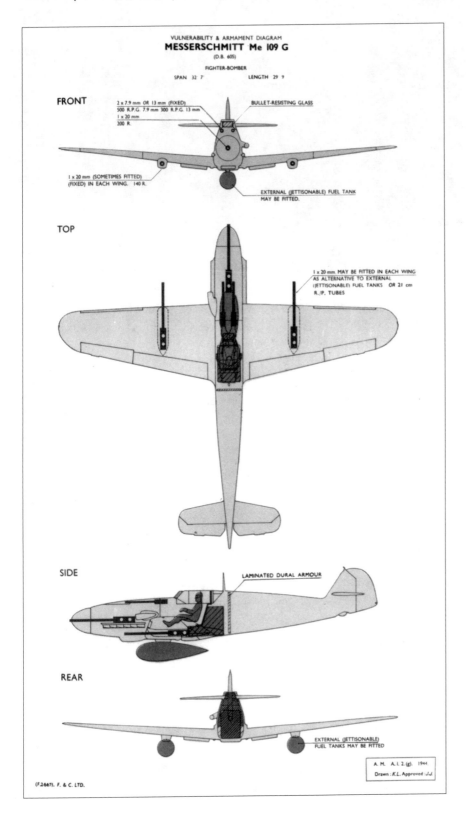

VULNERABILITY & ARMAMENT DIAGRAM
MESSERSCHMITT Me 109 G
(D.B. 605)
FIGHTER-BOMBER
SPAN   32 7'   LENGTH   29 9

FRONT

2 x 7.9 mm OR 13 mm (FIXED)   BULLET-RESISTING GLASS
500 R.P.G. 7.9 mm 300 R.P.G. 13 mm
1 x 20 mm
200 R.

1 x 20 mm (SOMETIMES FITTED)
(FIXED) IN EACH WING. 140 R.

EXTERNAL (JETTISONABLE) FUEL TANK
MAY BE FITTED.

TOP

1 x 20 mm MAY BE FITTED IN EACH WING
AS ALTERNATIVE TO EXTERNAL
(JETTISONABLE) FUEL TANKS OR 21 cm
R./P. TUBES

SIDE

LAMINATED DURAL ARMOUR

REAR

EXTERNAL (JETTISONABLE)
FUEL TANKS MAY BE FITTED

A. M. A.I. 2 (g). 1944.
Drawn : K.L. Approved : J.J.

(F.2667). F. & C. LTD.

A vulnerability and armament diagram of a Bf 109G. The drawings show the plane carrying drop tanks or additional 20 mm cannon under each wing. [AIR 40/5]

Two RAF officers examine the wreckage of a crashed Bf 109 in the Western Desert. The distinctive African woman and lion's head symbol of I/JG27 can be seen on the aircraft's nose. [AIR 40/127]

The German aircraft industry produced more Bf 109s in 1944 than in any other year. But by then the chronic shortage of experienced pilots and aviation fuel meant it was too late for the Luftwaffe to mount an effective challenge for air superiority. To combat the huge American daylight bomber formations, many combinations of extra cannon and 21 cm rockets were employed. While this may have helped to destroy bombers, the resultant extra weight impaired speed and agility; this made the aircraft more vulnerable to escorting P-51 Mustang and P-47 Thunderbolt fighters. The Bf 109K was the last variant to enter service; it was essentially a 109G with an improved engine and minor enhancements.

The Bf 109 fought on to the last day of the war. On 9 May 1945, Maj. Victor Gobulev of the Red Air Force shot down a Bf 109 over Prague; he was credited with the last kill of the war in Europe.

Intelligence History

September 1939. French capture a working Bf 109D with wooden airscrew and an armament of two machine guns. A French test pilot subsequently crashed it. Two further Bf 109s were captured intact by the French, including a Bf 109E. Their report concluded that the Messerschmitt plane featured many ingenious solutions to the problems of designing fighter aircraft. The clean lines of the airframe gave outstanding aerodynamic qualities, and the plane was easy to manufacture and service.

8 November 1939. Two Bf 109s are shot down by French at Antilly, in eastern France. They are badly damaged, but inspection shows they have two-blade propellers, suggesting an early version.

July 1940. The RAF carries out a comparative trial between a captured Bf 109 and a Spitfire. It claims that the Spitfire could outperform the Bf 109 in climb, speed, and maneuverability. The Bf 109 is also tested against the Bolton Paul Defiant fighter; the trial results (somewhat incredibly) state the Defiant could match the German aircraft in combat.

26 May 1941. AI acquires a memo from the RLM in Berlin that includes a copy of Messerschmitt's maintenance instructions for the Bf 109F.

20 July 1941. K Report states the Bf 109F has handling superior to the Bf 109E; however its wings are less stable. Hauptmann Balthasar, Commodore of the Richtofen Geschwader, is reported to have been killed when his wings tore off while chasing a Spitfire in a snaking dive. Other instances of wings tearing off Bf 109Fs are also reported.

June 1941. Another trial is carried out on a captured Bf 109 at the RAE Farnborough. This finds the German plane to be less maneuverable than RAF fighters. The report does acknowledge the Bf 109's better rate of climb, performance at high altitude, and diving ability, and its engine's ability to perform at negative "g." Report also notes the introduction of the Bf 109F. It was believed [wrongly] that changes to the airframe—rounding the wingtips and removing the tail struts—had been intended to make the Bf 109 closer in appear-

A row of Bf 109Gs outside a hangar. The aircraft in the foreground appears to be having its engine tested; other aircraft are undergoing various stages of engine and general maintenance by the "black men," as Luftwaffe ground crew were known. [AIR 40/127]

ance to the Spitfire. It was also thought [wrongly] that the Bf 109F had less armament than the E version.

7 December 1941. A tropical version of the Bf 109 is captured at Gazala, in North Africa. It features an air cleaner for desert flying, which when tested proved 40 percent less efficient than British filters.

13 April 1942. RAF Middle East reports shooting down a Bf 109F of 6/JG3. It is found with a container carrying ninety-two SD2 2 kg antipersonnel bombs, used for attacking supply convoys and soft targets. This indicates that the Bf 109 was being used in a fighter-bomber role. A Luftwaffe POW also states the Bf 109 to be an excellent aircraft but too sensitive for desert operations. Its high landing speed and narrow undercarriage resulted in many accidents.

June 1942. Several reports are received of Bf 109s using the "ha ha" process, by which the plane's engine had extra cylinders that forced gas through the engine. There was confusion in Air Intelligence as to whether this was designed as a power boost, which reportedly produced an extra 100 mph speed for five to ten minutes, or produced smoke to fool Allied pilots into thinking the plane was damaged.

21 July 1944. A Bf 109G-6 lands at Manston Airfield in Kent; the pilot had thought he was in Germany. The new Revi 16B gunsight is noted, as is a new sixty-six-gallon drop tank.

July 1944. A Bf 109 G-14 is shot down by antiaircraft fire at Fontenay-le-Pensel, Normandy. It had obviously been rushed from the factory with paintwork and wiring not completed to previous standards.

11 November 1944. A report is issued on the development of armament of the Bf 109. In 1937 it had 2 × MG 17; 109G has three times the engine power and up to 3 × MG 151 and 2 × MG 131, but added firepower detracts from handling and performance.

Prewar Bf 109

Messerschmitt Bf 110

This reconnaissance Bf 110 of Aufklärungs-gruppe 14 took off from Cherbourg on 21 July 1940, only to be shot down by RAF Hurricanes of 238 Squadron near Goodwood, southeastern England. It was then repaired and flown at Farnbourough. [AIR 40/127]

War Record

Before the war, Göring was convinced that a "heavy fighter," or *zerstörer* (destroyer) aircraft, would be a crucial weapon in any air war. A plane with the range to escort bombers deep into enemy territory and the armament to shoot down hostile bombers threatening the Reich would, he believed, be a trump card. The first campaigns of 1939 and early 1940 seemed to have proved Göring right. However, when pitted against more agile, single-engine modern fighters, the Bf 110 suffered badly. Despite its ultimate failure in its originally intended role, however, the Bf 110 continued in service through-out the war and was produced in great numbers, outlasting several aircraft designed to replace it.

Resulting from a 1934 RLM specification, the Bf 110 entered service in numbers in early 1939. Specially created *zerstörergruppen* took delivery of Bf 110C-0s, which featured cannon armament. During the Polish campaign the Bf 110s performed well, matching the kill rates of the Bf 109s. Indeed, the highest-scoring ace of the campaign was Hauptmann Hannes Gentzen, a Bf 110 pilot of I/ZG 2. December 1939 saw the *zerstörer* live up to its name. Twenty-four RAF Wellingtons raiding the Heligoland Bight were pounced upon by Bf 110s; nine were shot down, and three more failed to return. The aircraft showed that against bombers, its heavy armament and superior speed could produce results.

The Messerschmitt 110s also played a crucial role in the invasion of Nor-way in April 1940. Their range made them the only fighters capable of reach-

Data File

(BF 110 C) DIMENSIONS

Wingspan	53 ft. 4¾ in.
Length	39 ft. 8½ in.
Height	11 ft. 6 in.
Max. Speed	349 mph
Ceiling	32,800 ft.
Range	528 miles
Engines	2 × 1,100 hp DB 601A
Armament	2 × MG FF cannon, 4 × MG 17, 1 × MG 15
Crew	2

This Bf 110 took part in a little known action of World War II. It fought against the British in Iraq in support of German-backed rebels who sought to overthrow British rule. The Sonderkommando Junck aircraft crash-landed at Fallujah in the Iraqi desert. Having been repaired and painted in RAF colors, it was christened the "Belle of Berlin" and test-flown at Habbaniya and Heliopilis, Egypt. [AIR 40/127]

ing Norway until airfields there were overrun. The capture of Oslo's main air base involved the Bf 110 in one of the most audacious operations of the war. It was planned that Ju 52s would start the operation by dropping two hundred paratroopers to neutralize the ground forces stationed at the airfield. A second wave of Ju 52s would then land on the strip and disembark more troops and equipment to consolidate its capture. However, the first wave of transports encountered fog over the sea and decided to turn back to their base in Denmark. By this time the second wave had already taken off and was headed for Oslo. It ignored the recall order and pressed on. When the first Ju 52 attempted to land, the Norwegian defenses opened up, and it was forced to climb away. Bf 110s commanded by Hauptmann Hansen saw this and realized the plan had gone awry. Showing incredible bravery, the fighter pilots decided to land and neutralize the Norwegian defenses themselves. Using the rear machine guns from their planes, they managed to pull this off, so saving the whole operation from disaster.

The Battle of Britain proved a turning point in the Messerschmitt heavy fighter's career. When pitted against Hurricanes and Spitfires, the Bf 110's lack of agility, slow acceleration, and weak rear armament were cruelly exposed. During Luftflotte 5's disastrous raid on Scotland from Norway on 14 August

1940, the Bf 110 provided the sole escort, as the Bf 109 lacked the necessary range to take part. A third of the Bf 110s were shot down; the bombers were scattered and decimated by RAF fighters. As the Battle of Britain wore on, the ludicrous situation arose where the Bf 110 "escort fighters" had to be escorted themselves by Bf 109s. During September 1940 alone, 120 Bf 110s were lost.

Despite this setback, the aircraft continued to serve in all theaters. It was in the night-fighter role that the type achieved its greatest success. Away from opposition fighters, its "destroyer" capabilities could work once more. During 1942, Bf 110s shot down two hundred RAF night raiders. Innovations included fitting of airborne radar and the ingenious *schräge musik* (literally, jazz music). This consisted of an upward-firing cannon; the fighters could position themselves underneath a bomber for firing without the enemy's being aware of them. Many British bombers were shot down in this way without their crews ever having seen their opponent.

When USAAF B-17 and B-24 bombers started deep daylight penetration raids into Germany, the Bf 110 returned to its original day *zerstörer* role. Armament was progressively increased and often included 21 cm rocket tubes. While the American bombers' concentrated fields of fire made them harder opponents than Wellingtons, the Bf 110 performed creditably once more. That was to change when the plane's nemesis, single-engine fighters, returned to the scene. Early 1944 saw increasing numbers of long-range P-47s and P-51Ds escorting the bomber streams all the way to their targets and back. 16 March 1944 proved a disastrous day for the aircraft, as predatory

In-flight shot of a Bf 110C [AIR 40/127]

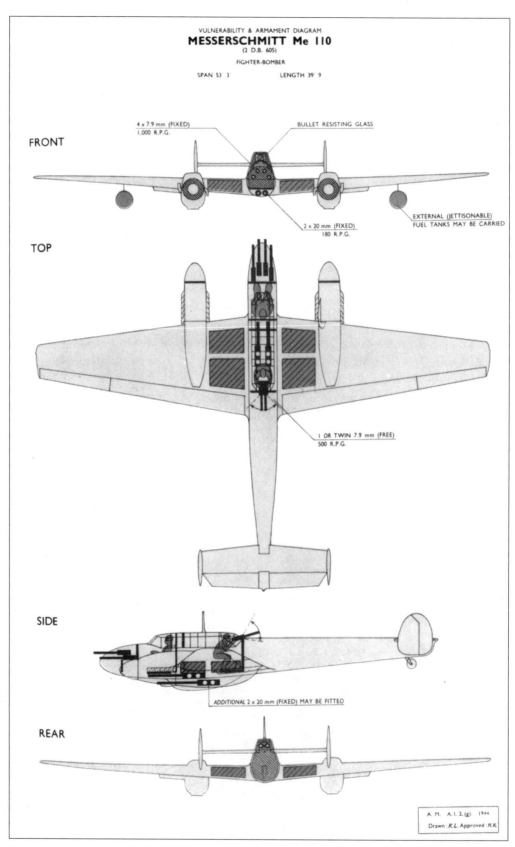

VULNERABILITY & ARMAMENT DIAGRAM
MESSERSCHMITT Me 110
(2 D.B. 605)
FIGHTER-BOMBER

SPAN 53' 3"   LENGTH 39' 9"

FRONT

4 x 7.9 mm (FIXED)
1,000 R.P.G.

BULLET RESISTING GLASS

2 x 20 mm (FIXED)
180 R.P.G.

EXTERNAL (JETTISONABLE)
FUEL TANKS MAY BE CARRIED

TOP

I OR TWIN 7.9 mm (FREE)
500 R.P.G.

SIDE

ADDITIONAL 2 x 20 mm (FIXED) MAY BE FITTED

REAR

A. M. A. I. 2. (g). 1944
Drawn : K.L. Approved H.K.

Vulnerability and armament diagram of a Bf 110G, featuring drop tanks,
four forward-firing 7.9 mm machine guns, plus a pack of two 20 mm
cannon under the fuselage and two rearward-firing 20 mm cannon
[AIR 40/5]

USAAF Mustangs shot down twenty-six out of forty-three of ZG 76's Bf 110s present. Shortly afterward the Bf 110 was forced once more to withdraw from the daylight air war. However, it continued in service at night and on the Eastern Front. In that theater the aircraft was increasingly used in a ground-attack role.

Intelligence History

1 May 1939. A Bf 110 crashes at Pontarlier, France, near the Swiss border. The crew was Luftwaffe noncommissioned officers in civilian clothes, possibly defecting. The aircraft featured one cannon and six machine guns for armament. It also featured a bomb-release mechanism for Lanzröhr 3 kg antipersonnel bombs, suggesting a ground-attack role.

1 August 1939. Just days before the outbreak of World War II, a British engineer visits the Messerschmitt development works at Augsburg, Bavaria. He is allowed to inspect a Bf 110 and speaks to Willi Messerschmitt, who is very open. He is told there were initial problems when all the Bf 110's forward armament fired simultaneously, due to vibration. This was rectified when the position of the armament was staggered and shock absorbers were fitted. At this stage there was no provision for bomb racks on the aircraft.

This Bf 110 features a large-caliber cannon under its nose and 21 cm rocket tubes under the wings. The lack of radar antennas suggests this to be a day *zerstörer* version. [AIR 40/127]

17 February 1941. A POW reports having been present at Rechlin test base when a mock combat was staged between a Bf 110 and a captured early-model Hurricane. The staff at Rechlin are said to have been very upset when the Hurricane clearly won the contest.

13 September 1941. The first report is received of the Bf 110 in use as a night-fighter.

1 December 1941. A report is received of Bf 110s operating in a ground-attack role, using a 30 mm cannon, in the western desert of North Africa.

16 January 1942. The Bf 110 is replaced in the reconnaissance role by the Bf 109, due to high loss rates.

16 March 1942. A Bf 110 that had crash-landed in England in July 1940 is repaired and test-flown at the RAE Farnborough. Following mock combats with Hurricane Mark 1s and Spitfire Mark Vs, it is ascertained that the Bf 110's rear armament had a limited field of fire. Attacking fighters were advised to attack from behind and below, or from the quarter or beam positions. Unsurprisingly, the single-engine fighters easily outmaneuver the Bf 110.

2 March 1943. A report is received from Russia of employment of fixed rear and downward-firing 30 mm cannon for ground attack.

27 October 1943. USAAF B-17 crews report sighting Bf 110s fitted with

Two Luftwaffe ground crew fit an ETC 500 bomb under the fuselage of a Bf 110. [AIR 40/127]

20 mm and 37 mm cannon as well as rocket projectors, opening fire from two thousand yards.

December 1943. AI interrogates a POW who had been an armament fitter with 3/NJG 1. He had fitted remotely controlled, upward-firing pairs of cannons immediately behind the wireless/telegraphy operator's position. They were designed so the aircraft could approach bombers from below and rake their undersides.

21 May 1944. A Bf 110 crashes in Switzerland. The crew tries to destroy the Lichtenstein radar equipment but is stopped by Swiss troops. The plane also featured *schrage musik* cannon behind the cockpit, angled upward at sixty degrees.

17 June 1944. The British diplomatic mission in Bern reports *schrage-musik* tactics. Night-fighters would fly below and slightly behind and to one side of their intended victims. They would aim for an aircraft's wings, to avoid detonating the bomb payload and being hit by debris.

This picture appeared in a German magazine with the caption "The new Messerschmitt bomber," as part of an elaborate hoax to fool the British into thinking the Luftwaffe possessed a new aircraft. It is in fact a Bf 110 with a glazed nose photographically superimposed. The hoax worked, to the extent that AI actually opened a file on the "Me 210 Jaguar"—the name the pretended aircraft was given. [AIR 40/127]

27 September 1944. Files captured following the fall of Paris show two Bf 110s fitted with retractable skis in the engine nacelles.

29 September 1944. A goods train is captured at Corbeil-Esonnes, France. It contains several truckloads of damaged Luftwaffe aircraft being returned to Germany for repairs. Among them is a Bf 110 G-4/R-3, featuring two upward-firing MG 81s bolted to the rear bulkhead of the cockpit. The guns were pointed fifteen degrees from vertical, confirming to AI the *schrage-musik* tactics.

December 1944. Nightfighters of 8/NJG 1 and NJG 5 participated in the German Ardennes offensive, by carrying out strafing attacks on railway trucks at dusk.

Messerschmitt Me 163 Komet (Comet)

Aerial reconnaissance shot of the Peenemunde test base, taken on 27 June 1943. An Me 163 can be seen on the left of the photo below the runway and two more in the bottom right, near the hangars and railway lines. Their white coloring shows they were prototypes; operational aircraft had darker camouflage paint. The dark streaks on the grass were believed to be evidence of jet or rocket engines being used. An He 111, Ju 87, Go 242, and various other aircraft can also be seen. A huge RAF night raid on Peenemunde was carried out during August 1943, causing extensive damage to the base and killing many technicians. Development of the Me 163 was then switched to Augsburg and Zwischenahn. [AIR 40/198]

War Record

Although an ingenious design, the Me 163—the world's first tailless aircraft—proved to be a great disappointment in combat. Deployed as a point-defense interceptor, it was the first and only rocket-powered aircraft to enter operational service.

The Komet's origins can be traced back to the DFS 194 rocket-powered flying wing, which first flew in summer 1940. Further development led to a historic test flight at Peenemunde West on 2 October 1941. The 623 mph reached that day stood as an unofficial world speed record until 1947. Following the death of Ernst Udet, the Me 163 fell from favor with the RLM. By 1944, however, the increasing penetration of Allied bombers and fighters into Germany resulted in a revival of interest in the aircraft.

It became operational in May 1944 with JG 400. However, its first kill, a B-17, would not come until 24 August. Though around two hundred *Komets* entered service, their final toll of Allied aircraft mounted to a paltry sixteen.

Although its speed and rate of climb were far superior to any Allied fighter, too many other factors weighed against the aircraft. Foremost of these was its rocket engines. The highly concentrated hydrogen peroxide that formed

Data File

(ME 163 B-1) DIMENSIONS

Wingspan	30 ft. 7 in.
Length	18 ft. 8 in.
Height	9 ft.
Max. Speed	596 mph
Ceiling	54,000 ft.
Range	62 miles
Engine	1 × 3,750 hp Walter HKW 509 A-2 rocket
Armament	2 × Mark 108 cannon
Crew	1

Shot from an air camera of combat between an Me 163 and RAF Spitfire IXF taken twenty-eight miles northwest of Dusseldorf on 27 August 1944 [AIR 40/198]

part of its propellant was extremely unstable; far more Me 163s were lost to accidents than to enemy action. Also, the engine tended to cut out as the aircraft leveled off from a climb—a crucial moment in air-to-air fighting. If the pilot managed to get into position to attack a bomber formation, his closing speed was so fast that accurate firing was extremely difficult. To counter this, the *Jaegerfaust* (fighter fist) was installed near the end of the war, ten vertically

Captured Me 163B-1a, factory number 191391, at a USAAF base. This aircraft was test-flown by the Americans in the presence of Dr. Lippisch, its designer. Towed to thirty thousand feet by a B-29, it glided down; the rocket engines were not started. [AIR 40/198]

mounted gun barrels in the wing roots. The Me 163 would fly underneath enemy bombers, triggering a photoelectric cell and firing the 2.2-pound shells upward. The *Jaegerfaust* was used once, destroying a B-17, the last victim of the aircraft.

In addition to these problems, when its small amount of rocket fuel was expended the *Komet* had to glide back to base, giving it only one chance at a landing and making it vulnerable to enemy fighters.

After the war all the Allies experimented with rocket-powered aircraft but rejected them.

Intelligence History

27 July 1942. AI notes that Messerschmitt files patent 723033 for apparatus for controlling tailless aircraft.

7 November 1942. A "new fighter aircraft" is reported being towed into the air by Bf 110, and as capable of 650 mph.

22 April 1943. First probable sighting of "tailless aircraft" is made.

23 June 1943. PR shot of Peenemunde shows four tailless aircraft. Discolored patches on the airfield are observed similar to those seen at Augsburg, with tailless aircraft.

July 1943. Informant reports seeing four to five tailless aircraft being towed into the air, gliding, then landing, with no sign of engine functioning.

1 November 1943. PR sortie over Lechfeld shows possible tailless aircraft, known to AI as "Peenemunde 30."

1 March 1944. Aircraft previously known to AI as "Peenemunde 30" is confirmed as the Me 163. POWs refer to it as the "Motte" (Moth). An informant at the Messerschmitt plant at Augsburg reports the aircraft being towed to ten thousand feet by a tug, then released. Luftwaffe designates the Me 163 as an "alarm fighter."

8 March 1944. "Peenemunde 30" confirmed as the Me 163.

20 April 1944. Report describes the Me 163 as "the mystery plane of the war." It has been spotted at Zwischenahan as well as at Peenemunde, and is apparently powered by a liquid-fuel rocket. Reports are received of lecture by Luftwaffe general Adolf Galland, who stated that the endurance of the Me 163 at full throttle would be eight minutes. The fuel is reported to be hydrogen peroxide and methyl alcohol, and maximum speed to be five to six hundred miles per hour. Its principal role is to attack bomber formations; it is almost ready to enter service.

25 April 1944. USAAF aircrew reports seeing a jet-propelled enemy aircraft fitting the Me 163 description at three to four miles.

View of the cockpit of an Me 163 [AIR 40/198]

29 April 1944. An RAF PR Spitfire pilot, Flight Lieutenant Crankanthorpe, on a sortie over Willhelmshaven, spots a white contrail two thousand feet away. He describes the enemy plane as "nearly all wing." The jet trail had started and stopped several times, suggesting it was being used intermittently.

11 May 1944. Me 163s are spotted at Zwischenahn in camouflage colors, suggesting the aircraft are operational.

4 July 1944. A POW who had served with Erprobungskommando 16 during 1943 is interrogated. He reports the unit had been formed at Peenemunde in August 1942 to develop operational tactics. Following the devastating RAF raid of August 1943, it moved to Zwischenahn. In early August 1943 a party including Göring, Galland, Willi Messerschmitt, and Hanna Reitsch visited the unit. It was rumored that the Me 163 would enter service in February 1942, but Messerschmitt had opposed this, wanting resources to go to further development of the Bf 109 instead. In January 1944 EP 16 started forming an "*ersatz schwarm*" of Me 163s, with the intention of using the aircraft against Allied PR aircraft, not bomber formations. Hauptmann Wolfgang Späte led the unit and all the pilots had operational experience. Their training included rigorous physical exercise and mountain training to prepare for high-altitude flight. EB 16 pilots would start on gliders, moving on to unpowered Me 163s, then fully powered Me 163s. Tactics developed involved gliding while engaging the enemy, as the rocket power seriously reduced maneu-

Sketch of Me 163 showing the details of the Walter rocket engines, given Luftwaffe designation HWK, or 109-509, 14 March 1945 [AIR 20/3286]

verability. One pilot had been killed on takeoff, having jettisoned his undercarriage too quickly; it had bounced up and hit his aircraft.

20 July 1944. USAAF P-38 Lightnings encounter an Me 163 while escorting a straggling B-17. The American pilots report managing to hit the Luftwaffe plane more than once, then losing it in clouds.

22 July 1944. PR confirms Me 163s at Peenemunde in summer 1943. The Luftwaffe is planning to speed up introduction of the aircraft. Ten airfield-servicing crews are being trained, each to service a *Staffel* of twelve aircraft.

28 July 1944. USAAF intelligence reports that a P-51 pilot has encountered an Me 163. The Mustang was escorting a formation of B-17s that had just completed bombing Meresburg. He saw two aircraft at five miles, with distinctive jet or rocket contrails. The escort fighter turned to confront the German aircraft, now totaling five. He estimated the Me 163s' speed to be 500–600 mph; he could not get in position for a shooting pass. The USAAF pilot commented, "The aircraft was a beautiful thing in the air. . . . These two pilots appeared very experienced, they were not aggressive and apparently were just up for a trial spin." He also stated the Me 163 had a fast roll rate but slow turning circle.

August 1944. Several reports are received of USAAF fighters dog-fighting Me 163s, with several probable kills claimed.

22 February 1945. A POW is interrogated who had worked at the Messerschmitt plant at Augsburg from 1936 to March 1943, when he had been drafted into the infantry. In winter 1940 an engineer called "Liebisch" [Lippisch] had been ordered to cooperate with Messerschmitt on the development of a rocket-propelled aircraft, referred to as the Me 163. Willi Messerschmitt ridiculed the whole project, deeming it a "step-child unworthy of interest"; there was little cooperation between his company and Lippisch. Only twenty men had worked on the Me 163 project, completing the first prototype, a glider, in spring 1942. It was towed by a Bf 110, then successfully flown for fifteen minutes by Flugkapitan Dittmar. In November 1942 the original Me 163 was taken to Peenemunde and flown under rocket power, again by Dittmar. During the same month Göring, Reitsch, Milch, and Messerschmitt inspected the aircraft.

14 March 1945. A full technical report on Me 163 gives details of its rocket motor and other features.

3 April 1945. Wreckage of several crashed Me 163s is recovered when the Americans capture Venlo airfield, in southern Holland.

Postwar

Civilian technicians interviewed Voigt, the Messerschmitt Director of New Designs, on behalf of the USAAF. He explained that engineers had identified problems of "critical speed" when approaching Mach 1. This had led to the development of swept wings for the Me 163, P1101, and P1112. Lippisch was also interrogated; he had designed the Delta IV in 1932, which had led to the DFS 39 glider. The Me 163 had originated when Antz of the RLM had initiated a project to put the Walter rocket into an aircraft. The DFS 39 was seen as the most aerodynamically advanced airframe at the time and was therefore chosen for the project.

When Adolf Galland was interviewed, he stated that the failure of the Me 163 had been due to a lack of fuel, not the rocket motor. He considered that it could have been a viable fighter; it was cheap to build and maintain. Development had been delayed by strife between Lippisch and Willi Messerschmitt.

A captured Me163 was flight-tested at RAE Farnborough as a glider only. The test pilot found the general handling to be very favorable.

Illustration showing how the fuselage of an Me 163 could be transported in a train carriage, October 1944 [AIR 20/3286]

Messerschmitt Me 210/410 Hornisse (Hornet)

The initial recognition drawing of the Me 210, produced by British Air Intelligence in 1942. RAF and USAAF aircrew would study these drawings to help them identify enemy aircraft and assess their fields of fire and weak points. [AIR 40/127]

War Record

First planned in mid-1937 as a replacement for the Bf 110, the Me 210 was a product of Göring's misplaced faith in the *zerstörer* concept. He believed heavily armed, long-range, twin-engine fighters could protect bombers over enemy territory and counter raids on Germany. In practice, the larger planes' lack of speed and maneuverability in comparison to nimble single-engine fighters put them at a distinct disadvantage in air-to-air combat.

One thousand Me 210s were ordered by the RLM before the project even left the drawing board. Dogged by stability problems, many Me 210 prototypes crashed; Erprobunsgesgruppe 210, scheduled to take part in the Battle of Britain using Me 210s, had to be diverted to other tasks.

The Me 210 was finally pressed into service, in the fighter-bomber role on the Eastern Front, in 1941 with II/ZG 1. However, the fatal accidents continued at an unacceptable rate, and production was halted in April 1942, with a huge financial loss to Messerschmitt. Existing Me 210s continued in service and were used in raids on Britain in late 1942.

Messerschmitt decided to salvage something from the project by developing the Me 410 *Hornisse*. Although very similar in appearance to the Me 210, the Me 410 incorporated many modifications, including more powerful engines and an adapted tailfin, to overcome the former's longitudinal stability problems. The result was a greatly improved aircraft. May 1943 saw the first Me 410s in operational service. One unit undertook night bombing raids on England, and two more were deployed in reconnaissance and

Data File

(ME 410A) DIMENSIONS

Wingspan	53 ft. 7¾ in.
Length	40 ft. 10 in.
Height	14 ft. ½ in.
Max. Speed	385 mph
Ceiling	32,800 ft.
Range	1,447 miles
Engines	2 × 1, 1750 hp DB 603A
Armament	2 × MG 131, 2 × MG 151/20, 2 × MG/17
Bomb load	2,204 lb.
Crew	2

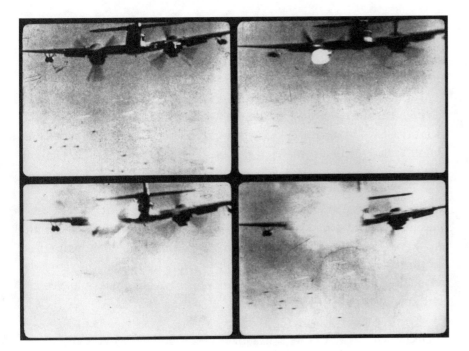

"Killing an Me 210." Four cine-camera stills dramatically show the last moments of an Me 210. The aircraft was shot down by a USAAF P-47 piloted by Sergeant Gregory on 5 September 1942. Strikes can be seen on the port engine, which then appears to blow up. Two 21 cm Wurfgranate 42 rocket tubes can be seen under each wing, indicating this Messerschmitt was operating in the *pulk-zerstörer* (formation destroyer) role. [AIR 40/127]

bomber-destroyer roles in Sicily. As a fighter, the Me 410 lost out in dog-fights to Spitfires and P-38s over Sicily. It found most success as a night raider, where its speed often allowed it to avoid interception. Following the Normandy landings, Me 410s were pressed into a day ground-attack role, but after six weeks of unacceptably high losses they were withdrawn.

An Me-410 in British decals but with spiral markings on the propeller hubs. These were introduced to help Luftwaffe crews distinguish friend from foe in the confusing maelstrom of air-to-air combat. [AIR 40/127]

Intelligence History

10 January 1942. A preliminary report is produced. AI had first identified the plane in 1941.

6 September 1942. An Me 210 is shot down by two RAF Tempests over Redcar, Yorkshire. The aircraft's wreckage was taken to Farnborough for examination. It had the first completely flexible fuel tanks found on any German aircraft.

Fall 1942. A prisoner is interrogated who saw a test flight of the Me 210 at Augsburg. He saw a new pilot volunteer to test-fly the aircraft. He put the aircraft into a shallow dive, then attempted a dive from nine thousand feet, but shortly afterward the tailplane broke off, and he crashed into a nearby wood. The Me 210 project was then abandoned; two hundred completed aircraft were dismantled.

24 December 1942. A POW states that the rear gun barbettes' sighting and remote control mechanisms are too complicated and difficult to use. This is corroborated by Allied pilots' combat reports that the fire from the rear guns is very inaccurate.

30 March 1943. AI report on development of Me 210: Arado engineers were bought in to work on the project to speed up development and ensure the plane was more suitable for mass production than other Messerschmitt types. AI describes aircraft as having a Messerschmitt fuselage with Arado wings. The failure of the project caused much tension

Captured photograph of a radio-controlled model of an Me 210 in flight. Instability problems dogged the aircraft throughout its development and operational career, leading it to be abandoned. Tests led to a slight lengthening of the fuselage and adaptations to the tailplane, resulting in the more successful Me 410. [AIR 40/127]

British troops and RAF personnel guard the mangled wreck of an Me 410. The rear-firing barbette can clearly be seen. Luftwaffe POWs claimed that this weapon was complicated to use and ineffective in combat; this was corroborated by RAF pilot combat reports, which stated that defensive fire from the barbettes was inaccurate. [AIR 40/214]

between Messerschmitt and Hitler, who threatened to put the company under state control.

30 April 1943. A POW reports that the Me 210 performed well in the air but was very fragile and prone to accidents on takeoff and landing. He states having seen one aircraft make a good landing approach, bounce slightly, and disintegrate in midair.

22 October 1943. USAAF B-17s report Me 210s attacking them using 37 mm guns and rocket projectors.

22 November 1943. Me 410 pilot makes a hundred-degree mistake in navigation and attempts to land at RAF airfield at Monte Corvino, Italy. Antiaircraft guns opened up on the plane, causing it to fire recognition flares. AA guns then ceased firing, and the German aircraft made a normal landing. The pilot, then realizing his mistake, tried to take off. Two British officers then drove a truck into the aircraft's path. As the pilot attempted to swing clear of the truck, an RAF officer threatened him with an automatic. At this point the Me 410's radio operator jumped out of the aircraft, but the pilot still tried to escape. The RAF man then jumped into the radio operator's seat and pointed the gun into the pilot's neck, so capturing the aircraft intact.

17 June 1944. First report is received of a 50 mm modified PAK 38 antitank gun being mounted. It is used for attacking bombers and tanks.

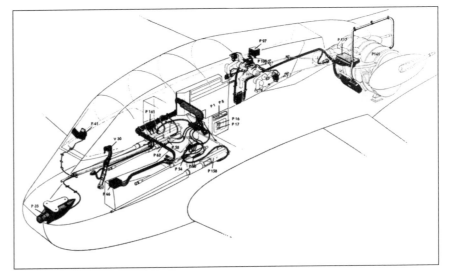

Captured technical drawing showing the armament layout of the Me 210/410 [AIR 40/127]

Messerschmitt Me 262 Schwalbe (Swallow)/ Sturmvögel (Storm Bird)

Head-on view of an Me 262, clearly showing the four-cannon armament in the aircraft's nose [AIR 40/201]

War Record

In the summer of 1944, the Me 262 became the first jet in the world to enter operational service. It was over 100 mph faster than its Allied piston-engine contemporaries. It was used as a fighter, fighter-bomber, night-fighter, and reconnaissance aircraft. When Adolf Galland, the legendary ace and fighter general, first flew it, he declared he felt like he was "flying on the wings of angels."

The origins of the Me 262's design go back to before the war. The RLM commissioned Messerschmitt to design an airframe for the jet engines being developed by BMW in 1938. The initial design, by Dr. Woldemar Voigt, was completed by 1941, and a piston-engined version of the airframe flew the same year. The project was dogged by delays, frequently attributed to Hitler's insistence that the Me 262 be developed as a bomber rather than a fighter. The impact of Hitler's meddling has been much exaggerated. The real holdup with the Me 262 was the failure of the German aircraft companies to come up with a reliable jet that could be used in operational service. The key problem was a shortage of the essential metals, nickel and chromium, needed to produce alloys. The fins of the jets were subjected to extremely high temperatures during flight, and insufficiently strong alloys would warp and bend after a few hours' flying. Indeed, the Jumo 004s used on the Me 262 had to be completely overhauled after only twenty hours of flying.

Data File

DIMENSIONS

Wingspan	40 ft. 11½ in.
Length	34 ft. 9½ in.
Height	12 ft. 7 in.
Max. Speed	540 mph
Ceiling	37,565 ft.
Range	650 miles
Engines	2 × Jumo 004B turbojets
Armament	4 × Mark 108 cannon
Crew	1

The first production Me 262s to be delivered to the Luftwaffe arrived in April 1944. In July 1944, Erprobungskommando Schenk finally flew the Me 262 in combat. Initially it was used for bombing missions from thirteen thousand feet, a task the plane had never been designed for. As the Germans retreated through France a few further Me 262 bombing missions were carried out, but to little effect. Meanwhile, in Bavaria, the ace Walter Nowotny was building up a unit of Me 262 fighters. In August 1944 this unit started attacking Allied aircraft over southern Germany, claiming five kills that month. During the rest of 1944 more Me 262s entered the battle, accounting for small numbers of Allied fighters and bombers. Ironically the Me 262's greatest asset, its speed, was proving to be a problem in air-to-air interception. The differential in its speed compared with American heavy bombers was over 250 mph. This meant that the time a pilot had to aim and fire at his target was minimal. An alternative tactic was for the Me 262s to go after the USAAF fighter escorts, forcing them to jettison their drop tanks and allowing Luftwaffe piston-engined aircraft to attack the bomber formations. Nowotny was killed in November 1944, and his unit disbanded to form the nucleus of JG 7.

The most famous unit to operate the Me 262 was Jagdverband 44, initially led by Adolf Galland. The experienced pilots and aces left alive in the Luftwaffe formed this unit at the end of the war. It included legendary aces such as Gerhard Barkhorn, Heinz Bär, and Walter Krupinski. As German airfields were increasingly bombed and constantly patrolled by Allied aircraft, Jv 44 had to use Bavarian motorways and improvised secret bases.

The final role adopted by the Me 262 was that of night-fighter. The Lichtenstein SN-2 radar was fitted to the nose of the aircraft, which served in this configuration in small numbers with Kommando Welter in the defense of the night skies over Berlin during the last few weeks of the war.

The overall combat record of the Me 262 was not spectacular. In air-to-air fighting, Allied records confirm around 150 kills for the loss of around 100 of the jets. However, combat losses accounted for only about a third of the

Aerial reconnaissance shot of the Messerschmitt development base at Augsburg, taken in February 1944. The Me 262's white paintwork shows it to be a prototype. [AIR 40/201]

Me 262s destroyed. Engine and undercarriage failure each accounted for roughly as many crashes, signs of an aircraft put into service with insufficient development and pilot training. An even more revealing statistic is that though 1,400 Me 262s were constructed, at any one time only two hundred were in operational service, generating an average of just sixty sorties per day. The circumstances that surrounded the career of the aircraft—the chaos of a collapsing Germany—meant despite its undoubted qualities the Messerschmitt jet was always fighting insurmountable odds.

The Me 262 was undoubtedly one of the major landmarks in aviation history. Its speed and firepower made it superior to any other fighter of World War II. Despite these advantages, the lack of experienced pilots, aviation fuel, and adequately defended bases allowed it to do little more than scratch away at the Allies' overwhelming air superiority during the last year of the war.

Intelligence History

19 November 1943. AI report states the Me 262 has surpassed the He 280 and been selected for series production. The informant had spoken with Willi Messerschmitt, who said the aircraft was being designed at Augsburg and tested at Lechfeld. Messerschmitt stated it was ready for series production and easy to build. The RLM had asked Messerschmitt how long it would take before it would be possible to build 1,500 per month.

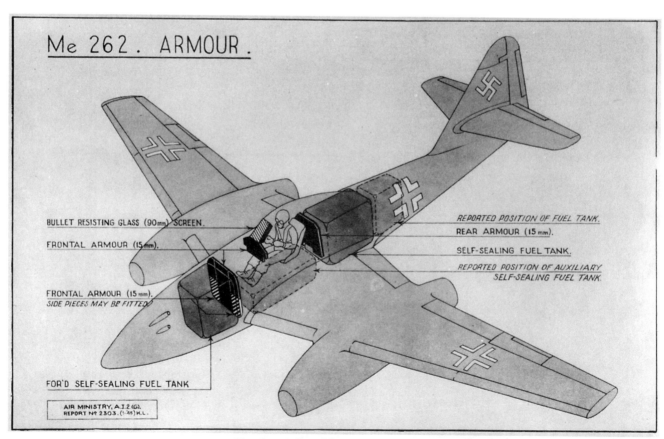

Sketch produced by AI showing the positioning of the Me 262's armament [AIR 40/201]

A U.S. officer inspecting a captured Me 262. The location of the aircraft in woods illustrates how the Germans used natural cover to help conceal their aircraft from Allied surveillance. [AIR 40/201]

1 December 1943. An official Spanish report is obtained of an interview with Lucien Pericaud, a French draftsman who had been working for Messerschmitt until September 1943, when he escaped to Spain. He reports that the twin-engine jet had been flying at up to 500 mph near Berlin in October 1942. Also a POW reported seeing an Me 262 in a mock combat with a Bf 109G at Lechfeld in October 1943; he stated the Me 262 was faster and more maneuverable.

11 December 1943. 3811st Bomb Group, Eighth U.S. Air Force, reports seeing an unidentified enemy aircraft the size of a P-47 flying at great speed under the bomber formation with a white vapor trail. Crews thought it was a jet but that it did not fit the He 280's description.

3 January 1944. PR shows Me 262s at Lechfeld and Augsburg.

27 February 1944. A PR image captures the "Lechfeld 42" (initial AI code-name for the Me 262) on film at Lechfeld.

1 March 1944. A general description of the Me 262 is released, describing it as capable of 527 mph and [wrongly] extremely maneuverable, especially in tight turns. It is assessed as likely to be operational within six months.

26 June 1944. In an interview, Lieutenant Colonel Torre, Italian air ministry, refers to an RLM meeting of June 1943 where series production of the Me 262 was discussed but a decision was delayed due to problems with development of the jet engines.

30 June 1944. A German fighter pilot is captured and interrogated. He had spent three weeks with Erprobungskommando 262 at Lechfeld. The Me 262

Initial AI sketch of the Me 262 by H. Redmill, produced in December 1944 [AIR 20/3286]

was being tested to establish whether it should be used as a bomber-destroyer or against Allied fighters. Dual-control Messerschmitt Bf 110s and Me 410s were being delivered to Lechfeld for conversion training for fighter pilots to twin-engined aircraft. Pilots thought the Fw 190 to be far more maneuverable than the Me 262.

29 July 1944. The first report of combat between Me 262 and Allied aircraft is received. An RAF PR Mosquito flying over Munich was hit by cannon shells but returned safely to Firmo, Italy. The crew reported the jet to be 100–120 mph faster than the Mosquito but with a larger turning circle. The Luftwaffe plane managed to get on the tail of the Mosquito several times using its superior speed, but each time the RAF plane went into a turn and lost it. The crew also stated that the high speed of the Me 262 disadvantaged the Me 262, by giving its pilot little time to aim and fire.

9 September 1944. The first example to fall into Allied hands is shot down by antiaircraft fire near Diest, Belgium while strafing troops. The plane was badly damaged but the two jet engines were sent to RAE Farnborough.

5 October 1944. An Me 262 is shot down by Spitfires nine miles southwest of Nijmegen, Holland. One jet engine is found intact, sent to the UK for analysis.

December 1944. A POW tells of experimental air-to-air bombing carried out by Me 262s at Rechlin. He is convinced the tactic could work if tried operationally.

Postwar

AI interviewed a selection of JV 44 Me 262 pilots, including Adolf Galland and Gerhard Barkhorn. The pilots stated that they rarely had more than sixteen aircraft available on any one day. Their primary objective was to destroy Allied bombers, and they only engaged fighters when strictly necessary. However, the pilots felt that the Me 262 was better suited to attacking fighters, where speed and rate of climb were decisive factors. They believed that a few hundred Me 262s deployed against Allied fighters could have gained air superiority.

The aircraft's great speed gave little time to aim and fire at bomber formations—unless they slowed down, which made them vulnerable to escort fighters. JV 44 flew in *kette* of three rather than the usual Luftwaffe *schwarm* of four. This was because the plane's speed and wide turning circle made it difficult to keep larger formations together. The aircraft would hold formation and attack the whole width of a bomber formation. The pilots believed this to be essential, to split the defensive fire of the bombers' guns.

Woldemar Voigt, designer of the Me 262, was also interviewed. Messerschmitt had received an order to investigate jet fighters in fall 1938. Initial drawings had been sent to the RLM in June 1939, and an order for prototypes was received in the same month. However, the project was not given priority by the RLM, because the aircraft would not be ready for the blitzkrieg. The project attained high priority in spring 1943, but government aid for manpower and materials was still not forthcoming. Willi Messerschmitt told AI that the plane had been designed in 1938. He had nine hundred Me 262s ready for service in early 1944, but they could be deployed only on Göring's personal order.

A neat row of eight Me 262s. The vertical stripe in front of the Balkankreuz on the fuselage was used by Kommando Nowotny. [AIR 40/201]

TWO BOMBERS

Arado Ar 234 Blitz (Lightning)

A U.S. soldier stands guard over the wreck of an Ar 234. USAAF P-47s shot down this jet at Julich, on the German-Belgian border, on 24 March 1945. U.S. troops overran the crash site the next day. [AIR 40/103]

War Record

The Ar 234 Blitz (Lightning) was the world's first operational jet bomber. It featured several innovations, including automatic pilots, landing-brake parachutes, and ejector seats, that are still used in military aircraft today.

The Blitz's operational debut took place in July 1944. It was first used, in its originally intended role, as a reconnaissance plane, making several flights over Britain. Flying at 30,000 feet, the Ar 234s were immune to interception by Allied fighters. Further reconnaissance units were set up at Aalborg, Denmark, in northern Italy, and at Stavanger, Norway. Aircraft from the latter continued flights over Britain up to the last days of the war.

The Ar 234 flew its first operational bombing mission during the German Ardennes offensive of December 1944–January 1945. However, the plane's most notable missions came in March 1945. When advance units of Gen. George Patton's U.S. Third Army seized the last remaining bridge over the Rhine at Remagen, Ar 234s joined Messerschmitt Me 262 jets in attacks on the crossing. The aircraft pounded the Ludendorff railway bridge constantly for ten days. On 17 March the bridge finally gave way, but it was too late to stem the Allied advance into the heart of the Reich. RAF pilots recalled the fast, low-flying jets as almost impossible to intercept.

Although a successful design, the small number manufactured and crippling shortage of aviation fuel meant the Ar 234 failed to make a significant impact on the course of the war.

Intelligence History

1941. USTAF has an informant in the Arado Drawing Office in Potsdam. Arado was then at work on a stratospheric bomber designated "Ar 238." The earliest blueprints are dated December 1941.

Data File

DIMENSIONS

Wingspan	46 ft. 3½ in.
Length	41 ft. 5½ in.
Height	14 ft. 1½ in.
Max. Speed	460 mph
Ceiling	32,810 ft.
Range	1,013 miles
Engines	2 × Jumo 004B
Armament	4,409 lb. bomb payload
Crew	1

May 1943. Prototypes are under construction at Brandenburg factory.

9 March 1944. The first probable sighting in aerial reconnaissance photograph is made.

May 1944. KG 76 aircrew and ground personnel are transferred to Alt Lönnewitz from Italy. British intelligence source confirm that pilots from II/KG 76 are being posted to Alt Lönnewitz at that time, confirming the prisoner's account. The prisoner had learned that the head of the Ar 234 pilot training program was a Colonel Sturm, a favorite of Göring.

25 August 1944. Three "Rechlin 46" (initial Allied code name for the Ar 234) jet aircraft are spotted with Me 262s at the Rechlin/Larz base, seen for the first time outside a hangar.

Fall 1944. A German prisoner interrogated by Allied intelligence had worked as a radio mechanic attached to the Arado development site from spring 1940 to August 1944, when he was transferred to an infantry unit and captured. He said the development of twin-jet Arado had taken place at Lönnewitz, near Leipzig. In early 1943 civilian engineers arrived with one or two jet aircraft. The cover name "Althahan G.m.b.H" had been painted on buildings the engineers were working in. Luftwaffe personnel at the base were denied access to this area. The prisoner had discovered the engineers were from Arado. By August 1944 there were around two hundred technicians at work on the project. He also described the aircraft in a way that fit the Ar 234's description.

8 September 1944. An informant working at SIPA of Paris tells the Allies the company had been designing wing flaps for the Ar 234.

5 October 1944. British intelligence borrows plans for Ar 234 obtained by USTAF.

A civilian oversees the dismantling of the Ar 234 that crashed at Julich. The aircraft was then transported to RAE Farnborough for evaluation. [AIR 40/103]

Initial sketch of the Ar 234, produced in December 1944 by H. Redmill [AIR 20/3286]

6 October 1944. AI receives the first reports of the Ar 234 becoming operational.

12 October 1944. "Rechlin 46" is confirmed as the Ar 234.

25 October 1944. Following the liberation of Paris, copies of technical drawings for Ar 234 are obtained from Arado's French drawing office. There are notes in French, showing that French designers worked on the project.

19 January 1945. Reports of Ar 234s being assembled at Kupper-bei-Sagan airfield in Silesia (now Poland) are confirmed. Aerial reconnaissance photographs show Ar 234s using hangars. Evidence of increased air activity in the site from September 1944 onward suggests it was being used for assembly.

24 February 1945. Three USAAF P47 Thunderbolts jump a German jet from above. The plane is forced to make a crash landing four miles south of Julich (on Belgian-German border), just behind the German front lines.

25 February 1945. U.S. ground forces overrun the village where the plane crashed. Troops examine the plane under fire from Wehrmacht forces. The plane is dismantled and taken to the RAE Enemy Aircraft Section at Farnborough for evaluation. One engine is sent to Power Jets at Pyestock, and one to the USAAF base at Wright Field, Dayton, Ohio. Samples of fuel are sent to the Anglo-Iranian Oil Company and ICI for tests.

27 March 1945. Wing Commander Proctor, AI, produces a ten-page technical report on the Ar 234.

7 April 1945. A pilot's handling notes for the Ar 234 are captured.

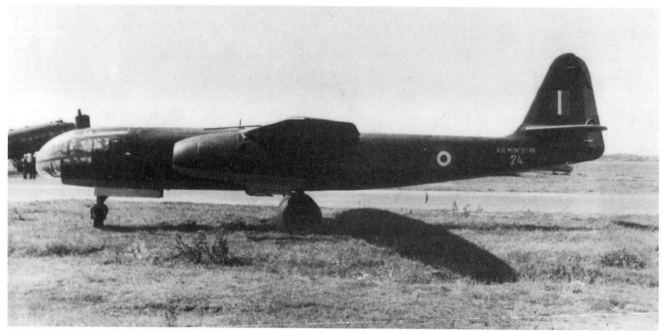

This Ar 234B-2, originally of Aufkl-Gr33, in RAF markings. It was given the designation "Air Ministry 24" by the British. At the end of the war some surviving Luftwaffe jets, including several surviving Ar 234s, made their way to Norway to avoid capture by the Allies. These were eventually surrendered to the British. Three *Blitzes* were subsequently taken to America for evaluation. [AIR 40/121]

Postwar

In June 1945, following the end of the war in Europe, a U.S. air interrogation officer, Colonel Folkin, interrogates Flugkapitan Joachim Carl, Arado's chief test pilot. Carl describes the Ar 234's first flight in November 1943 at Reine, Westphalia. He also states that the initial design was very successful with only minor alterations required for series production.

RAF aerial reconnaissance photograph showing an Ar 234 (center of picture) with two Me 262s outside hangars at the Rechlin/Larz base, fifty miles north of Berlin [AIR 40/103]

Dornier Do 17Z/Do 215

Early prewar version of the Dornier Do 17 "flying pencil." Following its successful demonstration at Dubendorf in 1937 and interest in the airplane from Yugoslavia, the Drazavna Fabrika Aviona factory at Kraljevo was to build Do 17Ks under license. [Air 40/123]

War Record

Dornier designed the Do 17 in response to Lufthansa's requirement for a passenger-postal service aircraft. Although rejected by Lufthansa, the design had military value, and the ninth prototype became the initial production variant, the Do 17E-1, which could carry a bomb payload of 1,102 pounds. Manufactured concurrently was the Do 17F-1 reconnaissance version, equipped with extra fuel tanks and cameras. Both types performed magnificently with the Condor Legion during the Spanish Civil War.

Owing to the slim design of the fuselage, the Do 17 acquired the nickname "flying pencil" soon after it was publicly displayed at Dubendorf, near Zurich, at the 1937 International Military Aircraft Competition. The Do 17Z, of which 1,700 were built, became the major production version for the Luftwaffe. It played a substantial part in the initial German blitzkriegs and was first used on 1 September 1939, during the invasion of Poland. The Do 17Z saw operational service in Norway, France, Belgium, Holland, Greece, Yugoslavia, Crete, and the Soviet Union. Additionally, Do 17Z-equipped *Gruppen* also played an extensive role in attacks upon British shipping in the English Channel, the Battle of Britain, and the 1940–1941 night "blitz" of British cities. However, by late 1941 the Do 17Z had been all but withdrawn from front line duties, as it was regarded as outdated, although some versions remained in the reconnaissance role.

Data File

DIMENSIONS

Wingspan	59 ft. 1 in.
Length	51 ft. 10 in.
Height	14 ft. 11 in.
Max. Speed	255 mph
Ceiling	26,905 ft.
Range	721 miles
Engines	2 × Bramo 323P
Armament	Up to 7 × 7.92 mm machine guns
Payload	2,205 lb./1,000 kg
Crew	4

Intelligence History

30 May 1939. Information from a reliable "source" informs AI that the Do 215 is in fact a twin-engine fighter version of the Do 17.

7 July 1939. The same source also states that the Do 215 can be used as a heavy bomber, a long-range bomber, a long-range reconnaissance aircraft, a combined reconnaissance-bomber, a ground-attack aircraft, and as a *zerstörer* plane, owing to its speed, maneuverability, and ideal flying characteristics.

12 July 1939. The assistant air attaché at San Sebastian declares that during the Spanish Civil War the Do 17's bomb payload was so insufficient that the

Two German propaganda photographs of the Condor Legion unit A/88 equipped with Do 17E-1s. Although the performance of the Do 17E-1 with the Condor Legion was excellent, it must be stated that the fighter aircraft that the Republicans could send up to oppose the Do 17E-1s and 17F-1s were, to say the least, "obsolete." [both Air 40/123]

A famous photograph of Do 17Z-2s over London's Docklands during the September 1940 daylight raids over the city during the Battle of Britain [Air 34/734]

aircraft were withdrawn from the bombing role and were instead employed as reconnaissance planes.

13 July 1939. AI Report 24870 relays an alarming assertion of French intelligence regarding the capability of the Do 215. The French believe that all new Do 215s being delivered to the Luftwaffe are equipped with special apparatus for the production of artificial clouds, a mechanism that can easily be transformed into a device for spreading poison gas.

17 July 1939. AI requests the British air attaché in Berlin to determine the degree of truth in the allegation that a 20 mm cannon has been fitted to fire through each air screw on the Do 215.

A Do 17Z-2 under ground attack. Although the intelligence file reveals no information about the attacking British aircraft, one can logically deduce that it was probably a Spitfire V. During 1941 Fighter Command was actively engaged in "fighter sweeps" over northern France, Belgium, and Holland, shooting up targets such as German airfields. Additionally, it will be remembered that the Do 17 was withdrawn from frontline service toward the end of 1941, a fact that encourages one to believe the earlier point. Gun-camera photographs were a useful source of intelligence, especially when new types of enemy aircraft were encountered. The terrain in this photograph would suggest the deduction is correct. [Air 40/123]

The Dornier Do 215 was the planned designation of the Do 17Z export version. Seen here are a prewar propaganda picture and a model, presumably meant to entice foreign customers. Originally ordered by Sweden in 1939, the first Do 215 to be developed was the A-1 variant. However, owing to the outbreak of war the Nazi authorities embargoed export of the eighteen aircraft. Subsequently they were converted to Luftwaffe requirements and entered operational service as bomber/reconnaissance aircraft.

4 January 1941. Air attaché Belgrade reports that the Do 17 was a highly versatile machine, well liked by Luftwaffe crews. In one engagement with four Spitfires, a Do 17 returned to base with 214 bullet holes, "which shows the constructional and qualitative value of this aeroplane."

21 May 1941. AI believes the Do 17Z night-fighter to have an armored nose with fixed, forward-firing machine guns and a crew of three.

27 February 1943. AI Report CSDIC 270 states that under interrogation a POW revealed that during October 1942 he saw a Do 215 at Mengen airfield with an enlarged nose. This feature was in fact a pressure cabin, as the Do 215 was being converted to work as a high-altitude reconnaissance aircraft. At the time the POW saw the Do 215, it was undergoing tests at the Dornier factory airfield at Friedrichshafen.

The final Do 215 variant was the B-5 night-fighter/intruder. With an unglazed nose, this type was armed with two 20 mm MG FF cannon and four MG 151 7.92 mm machine guns.

Dornier Do 217

On 4 December 1943, Second Tactical Air Force Typhoon IBs of 198 Squadron from Manston and 609 Squadron from Lympne supported a fighter sweep by P-47 Thunderbolts of the U.S. Eighth Air Force against German airfields in the Netherlands. While over Holland the Typhoons encountered a formation of four-teen Dornier Do 217s. These were probably E, K, or M vari-ants, as several were seen to jet-tison munitions suspended beneath their wings before combat commenced; one pilot confirmed that a Do 217 he engaged was carrying the Hs.293 anti-shipping missile. As a direct result of this engagement, on 19 December, Interpretation Report L.121 was issued. Referring to the combat photographs, this report drew attention to Photographic Reconnaissance Unit film taken in June 1943 identifying a Do 217 at the Garz/Usedom airfield with objects of a similar nature under the wings. The original PRU photograph depicts an aircraft outside a hanger with shadows that indicate the presence of objects under each wing, which AI considered to be Fritz-X or Hs.293 radio-guided bombs. AI photographic interpreters measured the distance between the wingtips and the shadows created by the objects and then correlated this data with the Typhoon pilot's estimation of the distance from the wingtip to the Hs.293. Thus, AI could determine from which German airfields these antishipping Do 217 squadrons were operating.

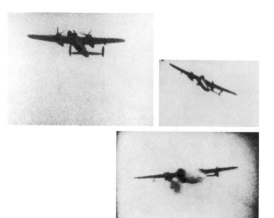

War Record

The Dornier Do 217 was a multipurpose aircraft, with roles ranging from long-range reconnaissance, bombing, dive-bombing, torpedo-bombing, anti-shipping missile attack, and service as a day and night fighter. Total production of the Dornier Do 217 (all variants) numbered 1,730. The first eight aircraft used operationally were employed in a reconnaissance role as early as 1940, though British air intelligence did not credit the Do 217 as being in service until the following year. Luftwaffe crews did not warm to the aircraft initially, as it had an alarming propensity to catch fire. However, after teething troubles with engines and streamlining of the fuselage, the Do 217 was a great all-rounder, especially in the various bomber roles. It was first deployed as a bomber in 1941 to II/KG 40.

Perhaps the most notable achievement of the Do 217 was in the antishipping missile role. Although the first Fritz-X radio-guided bomb was launched in an unsuccessful attempt on 21 August 1943 against targets in Augusta Harbor, Sicily, the Germans persisted with the weapon, and later variants

Data File

DIMENSIONS

Wingspan	62 ft. 4 in.
Length	55 ft. 5¼ in.
Height	16 ft. 4¾ in.
Max. Speed	348 mph
Ceiling	31,170 ft.
Range	1,336 miles
Engines	2 × DB 603A
Armament	2 × 13 mm,
	6 × 7.92 mm
	machine guns
Payload	8,818 lb./4,000 kg
Crew	4

improved its effectiveness. When Italy surrendered to the Allies on 9 September 1943, the Italian battle fleet at La Spezia, under command of Adm. Carlo Bergamini, left for the Allied port of Bone, in North Africa. German reconnaissance discovered the fleet on 14 September east of Sardinia and sent eleven bombers of III/KG 100 (Major Jope), operating from Marseilles. Believing the Do 217K-2s were friendly aircraft, the Italians left them unchallenged when they circled Bergamini's ships. Jope hit the battleship *Roma* with a Fritz-X, which blew the ship apart and took most of the crew, including the luckless Bergamini, to a watery grave. In the same attack Oberfeldwebel Kurt Steinborn badly damaged the battleship *Italia*. Missile-carrying Do 217s con-

While flying at ten thousand feet over London, on the night of 23/24 February 1944, during Oberst Peltz's *Unternehmen Steinbock,* this Dornier Do 217M was damaged by antiaircraft fire. Fearing the worst, the crew bailed out. They were later captured in the vicinity of Wembley. Remarkably, the aircraft flew on under its own control and proceeded to belly-land almost intact in a residential area near Milton Road, Cambridge. The markings on this machine were "U5+DK" and two white bands around the tail plane, identifying it as aircraft K from 2.l/KG 2 (Second Staffel, First Gruppe, Kampfgeschwader 2).

tinued to operate, though with restricted value, owing to Allied air superiority and electronic countermeasures, until the end of the war.

In defense of Germany, as a day or night-fighter, it was not particularly effective. Due to engine trouble, production of the Do 217N had to be suspended, but once these difficulties were overcome and the engine was

This detailed sequence of photographs illustrates the dive brakes on a Do 217. It was extracted from a German propaganda magazine published in Italian. Air intelligence about the Luftwaffe was taken from every means available.

switched to the He 219, the Do 217N night-fighter was abandoned. In the daylight role, once the Americans had developed and deployed P-51D Mustangs, long-range fighters to accompany daylight bomber raids, the Do 217 was easily picked off.

In early 1944, in reprisal for Allied bombing of German cities, Hitler ordered a bombing campaign, *Unternehmen Steinbock*, to commence against England. This was the last time Do 217s were massed in operations. Commencing 21 January, the offensive lasted until May 1944, at which time it was effectively over, due to severe losses.

Intelligence History

May 1940. AI learns of the existence of the Dornier Do 217.

14 January 1941. The Germans, it is learned, have produced about twenty Do 217s and are contemplating large-scale production. AI presumes that an air brake has been fitted for reducing air speed, since in dive-bombing and in losing height quickly it is considerably better than the Junkers Ju 88.

19 April 1941. A KG 26 Bordmechaniker POW reveals under interrogation that he has taken part in Do 217 flying trials and that it is the best plane in which he has flown.

18 August 1941. POW interrogation divulges new information about dive brakes for Do 217. They essentially consist of four fretted vanes, fitted at the tail of the aircraft, that open when required to form a cross. Some POWs say that these fold backward to form a pointed tail; others say that

A very rare picture of a Do 217 in the torpedo bomber role

Dornier Do 217E or J variant in the night-fighter role. It was unsuited to work as a night-fighter and proved unpopular with the crews, especially when compared to the Messerschmitt Me 110 and the Junkers Ju 88.

they fold forward along the sides of the fuselage, so that air pressure will assist in their operation. AI believes that the latter is more probable, because a number of POWs have said that the dive brakes can be jettisoned in an emergency.

16 May 1942. The Do 217, not popular with its crews to begin with, is now more favorably viewed, as problems have been resolved. Original variants were fitted with air brakes, but these have been removed, being so heavy that they unbalanced the plane.

7 August 1942. POW interrogation reveals that Do 217 is not well suited to torpedo work. Fitted with one weapon slung under each wing, due to difficulties experienced with internal stowage, the Do 217 was outperformed by Heinkel He 111s and Junkers Ju 88s in tests carried out at Grossetto, Italy.

October 1942. The Allies translate a captured German aircraft manual, *Do 217*. Dated March 1942, from the Dornier Werke GmbH Friedrichshafen, it begins, "The equipment of the Do 217E-2, E-4, Do 217K-1 and Do 217M-1 can be supplemented, to suit the various operational requirements, by the installation of additional fittings. These fittings include guns and bomb carriers, as well as photographic equipment and supplementary fuel tanks." This is confirmation for Allied intelligence that many variants of the Do 217 are to be expected.

2 October 1942. AI interest in Do 217 is stimulated after the Luftwaffe introduces the Henschel Hs 293 and Rheinstahl PC 1400 "Fritz" X radio guided bombs. Do 217s of KG 100 were adapted to carry these, with one slung under each wing.

13 May 1943. Allied photo-reconnaissance of the Dornier factory airfield at Lowenthal reveals that there is yet another new variant of the Do 217, designated by RAF Medmenham as "Lowenthal 90." At the same time confirmation is received that the Lowenthal 80 is the Do 217K-2, which was first spotted a year previously by PRU on 14 May 1942.

25 June 1943. AI report positively identifies nineteen known variants of the Do 217, in a wide range of operational roles.

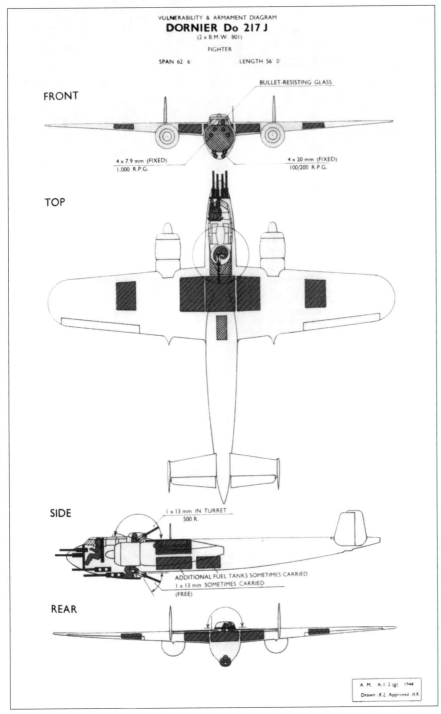

Dornier Do 217J vulnerability and armament diagram

11 July 1943. A POW reveals that at Herrsching, near Munich, experiments have occurred testing jet propulsion on the Do 217 to increase its speed. A colleague of the prisoner states that the tests were successful and that the jet apparatus is fitted above the nose of the aircraft. The conventional engines were still used for take-off and landing, but in flight the jet has enabled the Do 217 to reach a speed of 400 mph.

9 October 1943. A crew from the USAAF's 381st Bomb Group reports what it believes is a new, heavier-armed Do 217E fighter in operation.

> Heavy armament of some type, possibly rocket guns, was used against our aircraft again today. This armament was described as fitting on the twin-engine planes on the under-surfaces of the wing outboard of the engine nacelles, and firing outside of the air screw arc. It appeared to be about three to four feet long and hung down about one foot below the wing. The barrels appeared to have air-cooling jackets comparable to our 50 caliber machine guns. The muzzle was flared out and similar in appearance to a "pom-pom" gun. When fired, long flames came from the muzzle leaving a trail of whitish smoke with small flashes in it. The bursts from their explosions looked like small flak bursts. It was also observed that a large object would drop from the burst.

New tactics were also adopted, as twin-engine day fighters—Do 217s included—approached the bomber streams in line-abreast formations of five aircraft discharging their heavier armament into the densely packed American formations.

3 January 1944. The U.S. military attaché in Madrid receives photographs and a report from a Spanish soldier, taken in October 1943, of the latest German night-fighter, confirmed as the Do 217J. These are the first pictures of this type in Allied hands.

28 August 1944. AI is informed that production of the jet-assisted Do 217 has halted due to continued failures in testing.

September 1944. While engaged in a photo-reconnaissance sweep over Zoutjamp, Holland, a PRU Spitfire spots a Dornier Do 217 with a V-1 flying bomb mounted on top of the fuselage. Although unarmed, the PRU Spitfire dived to make a dummy attack, whereupon the V-1 was released. The pilot noted that the flame from the V-1 rocket engine appeared only after release from the Do 217, not before or during the procedure.

December 1944. POW interrogation reveals a new type of aircraft being employed by the Germans—an Me 163 mounted on top of the fuselage of a Do 217. The aircraft would be piloted from the Me 163 cockpit; the Do 217 would eventually be released. The POW was at the experimental trials carried out at Staaken airfield. The Me 163/Do 217 composite was manufactured at Lufthansa's Halle I in the summer of 1944.

Focke-Wulf Fw 200 Condor

Aerial reconnaissance photograph of the Trondheim Vaernes airfield in Norway. Nine Fw 200s can be seen with a Junkers Ju 52. Condors of KG 40 would often fly Atlantic patrols from Bordeaux round to Trondheim. [AIR 20/6245]

War Record

The Condor was originally designed as a long-range airliner for Deutsche Lufthansa. In 1938 it set a record for a nonstop flight from Berlin to New York.

The original military prototype came from a requirement from the Japanese for a long-range ocean reconnaissance aircraft. Shortly before the outbreak of the war, the Luftwaffe decided to set up a long-range antishipping unit. This was to be the Fw 200's most important role during World War II. KG 40, based at Bordeaux-Merignac, in southwest France, started patrolling the Atlantic approaches in June 1940. During the first year of the Battle of the Atlantic, Condors sank ninety thousand tons of Allied shipping, leading Churchill to dub the plane "the scourge of the Atlantic." Their most notable victim was the forty-two-thousand-ton liner *Empress of Britain*, crippled by Oberleutnant Bernhard Jope's aircraft off the north coast of Ireland and finished off by a U-boat. Condors would also act as scouts for U-boat wolf packs, spotting convoys and directing the submarines to their targets. By mid-1944 the Allied use of long-range coastal and escort-carrier-based interceptors had forced the Condor out of the Atlantic skies.

The Fw 200 was then relegated to the transport role. Two *Staffeln* were used to fly supplies into the Stalingrad pocket in early 1943. The Condor also made a brief appearance in the struggle against U.S. Eighth Air Force day-

Data File (Fw 200 C-0)

DIMENSIONS

Wingspan	107 ft. 9½ in.
Length	76 ft. 11½ in.
Height	20 ft. 8 in.
Max. Speed	224 mph
Ceiling	19,030 ft.
Range	2,206 miles
Engines	4 × 1,200 hp BMW Bramo 323R
Armament	3 × MG 15, 1 × MG 151/15, 1 × MG 151/20, 1 × MG 131
Bomb load	4,626 lb.
Crew	6

light bombers. B-17 crews reported seeing the aircraft flying alongside their formations, out of the range of the bombers' heavy armament. The aircraft would track the bomber formations and help direct Luftwaffe fighters intercepting the American raiders.

Another notable use of the Condor was as a VIP transport. Adolf Hitler used the fifth prototype as his personal aircraft, the "*Führermaschine*." Heinrich Himmler's version featured an armor-plated seat for extra protection.

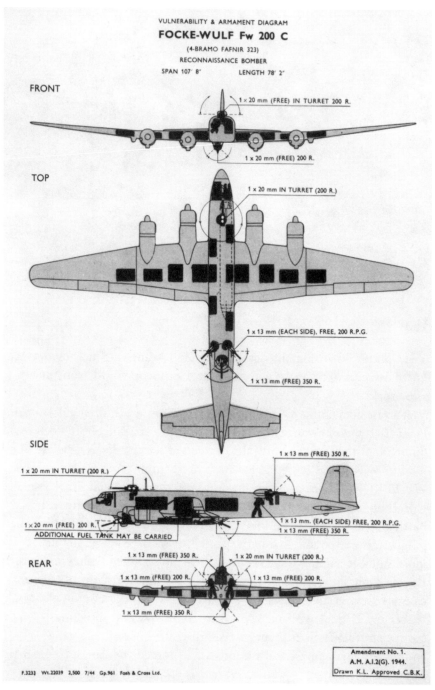

Sketch of Fw 200C showing positions of crew, armor, armaments, and fields of fire, produced in August 1944. These drawings would help Allied aircrew in their attacks on Luftwaffe aircraft. [AIR 20/963]

Intelligence History

27 April 1939. The Japanese press report that Dai-Nippon KK airline has ordered five Fw 200s. The personnel accommodation compartment is to be removed to house extra fuel tanks, suggesting the aircraft are intended for a military role.

December 1940. Two Fw 200s bomb Glasgow. Dublin is also bombed, having been mistaken for Liverpool.

10 January 1941. Fw 200 of KG 40 is shot down by HM Armored Tug *Seaman*, two hundred miles northwest of Ireland. Under interrogation, a POW reveals that a Major Petersen was the driving force behind the work of KG 40. Petersen had studied long-range antishipping attacks for years and had sent a memorandum to Jenschonnek suggesting the Condor be used in this role. The idea was rejected, but Field Marshal Albert Kesselring also saw the memo and passed it on to Hitler. Subsequently, Petersen was given a personal audience with the *führer* at Obersalzburg, resulting in the Luftwaffe extending its antishipping activity.

Based at Bordeaux, two *Staffeln* of KG 40 operated six Fw 200s each, with twelve officers and eighty other ranks. The crew consisted of two pilots, an observer, flight engineer, gunner, and wireless operator. Each crew would patrol once every three to four days. A typical trip would involve waking at 3 AM, taking off at 5 AM, then arriving over the patrol area at 9:30 AM. Planes would patrol singly but sometimes overlap with other aircraft taking over from them. There were four main routes from Bordeaux-Merignac, each involving 2,150-mile round trips. The routes were based on supposed convoy routes and extended to eighteen degrees west longitude.

Information on convoys was received from agents in the Americas, Spain, Portugal, and England, but KG 40 considered it unreliable. Intelligence also came from U-boats and Luftwaffe units based in Norway. There was little cooperation with U-boats, and KG 40 and aircraft could not communicate directly with the submarines.

A Condor in its original civilian version. Deutsche Lufthansa employed the Condor on the Berlin–New York route. The military version originated from a requirement from the Japanese navy, which ordered five Condors in 1939, through the airline Dai-Nippon KK. It intended to use the aircraft for long-range patrols in the Pacific. Although it never saw military service with the Japanese, Condors eventually fulfilled this role in the western Atlantic and off the North Cape. [AIR 40/124]

When attacking shipping, Condors would single out either the largest ship in the convoy or stragglers. Oceangoing tugs were considered particularly valuable targets. Bombing runs would be made at 275 feet from bow to stern, as it was believed most antiaircraft guns were positioned at the stern of merchant ships. A POW stated if four 20 cm antiaircraft guns were placed in bows of merchant ships, these attacks would become "suicidal."

10 February 1941. II/KG 40 carries out photo-reconnaissance flights over Greenland looking for potential U-boat bases.

29 November 1941. A report is received that a KG 40 crew trained in torpedo bombing at Grossenbrode in June 1940.

29 May 1942. A POW states that Rommel's advance in January 1942 was made possible by five Fw 200s ferrying petrol supplies from Catania, in Sicily, to Arae Philaenorum, three times daily.

7 August 1942. A K Report asserts that Fw 200s are being employed as torpedo bombers, with one weapon slung under each wing, although the Condor was not suited to this role.

1943. A POW reveals under interrogation that during spring 1942 a computer gunsight was tested but not put into service. Cement bombs are being used as markers to check bombsight accuracy before actual bombs are used. Crews are ordered to avoid air-to-air combat.

This gun-camera shot shows an Fw 200 caught on the ground by an Allied ground-attack plane. A hit on the inside port engine can be seen. [AIR 40/124]

Heinkel He 111

In October 1944 AI ordered PR sweeps of all airfields within range of London and those from which He 111s were known to operate, such as Barth, Boblingen, Garz, Griefswald, and Kolberg. He 111s that carried the flying bomb under the fuselage climbed to five to six hundred meters, then flew on the course to be taken by the bomb. When released, the bomb dropped thirty to forty meters, started its engine, then flew on its course. [AIR 40/10]

War Record

The Heinkel He 111 remained throughout the war one of the primary offensive weapons of the Luftwaffe's *Kampfgeschwader*. Before the war the German bomber wings had converted from the Junkers Ju 52 to the He 111, which had by then gone into series production. The first deliveries to an operational unit were made in late 1936 to 1/KG 154. In February 1937, thirty He 111B-1s were delivered to the Condor Legion's K/88 in Spain. By 1939, at the outbreak of war, the aircraft formed about three-quarters of the Luftwaffe's twin-engine bomber force, and throughout the war it served as a conventional medium bomber, torpedo bomber, photographic reconnaissance aircraft, and military transport. By mid-1940, after the successes of the early blitzkrieg campaigns, the He 111 formed the backbone of the Luftwaffe during the Battle of Britain and the night bombing campaigns. The He 111 *Gruppen* were largely withdrawn from the Western Front in preparation for Barbarossa, the invasion of the Soviet Union, and it was in this theater that the units operating the aircraft predominantly remained.

It was not until early 1942 that the Luftwaffe developed an effective torpedo-bomber arm. The He 111s of KG 26, equipped with one F5B torpedo slung under each wing between the engine housing and the fuselage, pioneered the force, and its bomber crews the tactics. Between twenty and forty aircraft, flying in four line-abreast formations of six to ten planes at 170 mph and at 150 feet, would each approach a convoy and release their weapons from about a thousand yards. Each crew chose a target, releasing both torpedoes at the same ship. The most notable success here occurred when roughly forty He 111s torpedoed eight ships in convoy PQ18 on 13 September 1942.

Data File (He 111 H-16)

DIMENSIONS

Wingspan	22.60 m
Length	16.40 m
Height	4.00 m
Max. Speed	227 mph
Ceiling	21,980 ft.
Range	1,212 miles
Engines	2 × Jumo 211F-2
Armament	1 × 20 mm cannon, 1 × 13 mm and 3 × 7.92 mm machine guns
Payload	2,205 lb./1,000 kg
Crew	4/5

Production of the He 111 continued during the war, chiefly because no satisfactory replacement was forthcoming. Additionally, it was easy to manufacture, economical in manpower and material, and remained reasonably effective in the less demanding Eastern Front, where it could also double as a transport (during the Stalingrad airlift, sixty-seven He 111s were shot down). By May 1944, seventeen bomber *Gruppen* were still operating the now obsolete He 111. Of these there were eleven *Gruppen* on the Eastern Front, in Luftflotte 6, and one *Gruppe* of KG 3, allocated to Luftflotte Reich, was training to air launch Fi 103 V-1 flying bombs. The last two He 111s produced were delivered to the Luftwaffe in September 1944.

Perhaps the last great success for the He 111 took place on 21 June 1944, when about two hundred He 111s drawn from seven *Gruppen* in Luftflotte 6 took off and attacked 162 USAAF Eighth Air Force B-17s that had landed at

On 4 July 1944, PR of Peenemunde showed FZG-76 flying bombs and He 111s at the experimental airfield. Using this image, photograph 106G/1201,4009, AI Interpretation Report L288 stated that "each of the He 111's has a small patch of light-spread on its fuselage between the dorsal turret position and the leading edge of the wing, which probably indicates either some marking or fitting at that point." These were believed to be above plane flying bomb carrier fittings. [AIR 40/158]

bases in the Soviet Union. They were the units assigned to Operation Frantic, the U.S. mission to destroy the oil refinery at Schwarzheide. Caught completely in the open at Poltava, forty-four B-17s were destroyed, and twenty-six were damaged; only two were left unscathed. Of the other U.S. and Soviet aircraft on the airfield, a further five were destroyed and twenty-eight damaged, and the 400,000-gallon fuel dump was blown apart. The Americans never again attempted shuttle-bombing operations staging through the Soviet Union.

Intelligence History

1 April 1938. AI Report 725 2-C/S states that "in spite of its relatively old design and its already obsolescent construction, the He 111 has had its equipment improved and, thanks to its first-rate armament and equipment, remains one of the best bomber types in commission in the German Air Force."

1940. AI learns that the two additional side blisters for extra defensive machine-gun armament reduce the speed of the He 111 by 15 mph.

17 October 1940. A POW states under interrogation that those *Gruppen* with Dornier Do 17s underwent He 111 replacement program during mid-July to mid-August. Although the speed of the two aircraft was roughly the same, the Do 17 was easier to handle. Icing was a massive problem with the He 111, and crews would not fly in high-altitude cloud formations. The service ceiling of the aircraft was 8,500 meters with a maximum operational payload of 1,000 kg, and about 9,000 meters without bombs.

18 February 1941. An He 111-H5 of II/KG 53 is shot down, the wreckage investigated, and the crew interrogated. The subsequent AI report (69/1941) reveals that the plane was equipped with extra tail armament for defense and a tube for ejecting grenades. The *Bordmechanikier* worked it electrically. He had two buttons to press; the first loaded the grenade into the tube, and the second ejected the munition. There were thirty to forty grenades in a drum magazine, all fused to explode sixty to seventy feet behind the tail plane. The POWs said the system was not popular with crews, because if the mechanism jammed when the grenade had armed itself it would explode in the aircraft. For this reason the *Gruppenkommandeur* of II/KG 53 had forbidden their use unless in an emergency.

This Heinkel He 111H-3 of 6/KG 26 radio code "1H+DP" was shot down on 8 April 1940 by two Hurricanes of 43 Squadron operating from Wick. The British fighters were on a routine patrol for RAF Coastal Command when they encountered this aircraft and another roughly thirty miles from Duncansby Head. One pilot, Sargent Hallowes, fired all his ammunition into this Heinkel, which crash-landed riddled with bullet holes near the flarepath of the RAF airfield. AI Report 42/1940 established that the He 111 "had a hole cut in the front of the lower gun tunnel and an MG fitted in this on a ball joint. A small window was provided for aiming. There is said to be a danger of bullets hitting the bombs as they leave the aircraft." Some of this information was undoubtedly gleaned from interrogation of the pilot, Leutnant Weigel, and the observer, *Oberfeldwebel* Rehbein, who survived. Both gunners, *Oberfeldwebels* Rost and Geerdts, were killed. [AIR 27/1568]

Heinkel He 111 in typical pose. It first flew on 24 February 1935, and over seven thousand of all variants were manufactured for the Luftwaffe. In addition to those produced at the Ernst Heinkel works at Marienehe and Oranienburg, He 111s were built by Norddeutsche Dornierwerke in Wismar, Allgemeine Transportgesellschaft in Leipzig, Arado in Babelsberg, and many other factories. [AIR 40/125]

14 April 1941. A POW from aircraft radio code "1H+ED," piloted by Oberfeldwebel Rose, shot down on 4 April, says He 111s of III/KG 55 are using longer runways to allow bigger payloads. The aircraft log reveals that the He 111 has on occasions carried a single 2,500 kg "Max" bomb.

20 June 1941. AI reports that all I/KG 54 crews have practiced at least two rocket-assisted takeoff flights. This reduces runway length requirement for takeoff by about 60 percent.

6 July 1941. AI Report 367 summarizes He 111 tactics for low-level antishipping bomb attacks. Usually made at night between 350 and 700 feet, reduced to three hundred feet during actual attack, the crews dive at a thirty-degree angle and fly into the moon to be as inconspicuous as possible during the approach run. The fuses are delayed to allow time for the He 111 to accelerate over the target and get out of the explosion radius.

9 July 1941. Rockets used by He 111 in assisted takeoff are three feet three inches long and two feet across, with one placed under each wing about two feet from the wing root. When fired the rocket canister quickly burns out, then parachutes into a nearby field, where it is recovered for recycling. The mechanism is initiated electrically by the observer, who presses a button about halfway through the takeoff run at the pilot's signal. The momentum gained during the one-kilometer burn time enables acceleration through three hundred feet in a very short period of time.

1 May 1942. The He 111Z is first spotted by a PR sweep after the second night raid on Rostock. AI is unsure of the aircraft's use but thinks it probable it would be employed as a heavy bomber, troop carrier, logistics transport, glider tug, or high-altitude research plane.

19 June 1942. AI learns that the He 111-H6 has fittings in the nose and tail for operations as a glider tug.

24 June 1942. AI acknowledges that the hooks, which would enable the He 111-H6 to be used as a glider tug, were "for catapult takeoff."

19 July 1942. He 111 torpedo-bomber carries two 750 kg weapons. The left is dropped first, followed a fraction of a second later by the right-hand weapon.

7 August 1942. The He 111 is favored as the first-choice torpedo-bomber of the Luftwaffe, due to its ability to absorb enemy fire and fly on one engine. I/KG 26 is to fly torpedo-bomber sorties against USSR-bound convoys with He 111s.

6 January 1943. AI discovers that He 111Z glider tug crews train at Rheims.

28 March 1943. SIS agent reports "a five-engine aircraft trailing a glider lands on the Longuevic airfield from time to time, leaving by night. The capacity of the glider is 150 men or two light tanks."

22 June 1943. POW confirms the designation of the He 111Z as a glider tug (Z is for *zug/zicher*, meaning tug). There is one towing hook, on either side of the center engine.

1 July 1943. AI is informed that the Lutfwaffe possesses seventy-eight He 111Z glider tugs, which can tow gliders large enough to transport heavy artillery.

22 October 1943. USAAF bomber crews report that He 111s armed with 20 mm and 37 mm cannon, and 21 cm underwing rockets, are attacking B-17 formations.

12 January 1944. An He 111 at Dijon/Longuevic aerodrome has undergone serious modifications. French specialists on site noted that it is armed with sixteen machine guns. Grouped together in a row of eight pairs and pointing vertically down through the bottom of the aircraft, each machine gun has 2,500 rounds of ammunition. Although an older He 111 variant, AI is bemused and notes, "It has not yet been possible to find out the purpose of this installation—machine-gunning roads, railway lines, trenches, towns, landing barges or attacking aircraft flying below."

27 August 1944. An interrogated POW was at Peenemunde in 1943 and witnessed He 111 trials with flying bombs. The weapon was slung under the fuselage between the wheels. He witnessed the first airborne launching of the weapon. Additionally the prisoner inspected the He 111 closely and saw that

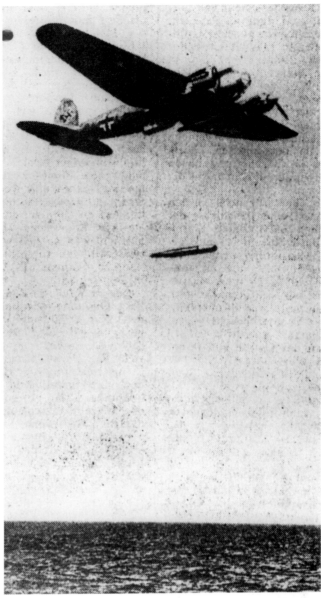

One photograph from a set of three that appeared in the German press portraying the He 111 as a torpedo bomber. AI sent all three images to the Admiralty on 30 October 1941. [AIR 40/156]

HEINKEL He ?

PR of Rostock-Marienehe Heinkel factory airfield on 25 April 1942 that accompanied AI Report 2057 of 1 May 1942 showed "an aircraft of extremely unusual design. Close study of this photograph indicates a very strong probability that this aircraft is built up almost entirely of standard He 111 components and on this assumption the attached composite silhouette has been made." [AIR 40/157]

The He 111Z indicated by the arrow at the lower edge of the picture was photographed at the Regensburg-Obertraubling Luftwaffe experimental station during takeoff. All five engines and both cockpits are clearly indicated by shadow. The other aircraft are the huge Me 323 six-engine transports and Me 321 gliders. The He 111Z was used to tow the latter. AI's Photographic Interpretation Unit regularly published photographs that it thought would be useful to aircrews in the journal *Evidence in Camera*. This image appeared in volume 3, no. 6 of the publication on 10 May 1943. [AIR 34/236]

a single wire running from the mother aircraft to the rear fuselage of the bomb constituted the control mechanism. The He 111 required the full length of the runway to get airborne but took off with no difficulty.

21 September 1944. RAE Farnborough informs AI that it estimates the range of the He 111 carrying the FZG-76 V-1 flying bomb to be about 1,120 miles at 296 km/h.

10 October 1944. AI believes that He 111/FZG-76s are being flown by 8/KG 3, based at Ahlhorn in Holland, and that a further *Gruppe* is to be based at Vasselbusch.

23 October 1944. He 111/FZG-76 minimum safety release height is five hundred meters. Pilots usually release from six hundred meters then fly on for a few minutes before banking away to port or starboard to avoid interception by night-fighters. When released the bomb dropped thirty to forty meters, fired up its engine, then flew on its course.

24 November 1944. A POW confirms that III/KG 3 is flying the He 111/FZG-76 flying-bomb combination.

2 March 1945. USAAF Technical Intelligence Report A.247 reports the installation of a top turret on the He 111-H armed with a single 13 mm MG 151.

12 March 1945. AI learns that III/KG 53 moved to Grottkau from Russia to train for air-launched flying-bomb operations against Britain. Active operations commenced in November 1944. Hauptmann Bischowski flew a pathfinder aircraft until the rest of 9/KG 53 could find its way in the dark. This *Staffel* had eighteen to twenty He 111s (H-16s or H-20s) available for sorties but only fifteen to seventeen trained crews. II/KG 53 was flying sixty aircraft about five times per week in combat operations. During mid-December 1944 II/KG 53 lost twelve planes in two operations, as a number of flying bombs exploded prematurely just after takeoff.

27 April 1945. Allied ground forces overrun Kohlenbissen airfield. Among the wreckage is an intact Fu 217 wireless set with FZG 76 launching equipment, which is salvaged and sent for analysis.

Gun-camera film of an He 111 shot up in dispersal at Laon-Athies airfield on 30 August 1943. The image appeared in volume 5, no. 1 of *Evidence in Camera*, published on 4 October 1943. [AIR 34/800]

Gun camera footage of an He 111 being engaged at low altitude. Not long afterward, the enemy bomber was shot down. [AIR 34/835]

Heinkel He 177

Five of twelve He 177s, photographed at the Rostock-Marienehe Heinkel factory airfield on 27 April 1942 by PRU aircraft. It was the thirteenth time He 177s had been captured on film. This image (photo number A/666, 5-92) formed part of "Interpretation Report L.63 Germany." The report recorded that this was the greatest number of He 177s to be photographed at the Rostock-Marienehe airfield on a single occasion. [Air 40/240]

War Record

Although this aircraft first flew in late 1939, it was beset with teething troubles and technical problems. By early 1941 it was apparent that the aircraft was experiencing serious difficulties that would render large-scale operational employment impractical until mid-1944. The fixation with dive-bombing did not help matters; indeed, when this was explained to Göring on 13 September 1942, he retorted, "What an asinine idea, to demand diving ability of a four-engine aircraft! If they had consulted me I could have told them right away that that was nonsense."

The Heinkel He 177 first saw active service in the Atlantic on 21 November 1943, when sixteen aircraft of II/KG 40 attacked convoy MKS.30/SL.129. Forty Hs 293 missiles were fired (of which only thirty worked), and three aircraft were shot down (18 percent losses) for the return of one 4,405-ton merchant ship sunk that had been straggling toward the rear of the convoy. The *Gruppe* then switched to the Mediterranean and on 26 November sank the 8,602-ton liner *Rohna*, with a loss of a thousand servicemen. However, four of the fourteen aircraft were shot down (28 percent losses), and another two crash-landed, leaving the unit seriously depleted.

Data File

DIMENSIONS

Wingspan	103 ft. 1¾ in.
Length	66 ft. 11¼ in.
Height	20 ft. 11¾ in.
Max. Speed	304 mph
Ceiling	26,245 ft.
Range	3,417 miles
Engines	2 × DB 610A/B (each comprising 2 × DB 605 close-coupled)
Armament	2 × 20 mm cannon, 2 × 13 mm, 3 × 7.92 mm machine guns
Payload	13,200 pounds
Crew	6

In late May 1944, equipped with about a hundred He 177s in three *Gruppen*, Oberstleutnant Horst von Riesen's KG 1 became fully operational and was the most powerful strategic strike force on the Eastern Front. Operating from airfields in East Prussia, flying in formations of up to eighty-seven aircraft, KG 1 began high-altitude daylight operations against supply centers, troop concentration areas, and Ukrainian railheads, in an attempt to stifle Soviet preparations for the forthcoming summer offensive. In the face of limited opposition—the Soviets possessed no high-altitude interceptor force—KG 1 achieved notable successes, such as hitting the Velikye Luki railhead, three hundred miles west of Moscow.

In the first week of July, because of the critical fuel situation, Luftflotte 3's He 177 *Gruppen* were withdrawn to Germany. Indeed, so serious was the problem that a single operational sortie by a *Geschwader* of He 177s required one day's output of aviation fuel from Germany's entire industrial base—about 480 tons—at a cost of suspending other types of flying, which the Reich could little afford. The only option was to disband the heavy bomber force. By the end of 1944 only one *Gruppe* of He 177s remained. An He 177 was modified at Letov airfield in Prague during 1943–44 to house a larger bomb bay that would be able to accommodate the planned German atom bomb. The bomb was never completed.

Intelligence History

20 January 1940. POW interrogation reveals that a new airplane, the He 177, is being produced. It is a four-engine dive-bomber capable of carrying two 1,000 kg bombs.

2 February 1940. POW interrogation of a KG 40 He 111 crew shot down on 13 January near Fifeness reveals that Germans are producing a very large four-engine dive-bomber. The first He 177 test model was ready at the Heinkel works in July 1939, but by this time the prisoner had ceased to be a test pilot.

23 May 1940. Air attaché Bucharest reports that an agent, a Romanian engineer recently returned from Germany, has disclosed that Heinkel has developed a new four-engine bomber, which has been tested and is now in production. He confirms that the aircraft has two engines housed together under each wing, both geared to one propeller.

12 June 1940. AI learns that He 177 has a 500 km/h cruising speed with a range of over 1,800 miles. Capable of operating as a dive-bomber, it is believed it will become operational in the autumn.

28 June 1940. AI produces the first estimates of the specifications for He 177. The figures are based on information provided by Heinkel.

8 August 1940. AI reports that unusually long runways constructed at the Rostock-Marienehe airfield were required for testing the new He 177 heavy bomber. AI declares that owing to problems experienced with the He 177's

A test version of the He 177. By May 1944, after a troubled history, the He 177 heavy bomber was in series production for the Luftwaffe. Several Gruppen of the Kampf-geschwader arm were in the process of reequipping with this type. The bomber had an excellent performance when everything worked, but the system of engine coupling resulted in overheating and frequent fires. Heinkel did actu-ally produce a four-engine, four-propeller version of the plane, the He 177B, or He 277, which experi-enced few difficulties and per-formed relatively well. Göring ordered two hundred per month in May 1944. However, within six weeks the decision had been reversed. [Air 40/240]

high-angle dive brakes, the RLM had conceded that a shallower angle of fifty degrees to the horizon would be adopted. The RLM did not like the idea of carrying bombs under the wings. Consequently, the entire bomb load was carried in the body of the fuselage. To facilitate bomb release during dive-bombing operations, ducts have been fitted that release the bombs at an angle to facilitate easy clearance of the aircraft. Heinkel has worked on a method of operating, sighting, and firing the He 177's defensive machine guns by remote control.

26 January 1941. POWs confirm that it was intended to equip their *Geschwader* with He 177 bombers. Doubts exist as to when the aircraft would be ready, as it was not performing well in dive-bombing tests.

17 February 1941. A POW under interrogation says that in recent tests one He 177 crashed, being unable to pull out of a dive. The same source gave his opinion that the He 177 "was not really a success," although "experiments were by no means completed."

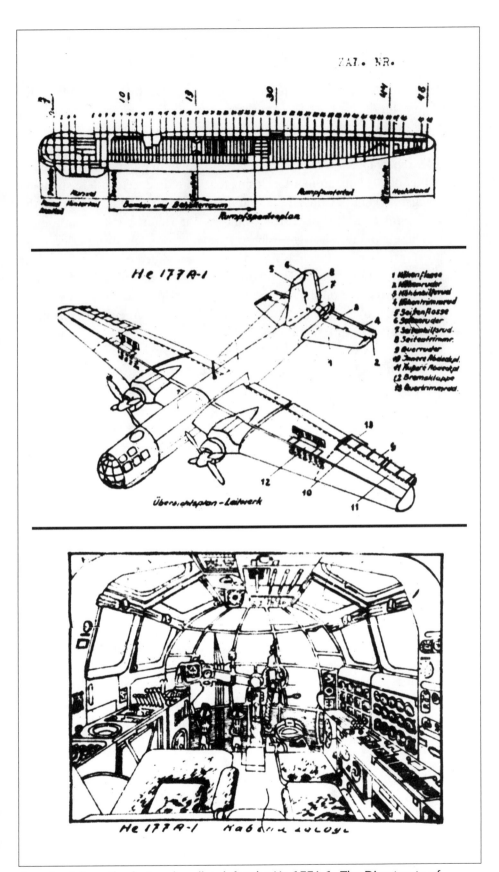

An extract from the factory handbook for the He 177A-1. The Directorate of
Air Intelligence acquired photostatic copies of selected entries of this publication from an SIS agent in the field in February 1944. [Air 40/165]

24 April 1941. AI learns that two He 177s "recently broke up while flying" and concludes that the bomber is not yet serviceable for operations.

25 April 1942. A POW states during interrogation that the problem with engines for the He 177 has not yet been resolved. The coupling of the engines in pairs still causes major difficulties with the firing sequence.

8 March 1943. An He 177 is claimed shot down in night action by a Beaufighter of 604 Squadron. After closing to six hundred feet, both the pilot and navigator (Flight Lieutenant Hoy and Flying Officer Dalton) observed that the enemy aircraft was an He 177 and gave it a short burst of cannon and machine-gun fire. Hits were visible on the wing roots and the fuselage, which burst into flames. The He 177 then slowed and glided toward the sea, flaming debris falling from it. The night-fighter crew then turned and observed flaming wreckage on the surface of the water. Upon debriefing, both crew are shown profiles and silhouettes of an He 177, which, they are adamant, was the aircraft type they shot down.

19 March 1943. AI summary of photographic intelligence on the He 177 reports that no major external modifications appear to have occurred since 1941. Since being first photographed at Rostock-Marienehe on 29 October 1940, an additional thirty-one PR missions have observed the He 177 at sixteen different locations. Measurements taken from "photographs of excellent quality" were given (in feet) as follows; wingspan 103–104½, length 66–68½, length of nose 20–22, tailplane span 31–31½. This example admirably illustrates the meticulous, painstaking work undertaken by the photographic interpretation units of the Directorate of Air Intelligence.

16 June 1943. POW interrogation reveals that many He 177s have crashed during trials and that a large number of test pilots have been killed.

17 November 1943. Intelligence supplied by the Belgian Ministry of National Defense in London reports to AI from "an extremely reliable source" that the He 177 has proved a "fiasco."

17 February 1944. AI acquires photostatic prints from an SIS agent in the field of selected entries of the text, figures, and sketches taken from the Heinkel He 177A-1 factory handbook.

25 February 1944. A worker at the Luftwaffe's Lechfeld experimental station informs AI that the He 177 is being withdrawn from operations to undergo modifications aimed at improving speed and defensive firepower.

25 November 1944. AI receives a captured copy of the "Mission d'Information Scientifique et Technique" of the He 177, the complete specification for this aircraft, from the French air ministry.

Henschel Hs 123

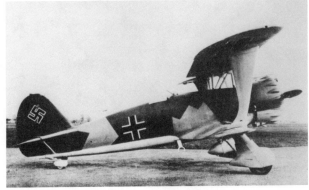

These photographs are taken from an Italian publication promoting the biplane dive-bomber. [AIR 40/122]

War Record

For a biplane to be serving with frontline Luftwaffe units in 1944 must seem anachronistic. The Hs 123 achieved this feat due to its robustness, reliability, and ability to operate in conditions that more modern, sophisticated aircraft found too harsh to withstand.

It was originally designed as a dive-bomber in 1933, the year the Luftwaffe was born. Although the famous Ju 87 Stuka won the RLM competition, the Henschel entry went into service as well. During the Spanish Civil War the Hs 123 operated with the Condor Legion, and it was here that Wolfram von Richtofen developed Luftwaffe close army support tactics that were to play a crucial role in the blitzkriegs of the Second World War.

The aircraft also bears the distinction of having completed the first close-support operation of World War II. Hs 123s of II/LG 2 attacked Polish positions in the village of Pryzstain in cooperation with an army attack. It went on to perform an important role in the advance into Belgium and France. During the first decisive tank battle, at Sedan, Hs 123s, alongside Wehrmacht panzer forces, wiped out two divisions of French tanks. Luftwaffe pilots discovered that the engine made a piercing shriek at 18,000 rpm and exploited this fact when attacking ground troops.

The type was mostly used on the Eastern Front. The extreme conditions of the Russian seasons often prevented other bombers from flying, but with its fixed undercarriage the Hs 123 could often continue flying. One senior German general even suggested the aircraft should return to production in 1943, such was its value. The suggestion was declined, but the type continued in operational service well into 1944.

Data File

DIMENSIONS

Wingspan	34 ft. 5½ in.
Length	27 ft. 4 in.
Height	10 ft. 6½ in.
Max. Speed	214 mph
Ceiling	29,520 ft.
Range	530 miles
Engines	1 × 880 hp BMW 132
Armament	2 × MG 17, 440 lb. bomb load
Bomb load	4,626 lb.
Crew	1

Henschel Hs 129

Initial rough sketch of the Hs 129 produced by Captain Sect for AI. The illustration features an Hs 129 variant, with a large-caliber cannon under the nose. [AIR 40/171]

War Record

The Hs 129 has become synonymous with the shark's teeth painted on its nose, and with a later version that featured a long-barreled antitank gun. It was designed specifically for the ground-attack role, in response to an RLM specification of April 1937. The specification stipulated that two small 465 horsepower Argus engines should power the plane. This caused the original Hs 129 to be severely underpowered; the Luftwaffe rejected it in 1940.

Henschel persevered with the project, and designer Friedrich Nicolaus completely revised the aircraft, making use of Gnome-Rhone 14U engines available from occupied France. It also featured a cockpit boasting three-inch-thick armored glass to protect the pilot from ground fire. The resulting Hs 129B showed a marked improvement in performance, and the Luftwaffe adopted the aircraft in 1942.

The plane was predominantly used on the Eastern Front, in the "*panzer-knacker*" tank-busting role. Its standard armament was quickly increased; a typical Hs 129 would carry 2 × 20 mm cannon, two 7.9 mm MGs, a 30 mm cannon, and forty-eight two-kilogram antipersonnel bombs. As Soviet tank armor improved, even this package proved inadequate, leading the Hs 129s to carry huge twenty-foot-long 75 mm guns under their noses. Toward the end of the war, Hs 129s even featured flamethrowers and an extraordinary downward-firing rocket mortar that was triggered by a photoelectric cell passing over a tank.

The aircraft made a brief appearance in North Africa, but engine reliability problems and the lack of an adequate sand filter prevented them from being fully deployed.

Data File (A and B series)

DIMENSIONS

Wingspan	46 ft. 7 in.
Length	31 ft. 11¾ in.
Height	10 ft. 8 in.
Max. Speed	253 mph
Ceiling	29,530 ft.
Range	547 miles
Engines	2 × 690 hp Gnome-Rhone 14M
Armament	2 × MG 131, 2 × MG 151/20, 550 lb. bomb load
Crew	1

The zenith of the Hs 129's career came during Operation *Zitadelle*, the 1943 German offensive at Kursk on the Eastern Front. The Luftwaffe claimed 1,100 Russian tanks destroyed in this campaign. Although this was an undoubtedly inflated figure, Hs 129s accounted for much of the destroyed Soviet armor. In one notable episode, a Russian armored breakthrough near Belgorod was headed off by Captain Bruno Meyer with four *staffeln* of Hs 129s.

Certain faults blighted the Hs 129's career, notably engine failure and poor visibility, but it did achieve limited success in the antitank role despite the small numbers built.

Intelligence History

30 September 1941. Air attaché Lisbon unofficially reports the Germans are designing a new dive-bomber, thought to be designated Hs 124 and intended for use attacking warships.

23 November 1941. An initial report on the Hs 129 describes it as very similar in concept to Italian Savoia-Marchetti S.M.86 dive-bomber. Luftwaffe classifies the aircraft as a "*schlachtflugzeug*" (ground-attack aircraft).

19 September 1942. A report from the Russians on tactics of the Hs 129 is received. The aircraft would take off and approach targets in *schwarm* formation. The *schwarm* would tighten if Russian fighters were present; Hs 129s would always have their own fighter escort. They would dive on target at a forty-five-degree angle from the sun to hamper antiaircraft fire.

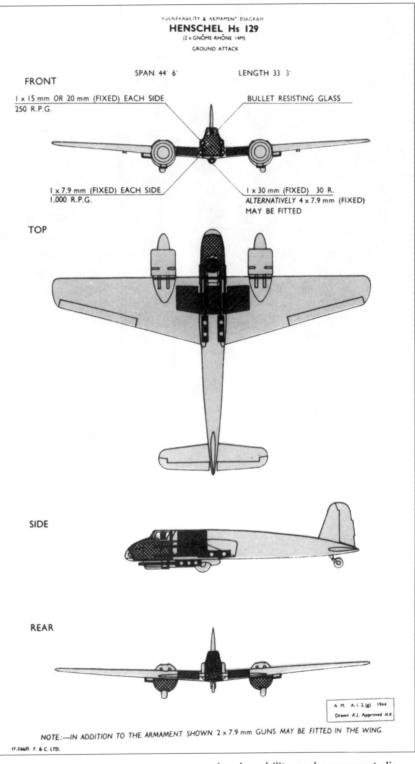

A vulnerability and armament diagram of the Hs 129 produced in 1944 [AIR 40/5]

4 December 1942. An engineer serving with Free French forces is interviewed. He had worked on Gnome-Rhone engines used on the Hs 129; he stated they were very good for the first twenty to twenty-five hours but then deteriorated completely and were "a disgrace to French manufacturing."

A distinctive "tankbuster" logo can be seen on the nose section of Hs 129 B-1 0297, photograph dated August 1943. The Italian markings on the wing in the top right-hand corner of the photo suggest this photograph comes from the Mediterranean theater. [AVIA 6/9076]

21 May 1943. AI obtains a report from an RLM expert who had visited frontline Hs 129 units in Russia. June 1942 saw SG 1 begin using the Hs 129 in the antitank role using 3 cm cannon. Russian POWs stated the Hs 129 had been successful during the battle for Kharkov, destroying many tanks and causing panic among troops. SG 1 claims twenty-three tank kills during the Soviet retreat from Kharkov to Voronezh.

From August to September, pilots begin to doubt the suitability of the Hs 129 for the tank-killing role. They disliked the 3 cm cannon and started to use bombs instead. The official also visited JG 51, which included a *Staffel* of Hs 129s. During training this unit achieved a 60 percent hit rate against dummy tanks. Between September and November it claims twenty-nine tank hits for three aircraft lost. During the Soviet breakthrough on the Don River, only the Hs 129 was effective against advancing tanks, claiming ten kills.

The report is not convincing as to the success of the Hs 129. There were problems with serviceability, with an average of only two aircraft per unit available on any one day. Also, the armorers were not trained on the 3 cm cannon. The plane was most effective against tanks that had broken through and were clear of other friendly forces. Another report from a POW in North Africa claims that eight Hs 129s had arrived in Tripolitana and within a week only two remained. It was estimated that only forty to forty-five Hs 129s were in operational use on all fronts. Reports that the Ju 87 is being developed for the antitank role suggests the failure of the Hs 129.

Hs 129 German propaganda picture. Apart from the distinctive crosses, there are no identifiable markings.

Junkers Ju 87

War Record

In January 1935, the Technisches Amt of the RLM gave Arado, Heinkel, and Junkers specifications for a new dive-bomber and tasked them each with designing and building a prototype. Within three months the Ju 87V-1 was undergoing test flights at Dessau. Thus was born the famous Junkers Ju 87 Stuka, from 1936 the backbone of the German dive-bomber arm. Elements within the Luftwaffe hierarchy thought the Ju 87 obsolete in 1939, owing to its slow speed and vulnerability, and wanted production ceased. However, the performance of the small number of Stukas in the Immelmann Gruppe sent to Spain with the Condor Legion reversed the view. Some 5,400 were built by the time manufacture halted in September 1944.

By the time war broke out on 1 September 1939, all nine *Stukagruppen* were equipped with the Ju 87B. They performed so well in Poland that Göring ordered production increased. Throughout the early blitzkrieg campaigns of 1939–1941 in Poland, Norway, France, Belgium, Holland, Greece, Yugoslavia, North Africa, and Russia, the Stuka spearheaded almost every assault of the *Panzertruppen* on the ground. One example of the astounding success this machine could achieve occurred at Sedan on 14 May 1940. While German engineers were constructing their bridges across the River Meuse, in full view of French artillery, they remained unmolested by hostile fire. This was largely because Stukas had been dive-bombing the French gunners for two hours and had made the dazed survivors bolt and run, such was their destructive

Data File (Ju 87D-1)

DIMENSIONS

Wingspan	45 ft. 3½ in.
Length	37 ft. 8¾ in.
Height	12 ft. 9½ in.
Max. Speed	255 mph
Ceiling	23,915 ft.
Range	954 miles
Engines	1 × Jumo 211J-1
Armament	4 × 7.92 mm machine guns
Payload	3,968 lbs.
Crew	2

A propaganda picture of a Ju 87B at an airfield in Poland during the very early stages of Operation Barbarossa, the 1941 invasion of the Soviet Union. The caption accompanying the picture states, "As soon as the sun stands high in the sky the bombers will set out for fresh attacks in order to prepare the way for German troops advancing to victory." [Air 40/126]

and psychological impact. The crossing of the Meuse at Sedan is widely held as the turning point in the Battle of France, and in its crucial phase—the crossing itself—the Ju 87s of the Luftwaffe's *sturzkampfgeschwader* achieved it.

Between 1 July and 9 August 1940, three *Stukagruppen* fought a strategic antishipping war in the Channel and the Western Approaches, flying 1,300 combat sorties. The result of their efforts was the suspension of Channel convoys by the British on 11 August. Well protected by fighter escorts over the Channel, the Stukas were not to fare so favorably in raids on the mainland radar stations. For example, on 18 August, during an attack on Poling radar station, four fighter squadrons pounced on the unfortunate crews of StG 77. Sixteen machines were destroyed, and two were damaged beyond repair (21 percent losses). As a result of the severe mauling during the Battle of Britain, the *Stukagruppen* were withdrawn by the Luftwaffe from operations over Western Europe.

On 10 January 1941, Hauptmann Paul-Werner Hozzel's I/StG 1 and Major Walter Enneccerus' II/StG 2 made a spectacular debut in the Mediterranean theater by putting six bombs into HMS *Illustrious*, as a result of which the stricken aircraft carrier spent a year being repaired in a U.S. dockyard. During

This unmarked and undated photograph of a Ju 87B was taken from a POW. The canopy of the Stuka is covered by a tarpaulin. Note also the technician standing on the wing root. [Air 40/126]

the assault on Crete, the Royal Navy suffered badly, the Stukas of Von Richthofen's Fliegerkorps VIII sinking nine warships; on 26 May 1941 they damaged the aircraft carrier HMS *Formidable*. It is worth noting the chivalry displayed by the Stuka crews during this (particularly brutal) campaign; they always ensured that hospital ships and columns of men retreating under the Red Cross flag were not attacked or endangered by their attacks on other targets. At the start of the North African campaign Rommel's Afrika Korps was provided with a *Stukagruppe* and came to rely on its excellent support

A Ju 87B in northern Russia fitted with snow skis in place of a wheeled undercarriage [Air 40/126]

The G-1 Stuka was a modified D-5 variant. Tests at Rechlin with the Ju 87D armed with two Flak 18 37 mm antitank cannon revealed that the best angle of attack against enemy tanks was sixty degrees. This improved the efficiency of the 37 mm H100Z shell in penetrating thick armor. The two underwing 37 mm Flak 18 BK37 cannon could be removed and replaced by conventional bomb racks. In Russia the Ju 87G-1 achieved astounding success; Hans Ulrich Rudel personally accounted for the destruction of 519 Soviet tanks. [Air 40/126]

throughout the two years of combat in the desert.

In the spring of 1941, the Ju 87D-1, possessing an increased payload and range, started to replace the B models in service. The Ju 87 upgrading program did not abate throughout the entire war, though the basic design remained hindered by its slow speed. For example, although Ju 87Ds armed with two 37 mm Flak 18 cannon were extremely effective as *panzerknacker* tank-busters, they continued to suffer heavy losses from ground fire and enemy fighter aircraft.

Perhaps the best method of illustrating the effectiveness of the Stuka is to briefly highlight the career of its greatest proponent. Germany's most decorated serviceman, Hans-Ulrich Rudel, flew all his 2,350 combat missions in the aircraft. Starting the war as a Leutnant, he finished an Oberst awarded the Knight's Cross with Oakleaves, Swords, and Diamonds in Gold, the highest award given by Hitler's Germany; he was the only man to receive it. He first flew in offensive operations on 22 June 1941 and is credited with destroying the Soviet battleship *Marat* as well as 519 tanks. Such was his reputation that Stalin placed a 100,000 ruble price on his head.

Intelligence History

1940. AI report states the Ju 87 has automatic apparatus for pulling out of a dive that works by barometric pressure. It has to be set according to weather conditions and is used as a safety device to prevent pilots diving from below five hundred feet.

August 1940. AI interrogates Gruppenkommandeur of I/StG 77, who states that armor taken from captured French Morane fighters had been fitted to one *Kette* of his *Gruppe*.

1940. AI interrogates a Stuka pilot from 4/StG 77, based near Caen, who reveals attack tactics. Units fly in *Staffel-Ketten-Vic*. The *Staffelkapitan* (number 1 aircraft) determines when to dive and commences the attack, followed by the left and then the right aircraft in the *Vic*. Then the left *Kette* dives in the same order, followed by the right *Kette*.

12 August 1941. AI is informed that the Revi bomb sight is still the standard for dive-bombing, and that the angle at which it is set during daylight attacks is based on a bomb release altitude of 1,600 feet. The automatic pullout mechanism on the Ju 87 is highly unpopular with the crews, as when it is in operation, the bombs can be released only once the aircraft has started to pull out. The pilots tend to feel that they are at the mercy of the machine. Consequently, the device has been removed from most Stukas in StG 1.

22 December 1941. AI Middle East acquires a copy of the German pamphlet *Einsatz der Panzerdurchschlagsbombe*, about a new rocket-bomb that POWs have frequently mentioned. The bomb is to be employed against shipping targets and dockyard facilities.

13 February 1942. A POW interrogated by AI Middle East attests that the Italians are manufacturing a new Stuka with a retractable undercarriage and other modifications.

A Ju 87D of III/StG 1 (Seventh Staffel), identifiable by the motif on the engine cover, being refuelled on the Eastern Front. Note that the mudguards have been removed.

23 February 1942. AI Middle East interrogates a POW who reveals much useful data on the Ju 87. The normal life of new engines in Africa was sixty to seventy hours flying, compared to 150–200 previously. The POW considers that maintenance standards in Africa were bad because there were too few ground crews for the necessary work in such difficult conditions. More important, the "rank and file were fed up with conditions in Africa." No machine was allowed to be returned to Germany unless it had flown 130 hours, as pilots were always wanting to take machines back in the hope of getting a few days leave at home.

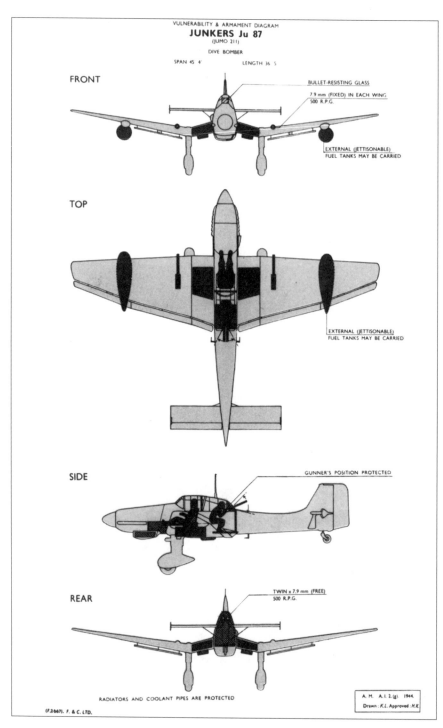

Ju 87B Stuka vulnerability and armament diagram

2 March 1942. AI interrogates a POW, formerly based in Italy, who saw a Ju 87D at Brindisi in December 1941. Its rear gunner was equipped with two MG 81 7.92 mm machine guns. The engine is a more powerful Jumo and permits an additional 60 mph. The aircraft is intended to carry a four-thousand-pound bomb, but the POW is of the opinion that the Ju 87 would have difficulty taking off with such a payload. Also, the oxygen bottles may have been moved from the rear of the Stuka, as they make a good target; the POW has heard stories of more than one Ju 87 having its tail blown off when these bottles were struck by enemy fire.

12 June 1942. AI interrogates *Unteroffizier* Rudolf Tuffek, who states that the engine on the Ju 87D-1 and D-3 is fully protected by armor, as are the petrol tanks. The D-1 can carry a four-thousand-pound bomb, but the D-3 can only manage 2,650 pounds, on account of the extra armor for protecting the crew. "The crew are completely walled round by armor plate and when in danger, they pull up sliding panels which enclose them completely into a kind of dome-shaped pillar box in which there are only narrow slits for the eyes."

26 June 1942. Middle East Command informs AI (in support of previous reports) that the Ju 87D can carry the 1,800 kg "Satan" bomb. A POW (a former fighter pilot based in Sicily) stated that he had seen these bombs at his airfield and that they were clearly marked "*Fur Ju 87 mit verstarkter Aufhangevorrichtung*" (For Ju 87 with strengthened bomb-rack).

12 November 1942. The British overrun El Daba airfield, North Africa, which is littered with sixty damaged enemy aircraft. AI gets its first opportunity to examine the Ju 87D.

1943. AI(k) Report 86/1943 on the Ju 87T is issued. AI learns from several POWs that the aircraft carrier *Graf Zeppelin* will be soon ready for service. One of the aircraft types mentioned for operations from the ship is the Ju 87T (T = *Trager*/Carrier), a specially adapted version of the Ju 87. The Ju 87T can jettison its undercarriage if it has to ditch in the sea. It was also reported that experiments had occurred at the Italian Torpedo School in Gosseto, using the JU 87 as a carrier-borne torpedo-bomber.

26 April 1943. Berne telegram 2053 informs AI that tests have occurred at Rechlin on a Ju 87D armed with two Flak 18 37 mm antitank cannon.

23 May 1943. AFHQ CSDIC Report 13 reveals details of POW interrogations regarding the Luftwaffe's Stuka arm. Prisoner "Duell" had heard of torpedo experiments but knew nothing of operations. He also declared that he had seen the ground-attack Ju 87D-3, which is armed with sixteen machine guns and can carry the 1,800 kg bomb in addition.

22 October 1943. USAAF B-17 crews mention that in combat operations over Germany Ju 87Ds armed with 20 mm and 37 mm cannon, plus rocket projectiles, have attacked their formations.

Junkers Ju 88

This Ju 88 was shot up on the ground by a Catalina flying boat from 210 Squadron. Taking off from Sullom Voe in the Shetland Islands on 26 June 1942 in a specially fitted out machine, to which extra fuel tanks had been installed, Flight Lieutenant D. E. Healy flew his Catalina to the Norwegian island of Spitsbergen in the Arctic Circle on a photo-reconnaissance mission. In the early morning of 27 June, this Ju 88 was spotted on the German airstrip at Banso, having been flown there by Leutnant Wagner two weeks earlier with supplies for a meteorological station on the island. The Catalina crew fired over 1,500 rounds of machine-gun ammunition. Such was the damage that the Germans abandoned the aircraft as a total wreck. [Air 15/470]

War Record

The Junkers Ju 88 was probably the most versatile German aircraft of the Second World War. Designed in 1935 as a high-speed bomber and tendered to the RLM, the Ju 88 fought off competition from Messerschmitt and Henschel. The first flight occurred on 21 December 1936, and succeeding prototypes set many speed records. In March 1939, the fifth prototype established a speed record of 321¼ mph over a thousand-kilometer circuit carrying a two-thousand-kilogram bomb load. Production aircraft were designated Ju 88A-1 and began to enter service in September 1939. However, not everything ran smoothly. At one stage, the Luftwaffe General Staff demanded that the Ju 88 be equipped for dive-bombing, which raised its weight from six to thirteen tons. As Generalfeldmarschall Erhard Milch sarcastically commented, this turned it into "a flying barn door."

During the Battle of Britain, Ju 88A-5s were equipped with fenders and cutters for dealing with cables hanging from the many barrage balloons over southern England. One of the key lessons learned during the air battles that raged over the summer skies of England was the need for more defensive firepower. Consequently, five 7.92 mm MG 81 machine guns were fitted.

Data File (Ju 88A-4)

DIMENSIONS

Wingspan	65 ft. 7½ in.
Length	47 ft. 2¾ in.
Height	15 ft. 11 in.
Max. Speed	292 mph
Ceiling	26,900 ft.
Range	1,696 miles
Engines	2 × Jumo 211J-1
Armament	7 × 7.92 mm machine guns
Payload	4,409 lbs.
Crew	4

However, Luftwaffe bomber crews held the Ju 88 in high regard; when proficient hands were at the controls, results were often impressive. For example, bomber ace Oberst Joachim Hellbig became the twentieth recipient of the "swords" to the "Knights Cross of the Iron Cross" as a Hauptmann commanding I/KG 1 after completing his five hundredth mission. His Ju 88–equipped unit was nicknamed the "Hellbig Flyers" by the British, as they were one of the Luftwaffe's most successful bomber units, especially in the antishipping role. Hellbig had personally sunk 180,000 tons of Allied shipping by November 1942. During the air siege of Malta in the first half of 1942, while in command of LG 1, Hellbig was stationed with his Ju 88s on Crete and was charged with intercepting convoys bound for the island from Alexandria, Egypt. Such was the ferocity of the LG 1 attacks that the Royal Navy nicknamed the waters south of Crete "Bomb Alley." To try to stifle the effect of Hellbig's unit, a British Royal Marine Commando raid was launched on Heraklion airfield where LG 1 was based; only seven of the unit's Ju 88s were destroyed.

The Ju 88C was designated as the fighter variant. The glass nose was replaced by solid metal and fixed forward-firing machine guns and or cannon. One hundred thirty Ju 88C-2 night-fighters were constructed and carried out night intruder operations over Britain between 1940 and 1941. It was the Ju 88C-6b that became the first radar-equipped night-fighter, with a Lichtenstein radar mounted in the nose. An improved version was the Ju 88G series, which additionally carried Flensberg aerials on the wings; these enabled the German aircraft to "home in" on RAF Lancaster and Halifax bombers, using their tail warning-radar emissions. The Ju 88G-4 was the first Ju 88 to be armed with the *schrage musik* featured on the Bf 110. As a night-fighter the Ju 88 was highly successful, especially when the latest radar was fitted. Between January and March 1944, 342 out of 3,759 bombers dispatched were shot down by night-fighters, largely thanks to the new radar. For example, on the night of 30/31 March 1944, during a raid on Nuremberg, Bomber Command suffered extremely heavy losses; ninety-five bombers were shot down, ten were written off on return, and fifty-nine were damaged, of an attacking force of 795 Halifaxes and Lancasters.

A Fourth Staffel, Second Gruppe Ju 88A-4, Kampfgeschwader unknown, preparing to take off on a mission. Just visible is part of the payload under the wing. This variant could carry four 550-pound bombs externally on racks under the inner wings. [Air 40/126]

The RAF was able to counter the German technological edge after two Ju 88s landed in Britain. First, in May 1943, a Ju 88R-1 defected, with, one suspects, the full knowledge and participation of MI6. Piloted by Condor Legion veteran Oberleutnant Heinrich Schmitt of NJG 3, the aircraft landed intact at RAF Dyce in Scotland, having been escorted part of the way by RAF Spitfires. R.V. Jones was telephoned by Jack Easton, one of the directors of Air Intelligence, and told that the Ju 88 night-fighter had landed at Dyce in Scotland. Jones went up to inspect it and found intact the Lichtenstein radar equipment.

Second, an inexperienced Ju 88G night-fighter pilot landed at RAF Woodbridge in Suffolk by mistake on the night of 12/13 July 1944. Once Professor Jones and his AI scientific/technical teams were able to examine the SN-2 radar and the "Flensburg" passive homing device, the RAF initiative in the night bombing campaign was reestablished.

A small number of Ju 88 aircraft were converted to the antitank ground-attack role. In 1942, a Ju 88A-4 was equipped with a 75 mm KwK 39 cannon mounted in a large bay underneath the fuselage. A small number of this variant, the Ju 88P-1, were delivered to Luftwaffe units. Other Ju 88Ps included the P-2 and P-3, each with a pair of 37 mm cannon, and finally the Ju 88P-4, armed with a single 50 mm BK5 cannon; 32 of the P-4s were manufactured. In all, total Ju 88 production (all variants) amounted to nearly fifteen thousand.

Intelligence History

17 October 1939. A POW under interrogation reveals that the Ju 88 is produced solely at the Dessau Junkers factory, from where the *staffel* collect the aircraft. The four-man crew compartment is especially cramped and uncomfortable. The Ju 88 is unarmored, carries a thousand kilograms of bombs, and has an all-in weight of 11,300 kg. The aircraft was originally intended to weigh just seven thousand kilograms, but as a result of an early experiment with dive-bombing in which a Ju 88 broke up in mid-air, Junkers was ordered by the RLM to reconstruct it with a better safety coefficient. This alone accounted for the substantial increase in weight, so that even when it dives at a top speed of 800 km/h the wings do not vibrate.

1940. AI learns that II/KG 26 is training in the antishipping fast-attack bomber role, practicing in the Baltic with Ju 88s on the target ship *Hessen*.

7 December 1940. A Ju 88A-5, radio code "F6+HM," of 4(F)/122 belonging to Generalfeldmarschall Kesselring's Luftflotte 2 is shot down near Skidbrook, in Lincolnshire. AI1(k) interrogates the crew and issues Report 970/1940 stating that Fernaufklarungsgruppe 122, based at Brussels-Evere since 23 May 1940, has been actively engaged in strategic reconnaissance over the UK. The Fourth *Staffel* is equipped with nine Ju 88 and three Bf 110 aircraft. The Ju 88A-5 had a greater altitude than earlier models and was the preferred aircraft of the *Staffelkapitan*.

4 January 1941. Air attaché Belgrade signals to AI that the Ju 88, capable of every type of bombing attack from horizontal to diving, medium and high

Three interesting gun-camera photographs of Ju 88s being shot up. The two on the ground were taken in the same attack. In the air-to-air-combat image, the attacking fighter is so close that the Lichtenstein radar fitted on the nose of the Ju 88C-6 is clearly visible. [Air 40/126]

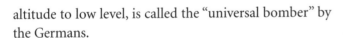

altitude to low level, is called the "universal bomber" by the Germans.

24 February 1941. Ju 88s and Do 17s have been fitted as night-fighters, operating from Amsterdam's Schipol airport. The Ju 88 has two 20 mm cannon in the nose, the glass of which has been replaced by steel.

6 April 1941. AI examination of a crashed Ju 88, radio code "5J+KN," belonging to II/KG 4, as well as interrogation of the POW crew, produces much useful data on the BZA1 automatic dive-bombing sight. The calculating mechanism is set in operation by a simple on/off switch, but it needs to be set four minutes prior to commencement of the attack dive, to give the gyroscopes time to run up. During this four-minute period it is not necessary for the pilot to maintain fore and aft trim, but steep banking turns should be avoided.

21 May 1941. Report K.281 states that the Ju 88 night-fighter has had its armament improved to accommodate three machine guns firing forward, in addition to the existing two 20 mm cannon.

11 June 1941. AI discovers from a POW under interrogation that Ju 88s of KuFlGr 606 (Kustfliegergruppe—Coastal Aviation Group) are being equipped with a free-moving, forward-firing 20 mm cannon, operated by the observer, to silence shipping antiaircraft fire during the attack run to the target.

1 October 1941. The Germans have about one hundred operational Ju 88s that are mounted on snow skis for missions in severe weather conditions.

20 December 1941. AI2(g) provides details of all the Ju 88 variants and their roles after capturing and translating all the relevant data from a captured Ju 88A-5 handbook.

22 December 1941. Middle East Command sends AI a captured booklet about the Ju 88A-4 that makes reference to a "Rauch-Gerate" rocket-assisted take-off apparatus. The booklet declares that the mechanism is switched on after "cruising along the ground for about 10 seconds, i.e., 100–150 meters," after which the thirty-second boost assists the heavily laden Ju 88 to achieve a reasonable height without running out of runway. At a height of no less than 150 meters the bomb-aimer jettisons the rocket apparatus.

16 January 1942. An AI report about the Ju 88 (PR version) discloses that aircraft of 1(F)/123 carry out missions over the Bristol Channel and the Atlantic Ocean. They also cooperate with fast attack motor-torpedo boats by circling convoys and acting as the *Fuhlungshalter*.

A Ju 88G-1 night-fighter from NJG 102 fitted with two 20 mm cannon in the dorsal position aimed forward at an angle of forty-five degrees. This configuration was known as *Schrage Musik* (see 21 July 1944 entry) and allowed night-fighters to attack bombers from below. Additionally the Lichtenstein SN2 radar aerial array is visible, as is the Naxos homing device, in a blister astride the cockpit. The Naxos was a passive system that homed in on the signals from the HS2 navigational radar used by RAF bombers. NJG 102 was formed in June 1943 from Nachtjagdschule 2, based at Stuttgart-Echterdingen [Air 14/2661].

24 January 1943. AI discover that the Rechlin Luftwaffe experimental unit is testing a Ju 88C *Zerstörer* in the night-fighter role. It is said to be heavily armed and armored.

7 February 1943. POW interrogation reveals that in the middle of 1942 experiments were successfully carried out at Okecie, near Warsaw, with Ju 88s of 4/KG 54 carrying three torpedoes each. The aircraft were assisted on take off by the "Krafteier" rocket booster device.

22 October 1943. USAAF B-17 crews report that Ju 88s have attacked them with 20 mm and 37 mm cannon as well as rockets.

22 November 1943. The crew of a 9/KG 26 Ju 88 torpedo bomber states under interrogation that the entire III Gruppe hopes to be equipped with Do 217s, as their current machines have not brought much success.

27 November 1943. AI Report P5/8546 states that a new Ju 88 was seen at the Okecie Junkers factory airfield equipped with a 37 mm cannon in the nacelle. This machine was first spotted at the airfield in September 1943.

2 December 1943. In AI Report 60095, a source at the Okecie Junkers factory airfield reveals that the main armament on the Ju 88C-6 night-fighter is three forward-firing 20 mm cannon.

11 June 1944. USAAF intelligence reports that a Ju 88 has been fitted with an 88 mm gun for antitank operations. Fitted underneath the fuselage, the barrel is 5.5 meters long and protrudes about one meter from the forward edge of the weapon's nacelle. It is loaded and fired automatically and is equipped with a special recoil system and muzzle brace. The shells are armor-piercing *Panzergranaten*; after three hundred rounds have been fired the Ju 88 becomes unsteady, as the rivets loosen owing to recoil.

13 July 1944. At 4:25 AM, a Ju 88G-1 night-fighter of 7.III/NJG 2, radio code "4R+UR," lands at Woodbridge emergency landing strip. Three days later AI compiles Report 242, designated Top Secret owing to the nature of the content, which declares, "This important capture is one of Germany's latest night-fighters and is fully equipped with up to date radar and radio." The Luftwaffe pilot had had his bearings confused and, thinking he was near Berlin, had landed at Woodbridge in error.

21 July 1944. AI2(g) issues Report 1612 concerning the fitting of two 20 mm cannon in the dorsal position at an angle of forty-five degrees in enemy night-

On 5 October 1943 this Ju 88 was shot down near Paris by RAF fighters of 609 Squadron, its two-hundredth enemy aircraft kill. The image was published in the 8 November issue of *Evidence in Camera*. Taken from a gun camera from one of the Fighter Command aircraft, it clearly shows that both engines are on fire. [Air 34/805]

fighters. Firing forward, Do 217, He 219, Ju 88, and Bf 110 night-fighters approach British bombers from below, guided by radar, and rake the entire underside from tail to nose. AI believes the advantage of this method is that the night-fighter can approach and attack from a position that ensures maximum safety and gives the least warning to the bomber crew.

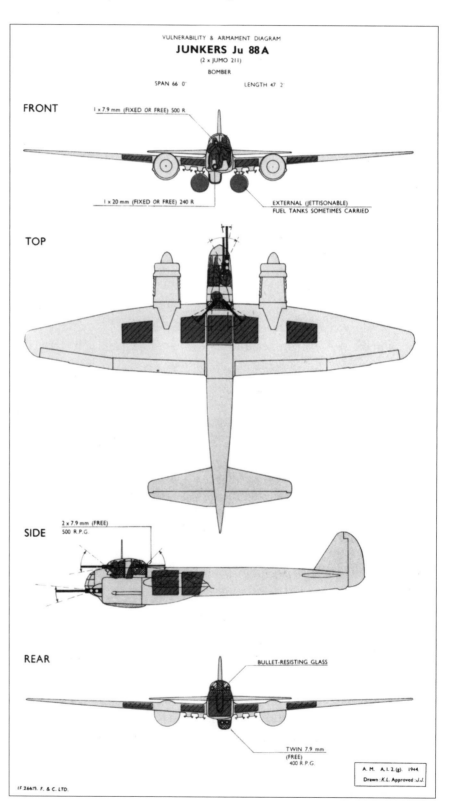

Ju 88A vulnerability and armament diagram

Junkers Ju 88 Mistel (Mistletoe)

This picture was included in AI Interpretation Report L.187 covering a PR sweep over Peenemunde on 26 April 1944. Circled are "two Ju 88s, each with a small aircraft mounted on top of its fuselage. The small aircraft, which have the appearance and dimensions of Me 109s, are mounted centrally above the larger aircraft, and shadow indicates that the tails of the small aircraft are raised well above the fuselages of the Ju 88s. The two 'composite aircraft' were seen in front of one of the main hangars." [Air 40/186]

War Record

The Mistel (Mistletoe) was originally the idea of Junkers's chief test pilot in 1941. While pondering possible military uses for outdated Ju 88 bombers, he proposed stripping the aircraft of interior fittings, replacing them with fuel tank and a 8,378-pound shaped-charge warhead in the nose, then attaching a fighter plane to the upper surface to pilot the combination. When both aircraft neared the target the pilot would put both aircraft into a shallow fifteen-degree dive designed to deliver the warhead with precision. Then he would release the Ju 88 and proceed to fly an accompanying parallel course making alterations to the bomber's flight path by radio control until it impacted upon the target.

The RLM was not receptive to the project at first, but by 1943 wartime demands had led to the concept's being put back into development. After the successful trial flight of a Ju 88A-4/Bf 109F-4 combination, fifteen sets were ordered by the Luftwaffe. Tests showed that the warhead could penetrate eighteen-meter-thick reinforced concrete.

This small Mistel force became operational in mid-1944 and commenced night attacks against Allied shipping in the Bay of Biscay from the St.-Dizier, France. Four ships were attacked and four hits registered, though none were sunk. Attacks were also made against Allied invasion shipping anchored off the Normandy beachhead, but without success.

Data File

SEE JU 88,
BF 109,
FW 190.

This photograph constituted only the third sighting of a Mistel and was included in AI Interpretation Report L.224. It was taken during a PR sweep over St. Dizier airfield in France on 17 July 1944, just prior to an attack by the U.S. Eighth Air Force. This "composite" is seen in a shelter in the southern dispersal area of the airfield. PR of the airfield after the attack showed that it had not been destroyed (see p. 137, entry for 17 July 1944). [Air 40/186]

This extraordinary photograph is of a Ju 88/Me 109 at St. Dizier was taken by a member of the French resistance and was one of four supplied to AI [Air 40/186]

Further Mistel missions were planned, including an attack on the Home Fleet at Scapa Flow in December 1944, from Grove airfield in central Denmark. At a range of 480 miles it was hypothetically possible that the minimum force requirement of forty *Misteln* would reach the Orkneys. However, they would probably have been shot out of the skies over the North Sea. The British had 160–200 night-fighters in the area, and radar would have detected the sluggish *Misteln*; their top speed was 236 mph.

In 1944, as the Allied armies advanced upon the frontiers of the Third Reich, an order was given for the production of a hundred Mistel-2s (later increased to 250). The Germans intended to use them in Operation Iron Hammer, the attack upon the advancing Allied armies. However, as with most of the Nazis' last-ditch schemes, the program came to nothing; the war ended before the force could be built. Some were used to strike at the Soviets during the Battle of Berlin in April 1945. When the Red Army crossed the Oder and Neisse Rivers on 16 April 1945, the Luftwaffe threw every available asset at it, including twelve Misteln from KG 200, in an attempt to destroy the bridges. Additionally, in what was probably the Luftwaffe's last attempt to relieve pressure on Berlin, Leutnant Eckard Dittmann led an attack by seven II./KG 200 Misteln against the Soviet-held bridge over the River Oder at Kustrin on 27 April 1945. Supported by three Ju 188 pathfinders and covered by a *Gruppe* of Fw 190 fighters, the attack was delivered in the face of withering Soviet antiaircraft fire. Dittmann, one of only two Mistel pilots to return to base, was unsure of the success of the mission, because the AA fire in the target area was too intense to allow him to loiter safely.

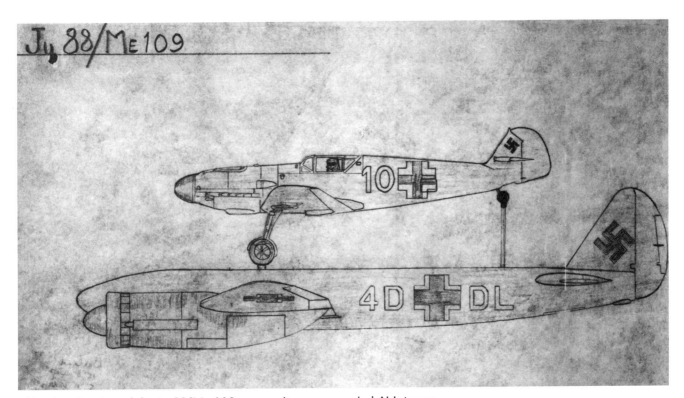

This plan drawing of the Ju 88/Me 109 composite accompanied AI Interpretation Report L.229, issued on 4 August 1944, listing all sightings of the Mistel up to that date. [Air 40/186]

The Ju 88/Fw 190 Mistel variant. It is interesting that the cockpit has not yet been removed and replaced with the powerful warhead. [Air 40/126]

Intelligence History

26 April 1944. A high-altitude PR mission to Peenemunde reveals the existence of "two Ju 88s, each with a small aircraft mounted on top of its fuselage," as declared by AI Photographic Interpretation Report L.187, issued by RAF Medmenham three days afterward.

6 May 1944. The director of Intelligence AI2(g), Wing Commander Proctor, issues Report 2237 about German composite aircraft. The report mentions a POW who "referred to a composite aircraft . . . and stated that the whole was controlled by the pilot of the Bf 109, the Ju 88 being without a crew. Although the POW reports all state that the smaller aircraft is piloted, it may prove to be a new type of glider bomb."

15 June 1944. Two 264 Squadron RAF Mosquito XIIIs on defensive patrol over the Normandy beachhead shoot down and destroy a "composite aircraft 25 miles west of Le Havre."

16 June 1944. An Admiralty flash message to all Overlord forces warns that the "Germans have developed a composite aircraft consisting of a bomber with a fighter mounted on top of its fuselage. The bomber is crewless and filled with explosive. . . . [P]robable combination is Ju 88 bomber and Me 109 fighter on top. Expected targets for these weapons are installations and heavy ships."

An Fw 190 cockpit, with an added center panel with automatic pilot control, propeller-pitch indicators, and combination boost gauge and tachometers. On the left side can be seen the Ju 88 throttles, undercarriage switches, and indicators.

27 June 1944. AI Report 2247 declares, "Fresh evidence supports the original POW story that the Ju 88 serves as a flying bomb. It is estimated that the weight of the complete warhead may be as high as 8,000 lb. There is good reason to believe that the penetrative force is exceptionally high, and that the enemy believes in its ability to sink a capital ship with one hit."

4 July 1944. A Ju 88/Me 109 composite aircraft is seen at Kolberg airfield, and again at the same location three days later. The Kolberg sighting led AI to order increased surveillance over known Ju 88 repair centers in case "repairs" being undertaken by the Germans were in fact conversions to this new role.

17 July 1944. AI PR over St.-Dizier airfield leads to the production of Photographic Interpretation Report L.224 two days later. The report states, "A 'Composite Aircraft,' consisting of an Me 109 mounted on a Ju 88, has been seen for the first time in France. It was photographed at ST.-DIZIER on 17.7.44 shortly before the airfield was attacked by aircraft of the U.S. 8th Air Force."

21 July 1944. Three Ju 88/Me 109 composite aircraft are photographed together at Nordhausen airfield, the greatest number seen together at one location.

18 August 1944. AI2(g) issue an internal memo assessing data so far acquired on the *Mistel*. Although it was believed the threat was initially exaggerated, PR sweeps over known Mistel airfields were to be kept up, as "the enemy will do all he can to hurt us."

28 January 1945. AI Report 86724 asserts that twenty He 177 composite aircraft with fighters mounted atop were spotted at Tirstrup airfield.

3 February 1945. USAAF Fifty-fifth Fighter Group P-51D Mustangs shoot down five composite aircraft near Hamburg. The pilots confirm that the composites comprised Fw 190/He 111 combinations.

21 March 1945. AI Photographic Interpretation Report L.749 issued, by RAF Medmenham, discloses that no sighting of composite aircraft at airfields and landing grounds between Hamburg and Brunswick occurred during a ten-day PR sweep, 9–19 March 1945. (The Allied Expeditionary Force had to keep this designated area clear, so *Misteln* would not attack Anglo-Canadian pontoon bridges across the River Rhine when Operation PLUNDER began on 23 March 1945.)

The Ju 88/Fw 190 Mistel in its RAE "Farnborough Luftwaffe" markings. This model is not equipped with the warhead; the glass canopy and nose are still conspicuously present.

Junkers Ju 188

Ju 188 radio code "N1+KQ." One POW interrogated by AI asserted that the crew compartment of the Ju 188 was more spacious than that of the Ju 88. He also claimed the Ju 188 was fitted with an emergency exit for the pilot on the port side of the cockpit, a section of which was jettisoned by an explosive charge. [Air 40/126]

War Record

The Ju 188 medium bomber, of which 1,076 were built, began as a private venture by Junkers to upgrade the aging Ju 88. When it became unequivocally clear in late 1942 that the problematic Ju 288 bomber would not enter service on time, the RLM needed an interim replacement. The Ju 188 featured a totally redesigned nose and forward crew compartment with a streamlined dorsal defensive gun turret, an increased wing span, and a new square-fin tail plane and rudder. This machine, having already flown in spring 1942, underwent further tests in January 1943 at the behest of the RLM. Satisfied with its performance, the RLM placed an order in February, and by the end of 1943 283 Ju 188s had entered service with the Luftwaffe.

On 18 August 1943 the aircraft saw its combat debut when Leutnant Hans Altrogge led three Ju 188 of I/KG 66 in a "*Piratangriff*" daylight surprise attack on Lincoln. Thereafter KG 6 re-equipped with the Ju 188 and from 12/13 October 1943 conducted harassment attacks upon London. The RAF first encountered the Ju 188 operationally in October 1943.

The Ju 188 performed many roles in the Second World War: medium-bomber, torpedo-bomber, night-fighter, fighter, and reconnaissance plane. Over 50 percent of the Ju 188s manufactured were reconnaissance versions. Throughout the Normandy campaign, though German field commanders received very little photographic reconnaissance intelligence, Ju 188s were employed in this hazardous role. Operating in darkness at twenty thousand feet, the Ju 188 crews dropped six-million-candlepower photographic flash bombs that lit up when they had descended to four thousand feet. Only five or six photographs could be taken before flak and night-fighter defenses, alerted by the powerful illumination, rendered loitering in the operations zone extremely dangerous. As already noted, three Ju 188 pathfinders supported one of the last offensive operations by the Luftwaffe when, on 27 April

Data File

DIMENSIONS

Wingspan	72 ft. 2 in.
Length	49 ft. ½ in.
Height	14 ft. 7 in.
Max. Speed	311 mph
Ceiling	30,660 ft.
Range	1,209 miles
Engines	2 × BMW 801D-2
Armament	1 × 20 mm cannon, 2 × 13 mm and 1 × 7.92 mm machine guns
Payload	6,614 lbs.
Crew	4

1945, seven II./KG 200 *Misteln* attacked the Soviet-held bridge at Kustrin over the River Oder.

Intelligence History

November 1942. It is reported I/LG 1 has the new Ju 188 and used them in attacks on Allied shipping employed during Operation Torch, in Algeria.

23 December 1942. The Ju 188 was ready for series production during the summer of 1942, but the RLM insisted on various changes. However, the Ju 188 would not go into series production, at the Junkers-Dessau factory, until mid-1943 and would not become operational until the end of that year. Difficulties were being experienced, such as a shortage of skilled labor and insufficient fuel stocks for the necessary flight trials.

8 July 1943. AI hears that the Ju 188 has become operational on the Eastern Front.

13 October 1943. AI learns Ju 188s at Toulouse are taking off with rocket boosters. AI believes that this is not a prototype but a fully operational unit, as rocket-boosters are being mass-adapted to heavy bombers.

18 October 1943. AI learns from a 3.I/KG 6 POW interrogation that the Ju 188 has a new system of electrically operated bomb doors. The bomb door switch simultaneously fuses the bombs, making it impossible to drop the payload unfused except by using the emergency-release lever.

30 October 1943. AI discovers that the knowledge the Germans gained from the Ju 88T was put into construction of the Ju 188, which was already serving in Russia.

12 February 1944. A POW reveals under interrogation that the Ju 188 has been fitted with the Jumo 213 engines, giving it a top speed of 338 mph, and is already in service in the high-speed reconnaissance role.

AI originally designated the Ju 188 as the "Rechlin 72" after these five were seen together with an He 177. The photograph was taken in a standard PR sweep over the Luftwaffe experimental airfield on 28 June 1943. [Air 40/173]

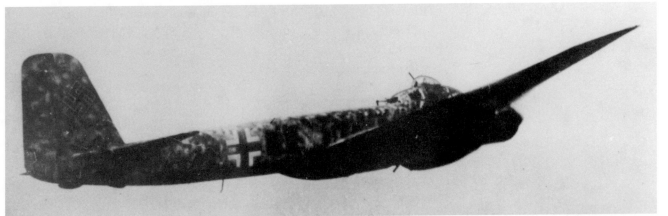

German propaganda photograph of a Ju 188 in flight. As with nearly all such pictures, the censor has obscured the unit markings. [Air 40/126]

11 May 1944. AI learns from MAAF (Mediterranean Allied Air Force) Technical Intelligence Report S31 that Ju 188 is operating in the naval reconnaissance role from airfields in southern France. Ten sorties were observed between 4 AM on 10 May to 4 AM on 11 May 1944, shadowing an Allied convoy off the coast of Algeria. The Ju 188s flew at various speeds and altitudes as low as sea level. Each time the Ju 188s were approached by RAF Mosquito aircraft, they evaded combat, one even entering Spanish airspace.

This reconnaissance photograph appeared in the 22 November 1943 edition (volume 5, number 8) of the RAF publication *Evidence in Camera.* The accompanying caption read, "Ju 188s (encircled) with Ju 88s (B) at BERNBURG. Compare the longer wing and nose shadows of the Ju 188 (A) with those of the three Ju 88s (B). Note the rows of wings (C) near the Assembly Shops." [Air 34/807]

21 June 1944. At 1:10 AM a Ju 188 reconnaissance plane flies into the side of a hill four miles west-northwest of Rothes, Scotland. The wreckage is partly buried in a peat bog. There is no fire, and the remains of the equipment are widely scattered.

24 June 1944. AI Report 75237 asserts the Ju 188 is being converted into a four-engine bomber with a lengthened fuselage. The new Ju 188 will be ready for testing in three months.

13 November 1944. A POW employed at the Luftwaffe Waffen Erprobungsstelle (Armament Research Establishment) at Tarnewitz between October 1943 and August 1944 stated he had seen a Ju 188 equipped with six upward-firing cannon in the fuselage. Experiments were conducted with this weapon configuration in the Ju 188 during April 1944.

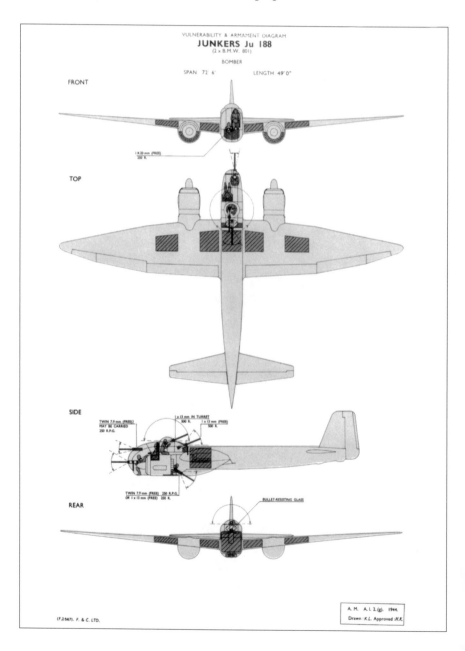

Ju 188 vulnerability and armament diagram

Junkers Ju 288

Ju 288
[PROVISIONAL DRAWING]

SECRET   ISSUED WITH A.I.2 (g) REPORT Nº 2287. NOV. 44.   P·E·C

The Junkers Design Bureau, ably led by Heinrich Hertel, had already developed a series of specifications for a series of twin-engine fast bombers that, as it transpired, closely fitted the requirements of the RLM for the B (for "Britische") bomber program. One of them, the Junkers EF73, was submitted to the RLM Technisches Amt and was selected. It became the Ju 288, as shown here in a set of provisional drawings produced by AI in November 1944.

War Record

In July 1939 the RLM issued a specification for a new bomber of advanced design able to exceed speeds of 400 mph carrying a payload of 1,102 pounds over distances of 3,355 miles. The Junkers response was the Ju 288. Although featuring a pressurized cabin for high-altitude flight, the entire Ju 288 program was beset with problems and technical difficulties. Essentially another derivative of the Ju 88 airframe, the Junkers Ju 288 differed in that its nose and twin tail fin and rudder configuration bore little resemblance to the other Ju 88 variants—the Ju 188 and Ju 388.

The maiden flight of the Ju 288V1 was originally scheduled for October

Data File

DIMENSIONS

Wingspan	51 ft. 6 in.
Length	52 ft. 9½ in.
Range	1,677 miles
Payload	6,612 pounds
Crew	2

1940, and series production was planned to begin in early 1942. By early 1941, development of the sophisticated Ju 288, initially selected as a bomber, was in serious trouble. The Ju Jumo 9-222 engine had failed to live up to expectations, and flight trials were deferred until mid-1942; even then the first prototype flew with less powerful BMW 9-801 engines, a change that confused the test evaluation process even further.

The program was eventually abandoned in June 1943, due to a variety of factors: a shortage of strategic materials, and the necessity for replacement engines, which were not forthcoming. The original twenty-four-cylinder Junkers Jumo 222 was rejected at the test stage. Of a total twenty-two Ju 288 prototypes built, seventeen crashed during flight trials.

Intelligence History

1940. AI describes the Ju 88Z as a fast "destroyer," with greater range than existing Ju 88s, a top speed of over 300 mph, nine hours' endurance, and a crew of three—pilot, radio operator, and flight engineer. The plane was too narrow to accommodate two men side by side, no bomb racks were fitted externally, and there were no dive brakes. Armament consisted of three machine guns and one cannon fixed in the nose to fire forward.

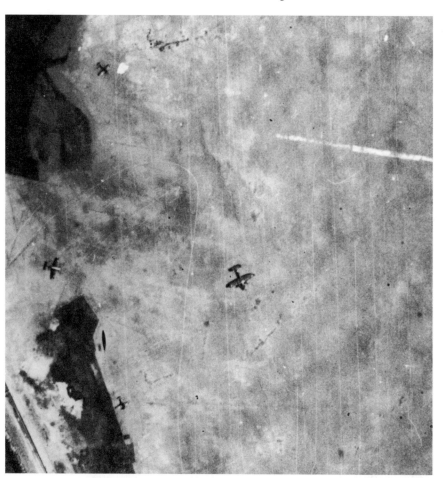

The Ju 288 was originally designated the "Dessau 62" by AI after it was first photographed on 1 August 1942 during a PR sweep over Dessau. This photograph is of the Ju 288 at Tarnewitz on 27 July 1943, only the second time it was seen.

1941. POW interrogation reveals in AI1(k) Report A.35/1941 that the *Geschwaderkommodore* and Gruppenkommandeur of III/KG 30 had visited Dessau to see the new Ju 288. This unit is to receive four Ju 288s by May and will eventually be totally equipped with the type. Göring recently addressed III/KG 30 in Amsterdam and promised that the complete reequipping of the unit would be concluded by September 1941. The same POW stated that the bomb load would be in the region of 6,600 pounds.

20 February 1941. AI learns the new Ju 288 will be armed with a pair of machine guns under the tail, fired by remote control by the radio operator, with a large arc of fire.

18 May 1941. A POW pilot, who claims to be a close friend of the Junkers factory's chief test pilot, Pieters, saw the Ju 288 in September 1940. The crew had been reduced to two men, as the observer was not needed—the pilot would do his work.

One of the many Ju 288 prototypes. After the RLM scrapped the entire B-bomber program, the Ju 288 project was officially abandoned. However, testing continued at Junkers until mid-1944. The program called for the design and building of a bomber force that could raid targets anywhere in Britain from bases in Germany.

3 November 1941. AI reports that KuFlGr 606 (a *Kustenfliegergruppe*) is to be equipped with the Ju 288. The aircraft is also to be fitted with a three-way autopilot.

13 December 1941. A top secret "M Source" mentions the new Ju 288 "Taifun" supersecret fighter. The Gruppenkommandeur of I/LG 1, who was always welcome at the Junkers factory, had already seen the aircraft.

4 January 1942. A pilot POW from KuFlGr 506 recently went to Dessau and saw the Ju 288. Unlike most Junkers aircraft, this one had twin tail fins. Because the cabin was tilted up in the front, with gun blisters in the glass at the sides, the forward end of the aircraft looked like a snake's head.

29 April 1942. K Report 86 declares that by mid-1941 Junkers Dessau factory had produced six prototypes, numbered V-1 to V-6 (V standing for *Versuchsmachine*, or experimental aircraft). It was believed that the final prototype, the V-6, would enter series production.

December 1942. A POW under interrogation says he believes the Ju 288 program had proven a failure.

19 February 1943. AI Report 258 asserts that series production of the Ju 288 has commenced.

9 June 1943. AI Report 50852 states that owing to the standardization of German aircraft types, production of the Ju 288 has been abandoned.

11 December 1943. Ju 288 is officially designated the "Dessau 62" by AI after several aircraft of the type are photographed in PR sweeps across German experimental airfields. Only four had been seen by the end of 1943.

Junkers Ju 388

Two views of the same Ju 388. Immediately after the war, the USAAF examined a captured Ju 388 and in TIR A-481 evaluated the pressure cabin. "The cabin was pressurized in flight to a differential pressure of about 31b./sq in. All windows were of double plexiglass construction; the outer pane withstood the pressure, and the two panes were separated by about 0.4 inch airspace. A silica gel type dehydrator was fitted in the inner pane of each window. The Junkers engineers indicated that considerable research had gone into the development of this window combination and that after initial troubles very little difficulty was encountered."

War Record

Following the unfortunate and untimely abandonment of the Ju 288 program, the Luftwaffe urgently required a replacement. Junkers, despite obvious problems, had continued development of high-altitude variants of the Ju 188—the Ju 188J, Ju 188K, and Ju 188L. All were modified to become Ju 388s. All were powered by BMW 801TJ turbo-supercharged radial engines. The Ju 388J all-weather fighter never really left the prototype stage, with only three of the model being constructed. More fortunate was the Ju 388K bomber, of which fifteen were manufactured before the program was terminated. However, a total of forty-seven Ju 388L high-altitude photographic reconnaissance aircraft were built. This was largely a result of the need for a high-altitude reconnaissance capability after the Allied invasion of France. The Luftwaffe received its initial complement of Ju 388Ls in August 1944. Production halted in December 1944 when jet fighter output assumed primary importance.

Intelligence History

18 April 1944. Under interrogation a POW informs AI that while serving as a Ju 188 observer he had heard rumors of the existence of a Ju 388. He said it was a twin-engine aircraft with twin tail fins designed for high-altitude long-range work. He gave the ceiling as between thirteen and fourteen thousand meters.

Data File (Ju 388L-1)

DIMENSIONS

Wingspan	72 ft. 2 in.
Length	49 ft. 10½ in.
Height	14 ft. 3¼ in.
Max. Speed	407 mph (assisted) or 382 mph (unassisted)
Ceiling	44,094 ft.
Range	2,159 miles
Engines	2 × BMW 801TJ
Armament	2 × 13 mm machine guns
Crew	3

2 May 1944. A top-secret "E source" reports the Ju 388 is a twin-engine bomber with twin tail fins and rudders.

24 May 1944. The same "E source" adds that the Ju 388 is like the Ju 188 and that it will probably be used for reconnaissance. The source saw one with turbo-charged Jumo 801 engines.

20 November 1944. AI discovers that there are three subtypes of Ju 388: the J (fighter), the K (bomber), and the L (reconnaissance). The Fokker factory in Amsterdam was producing Ju 388 fuselages at the rate of about ten per week.

16 January 1945. AI learns the Ju 388 had been ready for some time. It was also being asserted that racks had been fitted on top of the aircraft to fit V-1 flying bombs or Bf 109 fighters.

16 January 1945. AI is informed that the Ju 388 is the German Mosquito. As a twin-engine, long-range fighter or bomber, it can compete with the Mosquito in terms of speed.

26 January 1945. AI learns that in July 1944 there were four assembly lines established at Menibum for production of the Ju 388 fuselage.

A Ju 388L reconnaissance plane. In the rear of the bomb bay of this variant are mountings for the two cameras.

Captured drawings of the Ju 388 with the German annotations translated for the benefit of Allied air crew

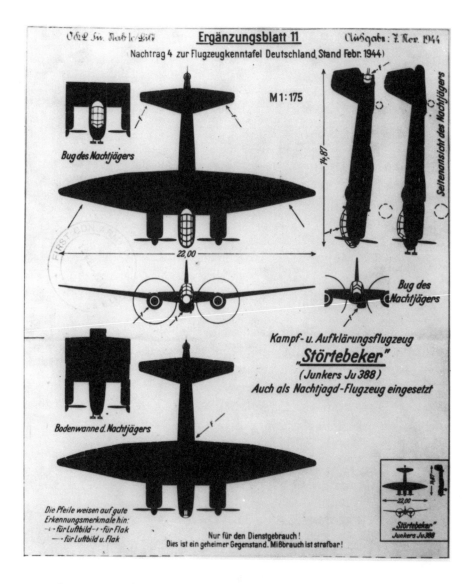

5 March 1945. ADI(K) Report 202/45 announces that the Ju 388 fighter program has received highest priority in production, "by decree of the Führer himself!"

21 May 1945. RAF Second Tactical Air Force Report B.143 on the Ju 388L/6 reveals technical information about the working mechanism of the remote-control machine-gun turret in the rear fuselage. This small revolving turret is remotely controlled and fired by a member of the crew in the cockpit. In the rear end of the cockpit is a control lever, and next to it a large periscope. The periscope projects above the fuselage, where it is covered by a glass bowl, and below the fuselage (forward of the bomb bay doors), where it is encased in an all-metal fairing. This gives the gunner all-round visibility.

5 June 1945. USAAF Tactical Intelligence Report A-481 asserts that "much of Junkers engineering effort has been devoted to the constant development and improvement of their basic Ju 88 series of airplanes. By design refinement and improvement of the power plant installation, this series was kept modern till the end of the war; the Ju 388L-1 version claimed a speed of 380 mph at an altitude of 41,000 ft."

Messerschmitt Me 264

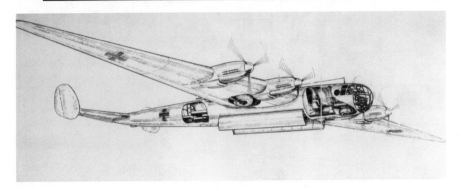

This illustration comes from the Me 264 prospectus produced by Messerschmitt in December 1941. The crew's sleeping quarters and WC can be seen toward the rear of the fuselage. [AIR 40/203]

War Record and Intelligence History

The giant Me 264 was known as the "*Amerika* bomber" and would indeed have been capable of flying to the East Coast of the United States and back from continental Europe. The plane could fly for up to eleven hours non-stop; the design featured sleeping quarters and lavatories for the crew. The prototype V1 first flew during December 1942. Due to a shortage of resources the program never developed any further. The one completed aircraft was transferred to Tranportstaffel 5 and was destroyed by an Allied air raid. (There is some contention over whether one or two Me 264 prototypes were built. As mentioned below, Willi Messerschmitt, when questioned by AI, stated that only one was completed.)

AI first heard of the Me 264 from a Dutch source at the Fokker company in April 1942. Fokker had been commissioned by the RLM to design part of

Data File

DIMENSIONS

Wingspan	141 ft.
Length	68 ft. 6¾ in.
Height	14 ft. 1¼ in.
Max. Speed	342 mph
Ceiling	
Range	9,321 miles
Engines	4 × DB 603H
Armament	4 × MG 131,
	1 × MG 151,
	4,000 lb. bomb load

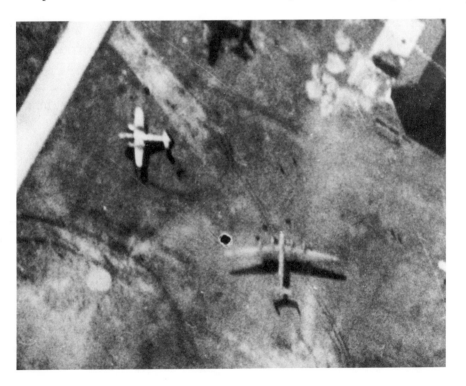

PR shot of the "Lechfeld 127," AI's code name for the Me 264. AI deduced from this photograph that the aircraft had tricycle undercarriage, as the tail unit is high off the ground. AI also calculated the length to be 68–69.5 feet, an extremely accurate measurement. Calculation of the dimension was aided by the presence of a Do 217 next to the Me 264 in the shot; AI would have known the Do 217's exact dimensions. [AIR 40/203]

Me 264 V1 on the ground at Neu Offing in late 1942 [AIR 40/103]

the wing for the Me 264. In May 1942, photo reconnaissance flights over the Messerschmitt development center at Augsburg produced shots of two aircraft with wingspans approaching a hundred feet. Nothing further was reported on the project until March 1944, when aerial reconnaissance photos of Lechfeld showed the aircraft again. It was given the code name "Lechfeld 127." AI confirmed the Lechfeld 127 to be the Me 264 a month later.

In April 1944 AI interrogated a German POW who had been at Lechfeld during summer 1943. He claimed the Me 264 had flown to Japan and back. He also stated that Fokker had been involved in the design of the Me 264, which gave credibility to his account, as this information was corroborated by a Dutch source. Another POW claimed the Me 264 had regularly flown to Japan with senior Nazi officials. He said ex-Lufthansa pilots flew the route from a base outside Leningrad. The aircraft certainly had the range to fly nonstop from Leningrad to Japan.

After the war, Messerschmitt designer Woldemar Voigt discussed the Me 264 with AI. He claimed the aircraft was intended for long-range submarine cooperation and leaflet-dropping over the United States. Willi Messerschmitt stated the aircraft could fly for eleven hours nonstop and would have been a "very good and cheap aircraft." He also stated the only prototype was destroyed during an Allied air raid on Memmingen. The Messerschmitt test pilot, Bauer, said he had flown the aircraft seventy times, diving to 652 mph without problems. Bauer stated, "Speaking personally, not as a Messerschmitt man, it would have proved an absolutely first-class aircraft."

Rare shot of the Me 264 V1 in the air [AIR 40/127]

THREE RECONNAISSANCE AND ARMY COOPERATION

Blöhm und Voss Bv 141

Correspondiendo a la construcción de la cabina en el plano derecho, también los timones tienen una forma asimétrica. El creador del nuevo modelo es el dirigente de economía defensiva Dr. Ing. Richard Vogt, constructor-jefe de las fábricas de aviones de Blohm & Voss, quien ya se ha hecho un nombre con el desarrollo de los hidro-aviones BV 139, que actuaron eficazmente en el tráfico aéreo del Atlántico Septentrional

War Record

Richard Vogt produced the radical design of the Bv 141 in response to an RLM specification of 1937. The experience of the Condor Legion had demonstrated the need for tactical reconnaissance aircraft to coordinate ground and air forces. A prime requirement of the specification was excellent all-round vision. Vogt addressed this in a unique way. By using an asymmetrical layout, the crew pod could be separated from the main fuselage, thus affording 360-degree vision. Despite its bizarre looks, the RLM decided the project was worth pursuing and ordered a further three prototypes. However, the program was dogged by minor technical problems. Lack of resources at Blöhm und Voss also hampered development; by the time a satisfactory prototype was completed, the Fw 189 had already entered service. Despite its problems, those who flew the Bv 141 found it to be a sweet-handling aircraft with excellent, all-round visibility.

Intelligence History

16 January 1939. AI report on Ha 141 states that series production began at Weser Fluzeugbau, Bremen about 16 December 1938.

15 May 1941. AI report states that a "sidecar aircraft" was seen at the 1938 Nuremberg Rally, reported [wrongly] as an Arado experimental aircraft.

23 August 1941. The Royal Observer Corps reports two witnesses having seen a strange, asymmetrical aircraft over Armscliffe, north Yorkshire, England, on 6 July 1941. From a sketch made of the sighted plane, AI believes it resembles the "Arado sidecar."

October 1941. A captured Luftwaffe handbook shows photographs and silhouettes of Bv 141 "offset" aircraft.

Data File (Bv 141A)

DIMENSIONS:

Wingspan	50 ft. 8¾ in.
Length	39 ft. 10¼ in.
Height	13 ft. 5½ in.
Max. Speed	248 mph
Ceiling	32,000 ft.
Range	708 miles
Engine	950 bhp BMW 132N
Armament	2 × MG 17, 2 × MG 15, 4 × 110 lb. bombs
Crew	3

10 October 1941. Air attaché Berne reports that a Swiss air force officer stated his staff saw a new reconnaissance aircraft undergoing trials. It was described as a monoplane with "pilot's cockpit in center of wing."

24 December 1941. An AI preliminary report declares that the Bv 141 has gone into limited production. The unusual layout gives very good visibility and a clear field of fire, except for the large blind spot to the right of cockpit. Luftwaffe classifies the Bv 141 as "*naherkunder*" (short-range reconnaissance).

7 May 1942. A German propaganda broadcast to North America describes the world's first "asymmetrical wonder-plane" and claims it has already been successfully operated on the Eastern Front.

June 1942. An Italian "political review" claims the "asymmetrical plane" has "proved its worth, one was attacked by a group of Soviet fighters over Kharkov which were Powerless against it." AI describes this claim as "doubtless optimistic."

18 June 1942. An article in *Luftwissen* (a German aircraft periodical) by Dr. Vogt, designer of the Bv 141, states it was designed in response to a 1937 RLM specification for a "single-engine monoplane with optimum vision characteristics." The unusual layout was produced to gain maximum visibility in a single-engine plane.

November 1942. AI reports that sixty Bv 141 aircraft are in use as trainers, that the type is not considered a success.

24 November 1944. AI reports Bv 141s being adapted to discharge mustard gas.

The lopsided design of the Bv 141 can clearly be seen in this photograph. [AIR 40/122]

Fiesler Fi 156 Storch (Stork)

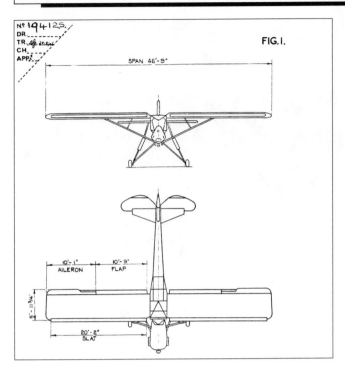

Postwar sketch of the Fiesler Fi 156 dated 29 August 1946. The *Storch* was not reported by Air Intelligence during the war, though examples were captured, but it was studied comprehensively after hostilities ceased. [DSIR 23/16054]

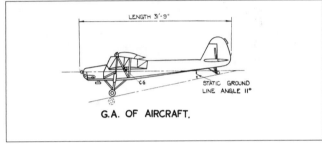

War Record

The Fi 156 proved to be the most successful multirole "go anywhere" aircraft of World War II. Designed in response to an RLM requirement of 1935, the *Storch* first flew in early 1936. Its great virtue was its ability to take off and land on the most limited of landing strips. Requiring only 185 feet to take off and sixty-five feet to land, it could be used all over the front and behind enemy lines. It proved such a success that by the end of the war over forty captured Fi 156s were being used by the Allies in preference to their own aircraft.

The *Storch* was used throughout the war in all theaters. The list of roles it was used in demonstrates its versatility: army cooperation, VIP transport, communications, reconnaissance, casualty evacuation, sabotage, and gunnery observation. In Russia they were fitted with skis and used to deliver saboteurs behind enemy lines. Rommel and Kesselring preferred Fi 156s to their grander official transports when visiting frontline units.

German paratroopers used an Fi 156 in the dramatic operation to rescue the Italian dictator Benito Mussolini from captivity in the Grand Sasso mountain Hotel following Italy's defection to the Allies. A *Storch* landed on the narrow plateau in front of the hotel, and Mussolini was crammed into the plane and evacuated.

The last notable mission performed by a Storch came when Hitler ordered the famous female test pilot Hanna Reitsch to fly Gen. Ritter von Greim into the ruins of Berlin. Greim was to be appointed the new commander of the Luftwaffe on 26 April 1945. Reitsch begged to be allowed to stay by the *führer*'s side to the end but was ordered to leave. She flew Greim back out of Berlin in an Fi 156 as Soviet troops closed in on Hitler's bunker.

Data File

DIMENSIONS

Wingspan	46 ft. 9 in.
Length	32 ft. 5¾ in.
Height	9 ft. 10 in.
Max. Speed	109 mph
Ceiling	15,090 ft.
Range	600 miles
Engine	1 × 240 hp Argus As 10C
Armament	none
Crew	2

Focke-Wulf Fw 189 Uhu (Owl)

An Fw 189 on the ground with its engines running. This particular aircraft does not have any armament in its dorsal turret (the circular glass pane directly behind the open hatch). [AIR 40/127]

War Record

Focke-Wulf's legendary designer Kurt Tank conceived the unorthodox Fw 189 design in response to a 1937 Luftwaffe specification for a short-range reconnaissance plane. The twin-boom configuration was used to maximize the field of view in the cockpit pod. The glazed cockpit resulted in the nickname "*Das Fliegende Auge*" (flying eye). Its maneuverability, stability, and excellent visibility made it a success in this role. An added bonus was the ruggedness of its airframe. One Fw 189 managed to return to base with one tail-base removed by a Russian ramming attack. They were also used in North Africa. Its ability to spot enemy units and report them directly to nearby army forces was an important tactical benefit.

In addition to the intended reconnaissance role, Fw 189s were used as ground-attack planes, employing 20 mm cannons. Field Marshal Kesselring and Colonel General Hans Jeschonnek, chief of the Luftwaffe General Staff, also used the aircraft as personal transports.

Intelligence History

13 August 1939. Initial report is filed by French sources summarizing the Fw 189's performance and dimensions.

30 October 1941. Report is received of six to ten Fw 189s spotted at Barce Aerodrome, Libya, bearing Italian markings and camouflage schemes.

18 May 1941. A POW claims a *Geschwader* is being trained in ground strafing at Krakow, Poland. The loss rate among pilots being trained was as high as 10 percent.

November 1941. In *Luftwissen* (a German aircraft trade journal), a Dr. Ing. H. Conradis of Focke-Wulf explains the aircraft's special design features. The twin boom was incorporated to maximize all-round visibility from the crew's pod. The observer's seat can slide forward, backward, and through ninety degrees to facilitate ground observation. The armament was added to keep

Data File

DIMENSIONS

Wingspan	60 ft. 4½ in.
Length	39 ft. 5½ in.
Height	10 ft. 2 in.
Max. Speed	208 mph
Ceiling	22,967 ft.
Range	416 miles
Engine	2 × 465 hp Argus AS410A-1
Armament	2 × 0.31 in MG 15
	2 × 0.31 in MG 17
	4 × 50 kg bombs
Crew	2

Aerial reconnaissance photograph taken on 7 May 1942 of Letov I, a factory airfield near Prague in Czechoslovakia. Fw 189s were assembled at this plant; the Germans made use of aviation industries in occupied Europe to help boost their domestic output. [AIR 34/234]

ground forces from hampering its reconnaissance work. He reports that the aircraft "successfully endured a baptism of fire" on the Eastern Front in fall 1941 and shot down a number of Soviet bombers in aerial combat.

6 December 1941. A POW from *Gruppe* 506 reveals that Fw 189s are being used to train *zerstörer* aircrew and for ground-attack missions against trenches.

2 February 1942. An AI preliminary report states that the Fw 189 was introduced in response to the shortcomings of the Henschel 126 in the short-range-reconnaissance role.

20 October 1942. A report in the Soviet military newspaper *Red Star* states that Fw 189s would fly four to five sorties per day, usually 70–150 miles behind enemy lines. Relays of planes would often remain "suspended" over one crucial spot in the battle all day long. As well as radio, they used colored smokes to communicate with ground forces. The aircraft's defensive capabilities were not rated by the Soviet report. Machine-gun fire aimed at the engines could bring them down. Antitank rifles could penetrate the cockpit at 1,800–2,400 feet, and rifles from 1,500–1,800 feet.

4 October 1943. The U.S. Eighth Air Force reports Fw 189s joining attacks on bomber formations over Germany.

20 February 1945. A captured German document reveals Fw 189s being used in the night reconnaissance role.

Henschel Hs 126

A row of neatly lined-up Hs 126s. The plane was used mostly on the Eastern Front and the Balkans, with only one unit serving in the North African campaign. [AIR 40/451]

War Record

The Hs 126 started the war as the Luftwaffe's main tactical reconnaissance and army-cooperation aircraft. The aircraft had good flying characteristics and, unlike its predecessors, could operate at night. A typical panzer corps would be assigned a *Staffel* of Hs 126s to act as its forward "eyes in the skies." An artillery regiment would usually have one aircraft for target spotting and damage assessment.

The design started life as the Hs 122, which was rejected by the RLM. Further development led to the Hs 126, which was accepted as a replacement for the He 45 and He 46. It first saw action in the Spanish Civil War. The Condor Legion operated six of the type, which also carried out light bombing raids; these aircraft were later handed over to the Spanish Nationalist air force. The aircraft's career continued successfully in the Polish campaign. During the "Phoney War" in the West, however, its lack of speed and armament made it easy prey for French fighters. This led to the cessation of production in January 1941 and its replacement in most roles by the Fw 189 from 1942 onward. Before this it served in the Balkan campaigns of 1941—on both sides. Henschel had sold a few Hs 126s to the Royal Hellenic Air Force in 1939. A trio of these was responsible for breaking up a large Italian column through constant low-level strafing.

However, even after its replacement the Hs 126 continued in service—usually behind the lines, particularly in the antipartisan war and in night harassment operations on the Eastern Front.

Data File (A and B series)

DIMENSIONS

Wingspan	46 ft. 6¾ in.
Length	35 ft. 7¾ in.
Height	12 ft. 3¾ in.
Max. Speed	221 mph
Ceiling	27,070 ft.
Range	360 miles
Engine	1 × 830 hp Bramo Fafnir 323A
Armament	1 × MG 17, 1 × MG 15, 110 lb. bomb load
Crew	2

An Hs 126 in one of its minor roles, as a glider tug. [AIR 40/122]

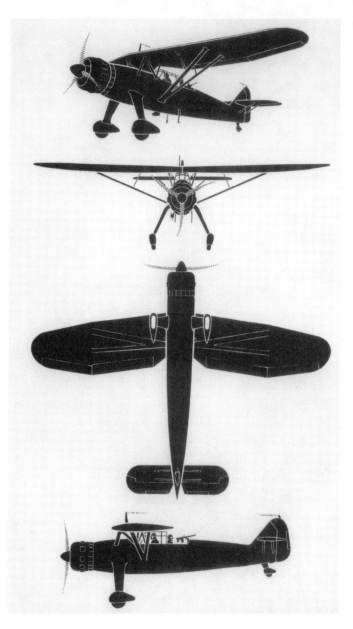

Air Intelligence sketch of the Hs 126.

Junkers Ju 86

War Record

The Junkers Ju 86 was obsolete before the start of the Second World War. Initially developed as an airliner and bomber, it originally flew in trials in January 1935; the first deliveries to the Luftwaffe were made in February 1936. Five aircraft were allocated to the Condor Legion, fighting with Nationalist forces in the Spanish Civil War, but they did not perform well, and their diesel engines were deemed by the Luftwaffe unsuited to combat conditions. By the time manufacture was halted in 1938, the Luftwaffe had already begun to withdraw many of its 390 Ju 86s from frontline formations. Occasionally it was necessary to recall the obsolete aircraft to service. For instance, Ju 86s based at Tatsinskaya performed transport duties in the Stalingrad airlift. Their contribution ceased after 1 January 1943, when Red Army soldiers liberated the airfield. The crews, drawn from training units, suffered appallingly high casualties.

However, the Ju 86 performed an important and unique role during the war. In September 1939, Junkers submitted to the RLM proposals for a high-altitude reconnaissance aircraft. Taking a modified Ju 86, Junkers installed high-altitude engines (which it had been experimenting with) and a pressurized cockpit, and removed the defensive machine guns, as no modern fighter would be able to reach its operational altitude. With the RLM's assent the project moved forward rapidly; prototypes were flown in February and March 1940, attaining altitudes of 32,810 and 39,700 feet respectively. The Luftwaffe ordered forty aircraft. They were produced in two variants—the P-1 bomber, with a 2,205-pound payload, and the P-2 strategic

Data File Ju 86D

DIMENSIONS

Wingspan	73 ft. 9¾ in.
Length	58 ft. 7½ in.
Height	16 ft. 7¼ in.
Max. Speed	202 mph
Ceiling	19,360 ft.
Range	932 miles
Engine	2 × Jumo 205C-4 diesels
Armament	3 × 7.92 mm machine guns
Payload	1,764 lbs.
Crew	4

reconnaissance plane, with three cameras. Undetected, one of these prototypes flew a reconnaissance sortie over England at forty-one thousand feet during the Battle of Britain. For almost two years no Allied fighter could touch the Ju 86P.

On 21 September 1940, Hitler ordered strategic PR of targets up to three hundred kilometers into the Soviet Union for the planning of Operation Barbarossa. Ju 86Ps in Aufklarungsgruppe Oberbefehlshaber der Luftwaffe, operating from East Prussian and Romanian airfields, initially covered the frontier region, but in the absence of Soviet fighter opposition, they gradually roved deeper into Russian territory; Stalin forbade interception of the German intruders. Operating up to 39,350 feet, these units covered much of European Russia, from the Murmansk-Moscow-Rostov line to the Polish frontier.

However, in the summer of 1942 the British found the answer to the Ju 86P; two were shot down on two separate fronts. A detachment of 2/(F)123 Ju 86Ps went to Libya in August 1942 to provide reconnaissance for Rommel's Panzerarmee Afrika. However, after modified Spitfires shot down Hauptmann Bayer's Ju 86P at forty-two thousand feet off the coast of Alexandria, the reconnaissance planes were swiftly driven from the skies over Egypt. Also, between June and October 1942 Ju 86P high-altitude reconnaissance aircraft of 1/ObdL identified targets for a strategic bombing campaign against Russian railway centers up to 190 miles behind the front. It was during this reconnaissance phase that one Ju 86P was shot down in the first action by British-supplied, Soviet-flown Spitfire VB fighters.

Even after production commenced in 1940, Junkers was continually experimenting with new methods to increase altitude. The upgraded Ju 86P-1 and P-2 aircraft were designated R-1 and R-2. Only a few entered service but during tests reached an incredible forty-seven thousand feet. It was during the "Baedeker Raids" that on 24 August 1942 the Luftwaffe commenced experimental high-altitude nuisance raids over England. Two Ju 86Rs each dropped a 550-pound bomb on Camberley and Southampton from forty thousand feet. Several more sorties were carried out, but they were aborted after 12 September, when Feldwebel Horst Gotz had to abandon his mission after his Ju 86R was nearly shot down by modified Spitfires.

Intelligence History

12 September 1938. The Society of Aircraft Constructors informs AI that "the retractable dustbin type of turret formerly employed on the Junkers 86 has been withdrawn."

1939. AI acquires a copy of the "*Handbuch der Luftfahrt*," which gives complete specification details on the Ju 86D.

21 September 1939. AI believes that the Ju 86, first constructed in 1936, is obsolete and inferior as a bomber to the new Heinkels and Dorniers.

1940. During interrogation a POW informs AI that the Ju 86 has a noise-reducing apparatus that makes the aircraft entirely inaudible at extreme heights.

Gun-camera photograph of a Ju 86P-2 over Alexandria. In this instance the aircraft got away and was not shot down. The vapor trail is quite evident.

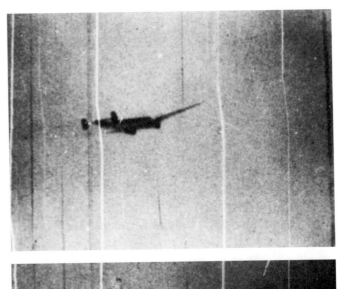

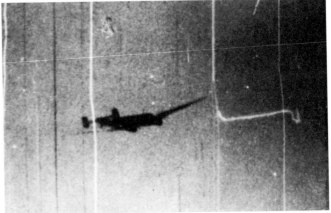

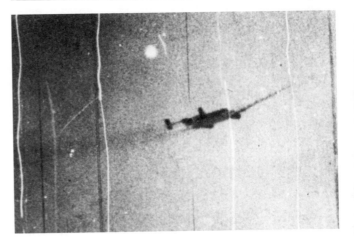

29 January 1941. AI2(g) estimates the ceiling of the high-altitude Ju 86 with no bomb payload to be thirty-nine thousand feet.

6 February 1941. The Ministry of Aircraft Production requests more information on the new high-altitude Ju 86. AI, it declares, "should endeavor by every possible means to get a stronger line on this aircraft."

February 1941. AI learns from a POW interrogation that experiments with the high-altitude Ju 86 are being conducted at Fritzlar, the headquarters of the

Oberbefehlshaber der Luftwaffe Aufklarungs (Reconnaissance) Gruppe. One Ju 86 reached forty-five thousand feet in a trial flight.

20 February 1941. AI Report K49/1941 claims that the high-altitude Ju 86 has a new telescopic bombsight, which the Germans are currently testing at thirty-six thousand feet.

18 May 1941. A POW discloses much useful data to AI on the high-altitude Ju 86 in Report K269. The prisoner declares he took part in a test flight at the Junkers works on 16 September 1940. The walls of the pressure cabin are 30 cm thick, and visibility is restricted, with just narrow strips of glass to the front and the sides. The ceiling is said to be forty-six thousand feet, and the aircraft has very great range; it can fly to New York and back from Paris and remain airborne for twenty-five hours. The purpose of the aircraft is unclear, though the prisoner claims it is high-altitude reconnaissance work, as the Ju 86 has been fitted with cameras using special infrared film.

22 December 1941. AI(2)g releases a short briefing paper about "German substratosphere bombers," the Ju 86P-1 and P-2. The paper is based on information "received from a reliable source giving details of new Junkers high-altitude bombers." The paper states the P-1 has no defensive armament and a crew of just two, and that the P-2 is fitted with three cameras for PR work from 39,400 feet.

4 January 1942. A captured pilot from Kustenfliegergruppe 506 claims that while at Dessau he saw a number of Ju 86 stratospheric aircraft. They were fitted with the Jumo 207 engine, said to be equipped with a supercharger fed by an exhaust driven turbine that enabled power to be maintained at great height.

5 June 1942. A Ju 86 is seen through a rangefinder above Alexandria at an approximate height of forty thousand feet and is immediately reported to AI.

13 July 1942. Two Spitfire pilots in Egypt, Flight Officer Reynolds and Pilot Officer Genders, engage a Ju 86 over North Africa. They attack it but a reserve booster enables the Ju 86P-2 to climb immediately a further two thousand feet and evade the British fighters.

August 1942. A 2/(F)123 Ju 86P-2 is shot down over the Nile Delta near Alexandria. The crew transmits a distress signal to Crete, and German aircraft are dispatched to rescue them, but the British pick them up first. The pilot, Hauptmann Bayer, was the Staffelkapitan and much of the material he manages to rescue from the downed aircraft is extremely valuable to AI.

15 May 1943. In Berne Telegram 2421 the British diplomatic representative reveals that a well placed Italian source recently visited Germany, where he saw a stratospheric bomber. The Germans told him that once they had a thousand of these aircraft they would use them to bomb the United Kingdom from altitudes of fourteen thousand meters.

Messerschmitt Bf 108 Taifun (Typhoon)

A Bf 108 in prewar civil livery [AIR 40/127]

War Record

The Bf 108 was the aircraft that made the Messerschmitt Company's name in aircraft design. It was produced to compete in the Challenge de Tourism Internationale race of 1934. Despite an early crash it went on to become a highly successful touring aircraft and an important milestone in German aircraft design. One notable flight saw the German female pilot Elly Beinhorn fly a Bf 108 from Berlin to Cape Town and back. Its success led the RLM to consider it in the fast transport and communications role. It went on to perform a variety of tasks during World War II, including target towing, rescue, and supply. It was even employed by the RAF after the war; it continued in production and service in France until the late 1940s.

Perhaps its most significant contribution to the German war effort came by accident. On 11 January 1940, one flew off course and landed in neutral Belgium. On board was a Luftflotte 2 staff officer carrying the plans for the planned German offensive on the Western Front. The Allies assumed they were a deliberately planted fake, but Hitler decided to cancel the attack. The subsequent revised plan of attacking through the Ardennes proved a master stroke.

Data File (A and B series)

DIMENSIONS

Wingspan	34 ft. 10 in.
Length	27 ft. 2½ in.
Height	7 ft. 6½ in.
Max. Speed	196 mph
Ceiling	19,685 ft.
Range	870 miles
Engine	1 × 240 hp Argus As 10C
Armament	none
Crew	1–4

FOUR   SEAPLANES AND FLYING BOATS

Arado Ar 196

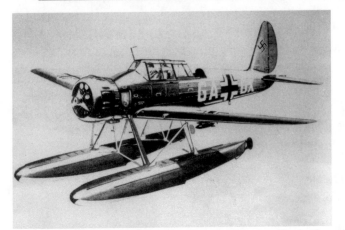

Two pictures portray the same aircraft. The sketch produced by AI is clearly based on the captured German midair photograph. The crew positions and markings in the two images are identical. [AIR 40/133]

War Record

The Arado 196 was designed in response to a 1936 RLM specification for a catapult floatplane to replace the He 50. It was intended for use on Kreigsmarine capital ships and large surface vessels. Employed in the long-range reconnaissance role, it could carry bombs for attacks on merchant vessels. Many famous German warships carried the Ar 196 including the *Bismarck*, *Scharnhorst*, and *Gneisenau*. The first Ar 196 to join a ship was taken by the ill-fated *Admiral Graf Spee*, scuttled off Montevideo Harbor in December 1939 following the Battle of the River Plate.

After this inauspicious start, the Ar 196 served successfully on many ships and from land bases in the Atlantic, Adriatic, Aegean, and North and Black Sea theaters, where it undertook coastal patrol duties. On one notable occasion two Ar 196s of I/Küstenfliegergruppe 706, based at Aalborg, Denmark, forced the Royal Navy submarine HMS *Seal* to surrender.

An excellent design, the Ar 196 even proved itself useful in air-to-air combat, shooting down eight Allied aircraft over the Bay of Biscay during 1942. This forced RAF Coastal Command to start Beaufighter patrols over the area. Around five hundred Ar 196s served with the Luftwaffe and the air forces of Rumanian and Bulgarian allies.

Intelligence History

26 April 1940. An Ar 196 crashes at Maee, with much damage to fuselage, tail, and wings.

10 May 1940. The Royal Navy issues a report on a captured Ar 196 flown by a British pilot from Sullom Voe, Shetland Islands, to Leuchars in western Scotland. He reports Ar 196 to be easy to fly, to handle well on water, and have good visibility.

Data File (Ar 196A-3)

DIMENSIONS

Wingspan	40 ft. 8¼ in.
Length	36 ft. 1 in.
Height	14 ft. 7¼ in.
Max. Speed	193 mph
Ceiling	22,960 ft.
Range	665 miles
Engine	1 × 960 bhp BMW 132K
Armament	2 × MG FF cannon, 1 × MG 17, 1 × MG 15 2 × 110 lb. bombs
Crew	2

3 December 1940. AI reports an Ar 196 armed with 250 kg bombs used on antisubmarine patrols from Aalborg, Denmark.

8 May 1941. The "Seilbombe" is reported used by Ar 196. It consists of a twenty-inch cylinder attached by hook to a seventy-to-eighty-foot cable, designed to carry away wireless aerials from merchant ships, preventing them from sending SOS signals.

24 June 1941. A POW claims that Ar 196s could be launched by the *Bismarck* when it was traveling at up to twenty knots and that all four aircraft could be launched within thirty minutes.

19 November 1941. The SNCA de l'Ouest Seaplane Factory at St. Nazaire, France, receives an order for assembly of ten Ar 196s per month, to start in 1942.

1 September 1943. A POW from German Raider 10 indicates that the Ar 196C has a different propeller from the Ar 196B. His ship was carrying twenty-four 50 kg bombs, six–ten "seilbombes," three thousand rounds of machine-gun ammunition, and twenty-four thousand liters of aviation fuel for use by the Ar 196.

Civilians crowd around an Ar 196 at the edge of a beach. The weather and clothing would suggest either the Mediterranean or Black Sea as the location for this photograph. [AIR 40/121]

Blöhm und Voss Bv 138

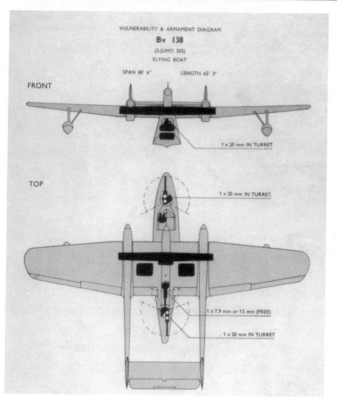

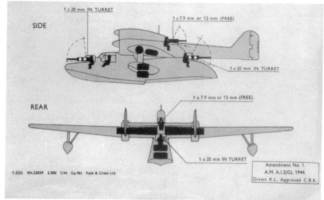

Sketch produced by AI in August 1944 showing the Bv 138's weak points and armament [AIR 40/963]

War Record

The Bv 138 was the Blöhm und Voss shipbuilding company's first prewar flying boat. The first prototypes, proven aerodynamically unstable, were radically redesigned. This modified version first saw action in the Norwegian campaign of 1940 with Luftwaffe reconnaissance units, earning the nickname "*Der Fliegende Holzschuh*" (Flying Clog). Its main military role was as a spotter and U-boat cooperation aircraft in the war against Allied convoys. In September 1942, a Bv 138 first spotted convoy PQ18 heading for Murmansk. Torpedo-carrying Ju 88s and He 111s proceeded to sink ten freighters. Luftflotte 5's use of antishipping aircraft over the Arctic forced the Royal Navy to introduce escort carriers. The year 1943 saw the final variant enter service as a minesweeper, the Bv 138MS. It was fitted with a circular loop of dural, field-generating equipment. The aircraft's final major act of the war came in 1945 as German forces abandoned the cut-off bridgehead in East Prussia and northern Poland. Twelve Bv 138s ferried three thousand people back to Germany proper.

Intelligence History

3 November 1938. A report in the German press describes the Ha 138 as a three-engined flying boat with an unusually short hull, twin boom, and three gunners' posts.

Data File

DIMENSIONS

Wingspan	88 ft. 7 in.
Length	65 ft. 3½ in.
Height	21 ft. 8 in.
Max. Speed	171 mph
Ceiling	16,405 ft.
Range	3,107 miles
Engines	3 × 880 hp Jumo 205D
Armament	1 × MG 151 cannon, 1 × MG 131 4 × 331 lb. bombs

This photograph shows a Bv 138 on a catapult ship. Two such ships operated in the fjords of the Norwegian ports of Tromsö and Trondheim. By launching from these ships rather than from the water, the aircraft could carry extra fuel and ordnance. [AIR 40/122]

24 November 1940. The Eire Air Corps reports a Bv 113A (in fact a Bv 138) force-landed off Blaskei Island, Southwest Ireland. When interrogated, the pilot stated he was on an armed reconnaissance mission in the North Atlantic and claimed he had previously made attacks on shipping. When questioned about flights over southern Ireland by German planes he claimed they were RAF pilots flying aircraft captured at Narvik, Norway. Irish intelligence officers felt the pilot had been carefully briefed on what to say if he crashed in Eire.

28 November 1941. An AI preliminary report indicates that the Bv 138 is used for long-range reconnaissance, U-boat cooperation, bombing, and possibly torpedo bombing and minelaying.

Bv 138 undergoing maintenance on the ground. A Bv 138 in flight can be seen just above the starboard engine. [AIR 40/122]

15 March 1943. A Bv 138 is shot down by the RAF, and the observer is captured and interrogated. He had launched from catapult ship *Bussard* in the Trondheim fjord, Norway. He had been on a mission to search between the Faroe and Shetland Islands for Allied shipping. Another catapult ship, *Schwanbenlami*, was operating at Tromsö, Norway. Catapults were being used as they allowed aircraft to carry heavier loads. The observer claimed he had completed thirty-eight operational patrols from Trondheim and had also carried depth charges.

Blöhm und Voss Bv 222/238

The one completed Bv 238 V1 flying boat making progress on the water. The heaviest aircraft completed during the war, it was sunk by USAAF P-51 Mustangs in late 1944. [AIR 40/122]

War Record

The Bv 222 was the largest flying boat to achieve operational status during World War II. Originally designed as a long-range passenger airliner for Lufthansa, it was used by the Luftwaffe as a transport capable of carrying up to seventy-six fully equipped troops. Its military debut came during the 1940 Norwegian campaign. Bv 222s also served in the Mediterranean, ferrying supplies to the Afrika Korps. In February 1942, Hitler ordered the aircraft to be deployed in the Battle of the Atlantic, but it did not enter this conflict until the summer. Although it extended the range of Luftwaffe patrols in the western Atlantic, it, like other converted civilian planes, was insufficiently robust to stand the rigors of combat aviation. The Bv 238 was planned as an even larger version of the Bv 222, with a wingspan of almost two hundred feet. One prototype was flown toward the end of the war but sank at anchor after being attacked by U.S. fighter-bombers.

Intelligence Reports

3 December 1940. K states that Blöhm und Voss is building a giant new flying boat destined for "colonial service."

20 October 1941. Aerial reconnaissance photographs show a six-engined flying boat at the Travemunde/Privall seaplane base.

6 December 1941. Correspondence between a Blöhm und Voss employee and a German pilot POW in Canada is intercepted. Letters (started on 2 July 1941) include references to the "22 year old swimmer Berta Viola" (the Bv 222), which the worker claims, "promises to be a great success." A letter of 30 August 1941 refers to a recent "defeat" at Trondheim (presumably a crash).

Data File (Bv 222C)

DIMENSIONS

Wingspan	150 ft. 11 in.
Length	121 ft. 4¾ in.
Height	35 ft. 9 in.
Max. Speed	242 mph
Ceiling	23,950 ft.
Range	3,787 miles
Engines	6 × 1,000 hp Jumo 207C
Armament	3 × MG 151, 5 × MG 131
Crew	10

Rare photograph of the giant Bv 238 in the air [AIR 40/122]

29 March 1942. An Italian Air Ministry weekly summary reports that the German air force is considering using the Bv 222 as a transport to supply Luftwaffe units in North Africa. One aircraft has recently been adapted for a military role (seven machine guns added). The report states that a series of flights has been made between Italy and Libya with 76–110 fully equipped soldiers.

February 1943. A report from Switzerland is received that a defected Luftwaffe meteorologist has been interrogated. He had been stationed at Athens-Tatoi airfield in early 1943. He had seen Bv 222s being used as transports between Greece and Sicily.

Postwar

AI reports that the Bv 222 successfully completed trials in July 1941, was allocated to Lufttransport in the Mediterranean and was used successfully until three were lost in March 1943. It was then handed over to *Atlantikführer* for reconnaissance work in North Atlantic. A POW also claims that a Bv 222 flew to Japan from the Baltic in 1943.

A Bv 222 on the water. The markings of the Blöhm und Voss company can be seen on the nose. [AIR 40/122]

Dornier Do 18

This Associated Press photograph of a long-range reconnaissance Dornier Do 18 was dated 4 April 1940 and was captioned "The weapon which carries the war to Britain's shore." Releases of photographs and information to the neutral and foreign press by the German Propaganda Ministry were to prove a consistently useful source of intelligence for the Allies throughout the war. [Air 40/144]

War Record

The Do 18 was a high-wing braced-monoplane flying boat originally developed in 1934 as Lufthansa's transoceanic postal service airplane. The Do 18 prototype originally flew on 15 March 1935. A Do 18 established a nonstop straight-line seaplane record of 5,214 miles in forty-three hours, flying from England to Brazil 27–29 March 1938. Thereafter it was used by German civil aviation for the regular South Atlantic air service, being catapulted from a depot ship on either side of the ocean.

Such was its capabilities that the Luftwaffe adapted it for use with coastal reconnaissance units. The first military versions were produced and entered service in September 1938. Further versions were developed, one of which was up-gunned; another stripped of all armament and converted for air-sea rescue operations; while some saw wartime service as long-range naval reconnaissance seaplanes.

Data File

DIMENSIONS

Wingspan	77 ft. 9 in.
Length	63 ft. 2 in.
Height	17 ft. 6½ in.
Max. Speed	162 mph
Ceiling	13,780 ft.
Range	2,175 miles
Engines	2 × Jumo 205D
Armament	1 × 13 mm MG 131, 1 × 20 mm MG 151
Payload	100 kg
Crew	4

On 26 September 1939, a Do 18 of 2./Kustenfliegergruppe 106 became the first German aircraft to be brought down by the British in the Second World War. Lt. B. McEwan of 803 Squadron (Fleet Air Arm) operating from the aircraft carrier HMS *Ark Royal* forced the Do 18 down in the North Sea.

A little more than a hundred Do 18s were built for the Luftwaffe, but production ceased in 1940, when the Bv 138 replaced it. It was then relegated to the air-sea rescue role.

Intelligence History

23 March 1941. An article in *Deutsche Berwerkszeitung* states that the new BMW 132 radial engines in the Do 18 give the seaplane vastly improved performance. Before the modification it was limited to an all-in weight of ten tons and required catapult-assisted takeoff. The new version could take off unassisted with a load of between 12.5 and 13.5 tons and was faster, while not losing seaworthiness.

10 May 1941. An article in *Flug Sport* attests that in terms of seaworthiness and stability the Dornier Do 18 is better than any other flying machine of its class.

3 February 1942. Captured Luftwaffe publications refer to the Do 18 G and H types as now operating with a rocket-assisted takeoff mechanism.

16 November 1944. POW interrogation reveals the new Do 318 is just an improved and updated version of the Do 18.

On 10 November 1939, two RAF Hudsons of 220 Squadron engaged this Dornier Do 18 in an air battle over the North Sea. From 3./Kustenfliegergruppe 406 (radio code "K6+DL") it was shot up, landed heavily in the sea, and then shortly overturned and sank. All the crew were saved except *Oberleutnant* zur See Lutjens. However, the engagement was not totally one-sided, as one of the two Hudsons, piloted by Flight Lieutenant Harold Sheahen, was so damaged by German fire from the Do 18 that it had to break off the attack and return to base at RAF Thornaby, leaving the second Hudson to continue the battle. [Air 28/828]

Dornier Do 24

Two views of the Dornier Do 24. Clearly visible is the power-operated dorsal turret housing the 20 mm MG 151 cannon. After the liberation of France a further forty Do 24s (T-1 variants) were manufactured by the Sartrouville factory for service with the French navy. [both Air 40/123]

War Record

An all-metal, three-engine, strut-mounted-wing monoplane with a shallow broad-beam hull and stabilizing sponsons, the Do 24 was designed to meet a Dutch navy requirement of 1935 for naval flying boats to serve in the Netherlands East Indies. It was first flown on 3 July 1937. The Dutch Aviolanda Company built forty-eight Do 24s under license but had only delivered twenty-five by the German invasion in May 1940. Aviolanda built another eleven, but these transferred immediately to the Luftwaffe, where they were employed in the air-sea rescue role. After Luftwaffe evaluation of the Do 24 in this role, the Dutch-built line was resurrected under the control of the German Weser Flugzeugbau Company, which produced a total of 159 Do 24s from its factories.

Predominantly serving in an air-sea rescue capacity with 1./ 2./ and 3./Seenotgruppe, these Do 24s were based in France at Berre, near Marseilles, and at Biscarosse, near Bordeaux. Another forty-eight Do 24s were manufactured at the SNCA du Nord factory in Sartrouville, France, between 1942 and 1944. The Do 318 prototype was a variant of the Do 24, designed and successfully tested by Weser Flugzeubau. However, only one machine was constructed, and this was scuttled in Lake Constance in 1945 at the end of the war.

Data File

DIMENSIONS

Wingspan	88 ft. 7 in.
Length	72 ft. 1/4 in.
Height	18 ft. 10 1/4 in.
Max. Speed	211 mph
Ceiling	19,355 ft.
Range	1,802 miles
Engines	3 × BMW 132
Armament	2 × 7.92 mm, 1 × 20 mm machine guns
Crew	5–6

Intelligence History

1 August 1936. AI1-13500/J reports that "the designers of the Dornier Works are working on a new type to be called the Do 24. This is a combined land and sea plane, but as it has not yet been passed outside the designing office into the works."

13 October 1936. AI1-13911/J reports that the Do 24 is still being tested but confirms it as a three-engine aircraft.

18 March 1938. Air attaché Brussels signals that the new Dornier has "a modern wireless installation, blind flying instruments, automatic pilot, directional apparatus, etc."

22 July 1939. Air attaché Bangkok declares, "I made a flight in one of these boats which climbed very slowly at 100 km/h and cruised at about 120 km/h. The view for bombing is poor whilst, owing to the tail construction, defense against air attack is not easy. However, they are easy to fly and have a good all round view for reconnaissance with a maximum endurance of about 11 hours."

On 19 October 1943, four RAF Bristol Beaufighter aircraft, two each from 227 Squadron and 603 Squadron, took off from Gamut, in Libya, as escorts to four B-25 Mitchell bombers from the 310 Bombardment Group on an offensive sweep around the north coast of Crete. While this operation was under way the Allied aircraft encountered this Do 24, which the Beaufighters duly engaged and shot down, leaving it disabled in the sea. [Air 34/239]

8 August 1939. Air attaché Bangkok delivers basic intelligence and technical specifications, thirty Do 24s having been sold to the Dutch for employment with the Netherlands East Indies air force.

17 November 1941. AI visits Norwegian air force headquarters to interview an agent just returned from Norway who claimed to have seen a Do 24 operating with a rocket-assisted takeoff mechanism. He said, "The effect of the rocket was to shorten take-off very considerably and after becoming airborne that boat seemed to climb at a very high rate. The rocket effect apparently ceased very shortly after take-off."

12 July 1944. The improved version of the Do 24 has a crew of six, three MG 151 13 mm machine guns, and can carry eight stretchers plus another twelve seated passengers.

1 August 1944. AI learns that the Do 24 is being manufactured by the French SNCAN Company at Sartrouville.

12 December 1944. A POW reveals that the Do 24 is the workhorse of the German air-sea rescue service. He has an extremely high opinion of the machine and states that the best pilot in his *Staffel* (Lange) on several occasions carried fifty-nine passengers during the evacuation of Crete.

Heinkel He 59

A prewar propaganda photograph of a Heinkel He 59 float plane [Air 40/251]

War Record and Intelligence History

The twin-engine Heinkel He 59 biplane first flew in September 1931, a year after it was designed as a reconnaissance bomber. It was the upgraded He 59B-2, armed with a 20 mm machine gun in the nose, that was sent with the Condor Legion to Spain, where it was employed on night bombing and antishipping patrols. By 1939 the He 59 was obsolete as a frontline aircraft but retained a role in the Luftwaffe throughout the war. A variety of versions were used in long-range naval reconnaissance, training, and air-sea rescue. Some were used in minelaying or air-sea rescue operations, but most were trainers.

It was perhaps in the air-sea rescue role that the He 59 is best known. At the start of the Second World War the Luftwaffe established the Seenotdienst to rescue aircrew who fell in the English Channel (Scheisskanal—Shitcanal or "Foul-water Sewer"). Thirty to forty obsolete He 59 floatplanes, Do 18s, and

Data File

DIMENSIONS

Length	17.4 m
Height	7.1 m
Wingspan	23.7 m
Max. Speed	137 mph
Ceiling	11,480 ft.
Range	1,087 miles
Engines	2 × BMW VI-6
Armament	3 × 7.92 mm machine guns
Payload	2,205 lbs.
Crew	3–4

A rare picture of the He 59 in the minelayer role [Air 41/10]

Do 24 flying boats, assisted by fast motor launches, were grouped into *Seenot-flugkommandos*. The unarmed aircraft, painted white with both civil and Red Cross markings, carried inflatable rubber boats, blankets, and medicines to recover survivors and provide first aid.

However, the chief of RAF Fighter Command, Hugh Dowding, was determined to deprive the Luftwaffe of valuable aircrew and authorized attacks on the rescue aircraft. Further attacks forced the Seenotdienst to arm its aircraft, and on 20 July a gunner from 1/Seenotflugkommando shot down a 43 Squadron Hurricane. Neither enemy action nor the elements prevented the Seenotdienst from operating, and during the Battle of Britain its crews rescued more than a hundred men (some of them British) at the cost of twenty-two aircraft and forty-nine casualties.

Heinkel He 115

Prewar propaganda photograph of a Heinkel He 115. In 1938 the He 115 set no fewer than eight floatplane speed records. [Air 40/251]

War Record

The Heinkel He 115 was primarily a torpedo-bomber in the Luftwaffe's *Kustenfliegergruppen*. It was also used as a conventional bomber and a long-distance naval reconnaissance seaplane. Originally developed as a replacement for the aging He 59, the first He 115 was flown in 1936. After evaluation the He 115 was put into series production and was widely used in coastal reconnaissance units.

Not long after the outbreak of the Second World War, He 115s were extensively employed dropping parachute mines into British coastal waters. Some bombed London during the 1940–41 night blitz, carrying a payload of bombs incendiaries. Improved variants continued to emerge from the Heinkel factories until 1941, when all outstanding orders for He 115s were completed. In its last guise, the He 115C-4, it was armed with a 20 mm cannon beneath the nose, 13 mm machine guns in each wing; it could carry a 1,760 lb. torpedo.

After it proved its worth as the Luftwaffe's most capable reconnaissance and attack floatplane, production of the moderately upgraded He 115E-1 was resumed in 1943. By the end of the war roughly five hundred had been built.

Data File

DIMENSIONS

Wingspan	72 ft. 2 in.
Length	56 ft. 9 in.
Height	21 ft. 8 in.
Max. Speed	220 mph
Ceiling	18,045 ft.
Range	2,082 miles
Engines	2 × BMW 132 De
Armament	2 × 7.92 mm machine guns
Payload	1,760 lbs.
Crew	3–4

Intelligence History

13 July 1939. The Swedish journal *Flygning* reports that the Swedish air force regarded the He 115 as the best available torpedo-bomber and has decided to acquire the machine.

6 June 1940. AI visits Dumbarton to examine an He 115 of the Norwegian air force. The Norwegians purchased the aircraft before the war. After the collapse of Norway the British hurriedly flew it to Scotland for analysis. Of particular interest was the torpedo and bomb gear.

1940. AI learns that the two fixed rear-facing machine guns are the invention of a *Nachtrichten Offizier* of 1.I./KuFlGr 506. The guns converge at a point behind the tail; the pilot aims by aid of a mirror, which effectively acts as a back sight, with a white line painted on the tail acting as a fore sight.

8 May 1941. Report K.215 on the He 115 reveals valuable intelligence about the torpedo attack tactics used. The speed of the German compressed air–driven torpedo is given as thirty-five knots at extreme range and forty-five

On 6 December 1939 this He 115, radio code "S4+BL," crashed in the sea near Sheringham in Norfolk after flying into a mast at the West Beckenham radar station. All three members of the crew—*Oberleutnant* zur See Wodtke, *Oberfeldwebel* Rodel, and *Oberfeldwebel* Ullmann—were killed. The wreckage became visible only after the tide had gone out. The AI report stated, "Portions of a Heinkel 115, type 'B.B' recovered from the sea at Sheringham 5–6 December 1939 would show this particular version to be a modified civil type with the non-transparent nose. Further, the trap door under the center section portion of the fuselage is of small dimensions to admit a torpedo as in the standard military version. It is probable that this aircraft might have been employed for mine laying, since a damaged portion of a substantial carrier found appears capable of accommodating a magnetic mine of dimensions 8ft × 25ins, and the strength of construction would show that a heavier projectile than the 928lb mine could be carried. It is thought that only one such carrier was fitted to the aircraft and that it was mounted externally underneath the fuselage." [Air 28/75]

One of a series of three photographs taken from the gun camera of a De Havilland Mosquito FBIV piloted by Lt. Hans Engebrigsten of 333 (Norwegian) Squadron. On 6 February 1944, while flying an armed reconnaissance mission to Norway, the Mosquito encountered this He 115B, of 1/406 Kustenfliegerstaffel, over Bremangerfjord and immediately engaged it. After first making sure the aircraft did in fact belong to the enemy, the Mosquito got behind the He 115 and opened fire, causing it to burst into flames and crash in the sea, killing all of the crew. The pictures taken by the gun camera were sent to the Directorate of Air Intelligence by Headquarters RAF Coastal Command. AI2(g) declared that they were of "considerable interest." It proposed to send them to the *Journal of Aircraft Recognition*. This image ended up in the 3 April 1944 edition of *Evidence in Camera*. [Air 40/240]

knots at close range. If the torpedo is released from too low a height it is liable to fall flat on the water and disintegrate. Additionally, three actions are necessary by the crew to ensure the torpedo is successfully released. First, they unlock the release gear; second, they arm the release gear; and third, they press the release button.

14 January 1942. AI learns that the Germans had started to fit specially designed ice skates to the floats of He 115s. The skates are made of a light metal and allow the He 115 to take off from ice-bound bases. In this way, the floatplanes need not be entered into the water, so reducing the danger of ice forming on the floats. The report declares that numerous He 115s equipped with skates have been seen in Norway.

7 August 1942. AI discovers that the He 115 is now regarded as obsolete and has largely been withdrawn from frontline torpedo-bomber work, except in northern waters. Here it is still useful to the Luftwaffe in finishing off ships that had been crippled by previous attacks.

FIVE TRANSPORTS

Arado Ar 232

AI sketch of a four-engined Ar 232B produced in January 1945 by P. E. Castle. The row of eleven extra wheels can clearly be seen; these were designed to support the fuselage during loading and unloading. [AIR 40/120]

War Record and Intelligence History

Unofficially nicknamed *tausendfüsser* (millipede) due to its multiwheel undercarriage, the Arado Ar 232 was designed as a replacement for the legendary Junkers Ju 52 trimotor transport aircraft. Design began in 1940, with the first prototype flying in 1941. The aircraft mainly saw service on the Eastern Front, but due to the demands of fighter production and problems obtaining sufficiently powerful engines, it never came close to replacing the Ju 52. In total, some twenty four-engine Ar 232Bs were produced.

A few Ar 232s were used in Kampfgeschwader 200 "special mission" units, sometimes picking up agents from behind Soviet lines.

One of the aircraft was fitted with skis for use in Norway. At the SIPA factory in Paris AI found a mock up of an amphibious Ar 232 variant.

Data File

DIMENSIONS

Wingspan	109 ft. 10¾ in.
Length	77 ft. 2 in.
Height	18 ft. 8 in.
Max. Speed	211 mph
Ceiling	26,245 ft.
Range	658 miles
Engine	4 × 1,200 bhp BMW Bramo 323R-2
Armament	2 × MG 131, 1 × MG 151/20 cannon, 1 × MG 15

An Ar 232 of the original design featuring two 1,600-hp BMW 801MA engines. The priority given to Fw 190 production meant this engine would not be available to the Ar 232, resulting in switching the four-engine Ar 232B to BMW 323R engines. [AIR 40/120]

This Ar 232B-0 of 3/KG200 surrendered to British forces at Eggebek at the end of the war. It was flown to the RAE for testing. [AIR 40/120]

Junkers Ju 52

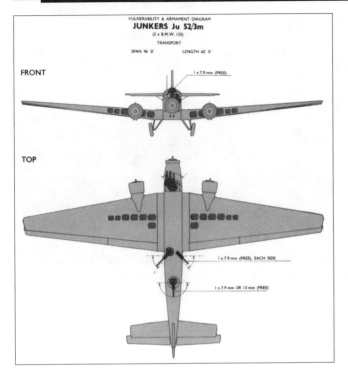

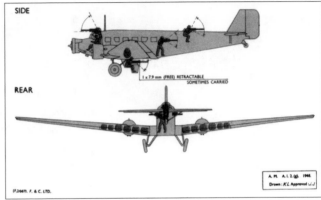

AI first learned about the increased defensive armament of the Ju 52 on 27 December 1941, when Middle East Command reported its findings after several Ju 52 crash wrecks were inspected. This AI technical drawing illustrates the defensive firepower of the Ju 52.

War Record

The Ju 52 was the transport workhorse of the Luftwaffe, remaining the leading aircraft of this type right up to the fall of Berlin. A prewar Lufthansa airliner, it also became the Luftwaffe's standard training plane for pilots of multi-engine aircraft. Produced in the thousands it proved to be a reliable and rugged airplane.

The Ju 52 began as a single-engine aircraft, the original prototype flying in October 1930. Characterized by the corrugated metal surface, only six single-engine aircraft were built before Junkers experimented with a three-engine model. First flown in April 1931, the Ju 52 proved a great success; it could operate on a standard wheeled undercarriage, floats, or skis. In spring 1932 Deutsche Lufthansa took delivery of its first Ju 52 airliners and was soon operating a fleet of fifty-one. Meanwhile the Luftwaffe, still in embryonic, clandestine existence, was evaluating the military capabilities of the Ju 52 as a bomber and a strategic transport.

It first made its operational debut during the Spanish Civil War in both roles. However, as a transport the Ju 52 was at the forefront of the spectacularly successful German airborne operations in Norway, Holland, and Belgium, either dropping paratroopers, towing gliders, or ferrying in regular infantry. Somewhat alarmingly, during the campaign in the West 37.5 percent of the Ju 52 force (162 out of 430 aircraft) was destroyed.

In Operation Merkur, the 20 May 1941 German assault on Crete, 504 Ju 52s took part. It was a Pyrrhic victory, as 121 Ju 52s were destroyed,

Data File

DIMENSIONS

Wingspan	95 ft. 11½ in.
Length	62 ft.
Height	18 ft. 2½ in.
Max. Speed	171 mph
Ceiling	19,360 ft.
Range	808 miles
Engine	3 × BMW 132A-3
Armament	2 × 7.92 mm machine guns
Payload	1,102 lbs.
Crew	2

A Ju 52 in flight during operations in the Mediterranean. On 17 January 1941 a POW informed AI that the maximum carrying capacity of a Ju 52 was twelve fully equipped paratroopers with four weapons canisters. [Air 40/126]

leading Hitler to comment that "the day of the paratrooper is over," thereafter the Ju 52 was relegated to the airlift role. In the three major airlift operations of the war conducted by the Luftwaffe—Demyansk, Stalingrad, and Tunisia—the Ju 52 fleets suffered badly.

In February 1942, during the airlifts to supply the surrounded German II Corps in the Demyansk pocket, a staggering 265 Ju 52s from the fifteen *Transportgruppen* engaged were destroyed, although this operation was a success. The Luftwaffe had to deliver 177 tons of supplies daily to the beleaguered 95,000 soldiers; it achieved peak deliveries of 182 tons in 110 flights on 22 February, and 286 tons in 159 flights on 23 February. Thereafter a combination of the weather, exhaustion among the flight crews, and the activity of the ever-attendant Soviet fighters contrived to reduce the average daily supplies delivered to less than half the necessary requirements. However, the success of this airlift mortgaged future German strategy; ten months later, at Stalingrad, Hitler decided on a similar policy.

During the winter of 1942–1943 at Stalingrad, Göring boasted that his Luftwaffe could supply the Sixth Army with all the supplies its 250,000 men required. It was estimated that five hundred Ju 52s would be required, but only 298 were available; of the Luftwaffe's twenty-three *Transportgruppen*, eleven were committed to North Africa. A total of 4,872 sorties were flown, delivering 8,250 tons of supplies in the operation, about 111 tons per day, when a minimum of three hundred tons was required daily. The eleven *Transportgruppen* evacuated 29,910 German troops but lost 266 Ju 52s.

The attempted relief of Tunisia completed the annihilation of the *Transportgruppen*. From the occupation of Tunisia on 8 November 1942 until the 10 May capitulation in the face of overwhelming Allied air superiority, 99,333 men and 32,270 tons of supplies were airlifted to North Africa. However, the losses were staggering. In April alone 123 transports were shot down.

Demand for new aircraft exceeded supply. In 1942, manufacture of the Ju 52 began in the French Amiot factory at Colombes and the Hungarian PIRT works in Budapest. When the new Ju 252 and Ju 352 transports entered series production in mid-1944, Ju 52 manufacture ended. As a postscript to

this magnificent aircraft, during the Battle of Berlin in 1945 an attempt was made to airlift infantry and supplies into the surrounded capital. In the early hours of 28 April, four Ju 52s took off from Rechlin intending to land in the center of Berlin. Only one aircraft completed the mission, and it was destroyed when it crashed on landing.

Intelligence History

3 December 1940. A POW under interrogation reveals the Ju 52 is being converted to a night-bomber, fitted to carry two "Satan" bombs.

This Ju 52, radio code "G6+JU," belonged to the Tenth *Staffel*, IV/Transportgeschwader 4. The complement of mountain troops, and the existence of only one defensive machine gun, would indicate that this early model JU 52 took part in the 1941 invasion of Greece/Crete. [Air 40/126]

On 30 August 1943, RAF Typhoons of Fighter Command shot up the Athies airfield at Laon in France. Caught out in the open, as the film from a Typhoon gun camera reveals here, was a Ju 52 preparing for take off. A sequence of still shots from the gun cameras of the attacking Typhoons appeared in the 1 November 1943 edition of *Evidence in Camera*. [Air 40/238]

18 August 1941. Several POWs under interrogation declare that they have seen flying tanks. They all stated that light two-man tanks were used, but that the mode of carriage had not been finalized. Some prisoners maintained that a special glider carried the tank, which effectively formed the fuselage and undercarriage of the glider. As soon as the glider landed, the fuselage and wing structure detached, leaving the tank ready to flight. The preferred transport to tow the glider was the Ju 52. Production of the tank/glider combination was in the thousands; they were being reserved especially for an invasion of England.

1 October 1941. The Ju 52 is to be fitted with floats and skids for operation on water and ice. AI discovers from a POW that two sets of experimental floats were produced in August 1941.

19 November 1941. Ju 52s are being manufactured at the Colombes factory, Paris, of the Societe Avions Amiot. AI learns that a "Mr. Felix AMIOT is the 'arch-collaborator' in the French aircraft industry and is believed to have been put in charge of the Junkers organization in France."

27 December 1941. Middle East Command informs AI that Ju 52 wreck inspections reveal that its defensive armament has been significantly increased. All the Ju 52s examined carried four 7.92 mm MG 15 machine guns.

25 February 1942. According to a POW interrogated by Middle East Command, the Italian Savoia 82 is being used by the Germans in increasing numbers for transportation duties as it can carry a considerably higher payload.

26 May 1942. Air attaché Berne reports it was widely acknowledged in the military hierarchy that the mass employment of the Ju 52 during the 1941–1942 winter had saved the German army in Russia (probably in reference to the Demyansk pocket).

9 December 1942. A Ju 52, radio code "C3+MH," was shot down and the *bordmechaniker* interrogated. He revealed that three Ju 52 aircraft were needed to tow a single Gotha Go 242 glider to Heraklion, Crete, from Kalamaki in Greece. The prisoner had also engaged in fuel transporta-

Following the 8 November 1942 Operation TORCH allied landings in French North Africa, the Germans rushed reinforcements into Tunisia. This PR photograph of the El Aouina aerodrome at Tunis four days after the landings shows the frantic activity the Axis forces engaged in to shore up their newly created western front in Africa. The A highlights an Italian-made Savoia SM 82 in German markings—see the 25 February 1942 entry—while the arrow points out a burned Bloch 174 of the Vichy French Air Force. [Air 40/234].

A Ju 52 during the Stalingrad airlift. The Germans made extensive use of Russian prisoners as forced labor throughout the Russian campaign.

tion operations to Tunisia and Tripoli, in which the fuel expended by the aircraft exceeded the amount delivered. Consumption was roughly 2,500 liters, whereas each Ju 52 could carry only ten oil drums of two hundred liters each.

May 1943. AI inspects a burned-out Ju 52 at El Aouina airfield, Tunis, and discovers that it is equipped with a magnetic ring for mine detonation. Unfortunately, the wreck was badly gutted by fire and no real technical data is gathered.

5 November 1943. Air attaché Berne reports that during the spring and summer of 1943 one-third of the Ju 52s produced by the French Amiot factory were fitted to carry wounded, while the other two-thirds were equipped as glider tugs.

6 November 1943. AI Report 58665 asserts that during the period 11–17 April 1943, fifteen Ju 52s were sent to the Luftwaffe *Feldluftzeugamt* near Warsaw to have bomb racks built into their fuselages. According to assembly workers and some pilots, these racks are for gas bombs. AI, while not dismissing the report, believes the racks were probably installed to enable the Ju 52 to carry external supply packs to drop by parachute.

11 February 1945. POW interrogation reveals technical data about the equipment used by Ju 52 aircraft for minesweeping. The magnetic ring on the Ju 52 was roughly fifteen meters in diameter, and a twelve-cylinder Mercedes Benz Nurburg petrol-driven dynamo produced the current. The observer had an amp meter and control mechanism, enabling him to maintain the current at a constant 300 amps. During the forty sorties the POW flew, when he was with the Fifth and Sixth *Staffeln* (II Gruppe), his aircraft exploded ten magnetic mines. This was considered a good average tally.

Junkers Ju 252/352

This is the photograph of the first confirmed sighting of a Ju 252, taken 28 June 1943 and released in AI Interpretation Report L.81, dated 29 July 1943. [Air 40/174]

War Record

For much of the war the Luftwaffe had to rely on the Ju 52 because its eventual replacement, the Ju 352 *Herkules* appeared too late. Prior to the Ju 352, Junkers submitted proposals for the Ju 252 to the RLM. The Ju 252 prototype was first flown during October 1941. It featured a stressed-skin surface, replacing the characteristic Ju 52 corrugated metal. The first Ju 252 entered service in January 1943 with Lufttransportstaffel 290; only fifteen were built, including the four prototypes. Owing to the shortage of raw materials plaguing wartime Germany, the new-look pressurized transport took a very low priority. Consequently, Junkers was tasked with redesigning the Ju 252 using more timber in its construction.

The redesign was completed, but as Junkers had no production capacity available because of the Ju 88/188 program, construction work on the Ju 352

Data File Ju 352

DIMENSIONS

Wingspan	112 ft.
Length	79 ft. 4 in.
Range	1860 miles
Engines	352 3 × BMW-Bramo 323R
Armament	1 × 20 mm cannon, 2 × 13 mm machine guns

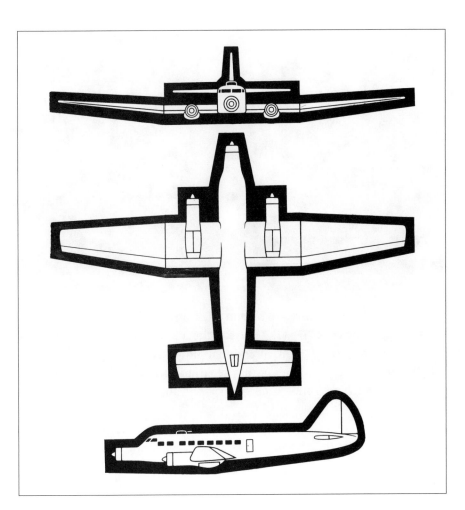

In August 1944 AI released these drawings of the Ju 252 to assist Allied aircrew in identifying this new enemy transport aircraft. [Air 40/174]

started at the Fritzlar airfield. The Ju 352V-1 prototype was flown on 1 October 1943. Considering it a substantial improvement on the old Ju 52, the Luftwaffe immediately ordered production to commence. By the time manufacture was halted in mid-1944, a total of forty-five Junkers Ju 352A-1 transports had been built. Featuring a hydraulically operated loading ramp beneath the rear section of the fuselage, the aircraft could be raised sufficiently off the ground to enable the carriage of some types of military vehicle. Another superb feature was its reversible-pitch propellers, designed by Messerschmitt and built by the Vereinigte Deutsche Metallwerke Company. The Ju 352 was the first German aircraft to be equipped with these propellers. They reduced the required runway length for landing by almost 60 percent.

Intelligence History

September 1941. AI hears that the Ju 252 is to be a stratosphere bomber or a troop transporter. It is reported that the aircraft will be ready and in service within a calendar year. AI labels the information "questionable."

1 June 1942. Middle East Command reports that the Germans place high value on the Ju 252 as a fuel transporter, as it has a carrying capacity of sixteen thousand liters.

In his interview by AI after the war, Professor Hertel stated that although the designs for Ju 352 were commenced in August 1942, some difficulties were experienced with the wood construction, and the first prototype did not fly until May 1943. [Air 40/126]

10 May 1943. AI3(e) Report 514 on a Ju 252 from 2/KGzbV 106 (Special Service Group), radio code "DF+BQ," reveals the full capacity of the aircraft. On one occasion in April 1943 this aircraft had flown from Pomigliano to Tunis with 4,000 kg of fuel, and on another separate occasion it had transported thirty-one infantrymen and a *Kubelwagen* jeep, amounting to 4,015 kg.

16 May 1943. A POW declares that the Ju 252 is an upgraded version of the Ju 52, modeled on the Italian Savoia SM 82, which proved invaluable in Tunisia.

28 June 1943. A PR sweep over Rechlin captures a Ju 252 on film. Although similar aircraft had been photographed at Dessau in August 1942 and February 1943, this was the first time AI was able to confirm it as the Ju 252.

26 August 1943. AI Report 54867 discloses significant data on the Ju 252. The flying duration is given as about eight hours, with a normal seven-ton load. The aircraft has also carried ninety fully equipped infantrymen. The

A Ju 352 with its hydraulically operated rear loading ramp down. This feature enabled much faster unloading of cargo, and it is indicative of German design and technology that the concept is still in widespread use today. [Air 40/178]

crew considers that the defensive armament is insufficient for its needs. The trap door at the rear is large enough for the aircraft to accommodate a light tank, half-track, or jeep. If the Ju 252 is employed in the paratrooper transport role, when the rear ramp is lowered in flight the full *Fallschirmjager* complement can be disgorged within one minute.

21 October 1943. The Ju 352 cockpit is learned to be large enough to accommodate eight to ten men. Additionally, it is pressurized to enable the aircraft to fly at high altitudes, and each crew position is fitted with oxygen mask installations.

25 January 1944. AI Report 66294 reveals from a source at the research office at St. Eloi, Toulouse, France, that there are no plans for the Ju 352 to be manufactured there. Those who had witnessed a Ju 352 land and then unload a jeep at the St. Martin du Touch airfield were amazed at the speed with which the entire operation was accomplished.

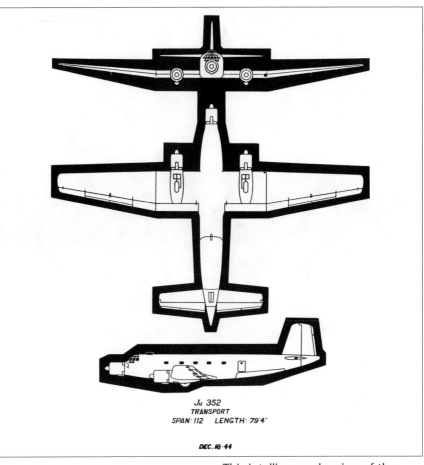

This intelligence drawing of the Ju 352 was published for use by Allied aircrew in mid-December 1944. [Air 40/178]

5 May 1944. AI Report 70469 confirms that a Ju 352 was recently at Okecie airfield, Warsaw. The report, from an unidentified source, revealed considerable information about the construction of the aircraft. Only the cockpit and the rear portion of the fuselage and the tail unit are made entirely of duralumin.

10 October 1944. According to a secret report, GER 333/44, AI has learned from an undisclosed source that production of the Ju 252 stopped after only five or six had been manufactured. A modified version was expected to "appear shortly."

7 March 1945. In ADI(k) Report 211A/45 AI discloses learning from a "secret" undisclosed source that the Ju 352 was operational with the Seventh, Eighth, and Ninth *Staffeln* (*Geschwader* unknown). It was only used in daylight operations to supply airplane engines and spare parts to airfield workshops and to transport wounded soldiers back from the front.

8 June 1945. CIOS Evaluation Report 69 states that only about fifty Ju 252s and fifty Ju 352s were manufactured and left the production line for service with the combat commands of the Luftwaffe.

Junkers Ju 90/290/390

The Ju 90, converted prewar civilian airliner. The radio code is "DJ+YE."

War Record

The Ju 90 began life as the Ju 89, Junkers's attempt at a four-engine bomber. Even though a prototype was built and test-flown, the RLM ordered a halt to further work, as the Luftwaffe did not require such aircraft. Determined to salvage something from its work, the RLM granted Junkers permission to convert the Ju 89 into a transport; the inaugural prototype flight trials occurred on 28 August 1937. The Deutsches Lufthansa Airline placed an order for eight Ju 90s equipped as airliners, with a capacity of thirty-eight passengers. When war broke out, Lufthansa's Ju 90 airliners were incorporated into the Luftwaffe's transport fleet.

The fourth prototype developed by Junkers, featuring modifications to the fuselage, wings, and tail plane, officially designated the Ju 290, made its maiden flight in July 1942. From the beginning of series manufacture until production ceased in July 1944, a total of forty-eight Ju 290s were delivered, in a variety of configurations depending on the intended operational role. They were originally employed in a host of theaters as military transports. Two even took part in the Stalingrad airlift, where one, piloted by Lufthansa's experienced "old hand" Flugkapitan Haenig, crashed during takeoff with a full cargo of wounded soldiers aboard.

However, from 1943 onward, most served in the maritime-reconnaissance role. On 8 March 1943, the Oberbefehlshaber der Luftwaffe agreed to supply Admiral Doenitz with a small force of long-range naval-reconnaissance Ju 290s to assist the U-boat campaign. These were assigned to Fliegerfuhrer Atlantik. In July 1943 they constituted the operational elements of Hauptmann Hermann Fischer's newly formed Fernaufklarungsgruppe 5 (FAGr5), based at Monte de Marsan, near Bordeaux. In September 1943 the land-based Ju 290s of FAGr5, equipped with the new FuG 200 Hohentwiel high-resolution sensor (possessing an 80 km detection range), became fully operational. With

Data File Ju 290A-7

DIMENSIONS

Wingspan	137 ft. 9½ in.
Length	95 ft. 7¾ in.
Height	22 ft. 4¾ in.
Max. Speed	273 mph
Ceiling	19,685 ft.
Range	3,784 miles
Engines	4 × BMW 801D
Armament	7 × MG 151,
	1 × MG 131
Payload	6.614 lbs.
Crew	6 (military transport)

This photograph of a Ju 290 at an unidentified airfield admirably illustrates the rear loading ramp mechanism in operation.

their ability to fly even farther westward than the Fw 200, FAGr5's Ju 290 aircraft consequently became FlFu Atlantik's extreme long-range reconnaissance aircraft. In the context of the overall Battle of the Atlantic, it was too little too late, and by 1944 the Luftwaffe was failing to detect suitable targets for the U-boats. In the Western Approaches during January and February, only four convoys were detected, and fighters from the escort carriers and long-range Beaufighters prevented the Luftwaffe from shadowing targets. For example, while shadowing convoy ONS.29 in February FAGr5 lost three Ju 290s to Allied aircraft; this action represented FlFu Atlantik's last major achievement in locating convoys.

The final variant in this line to evolve from Junkers was the Ju 390, which first flew on 21 October 1943. Powered by six BMW 9-801E engines, the Ju 390V1 prototype could fly at 294 mph to a maximum range of 7,452 miles. In January 1944, with additional fuel tanks, it took off from an airfield near

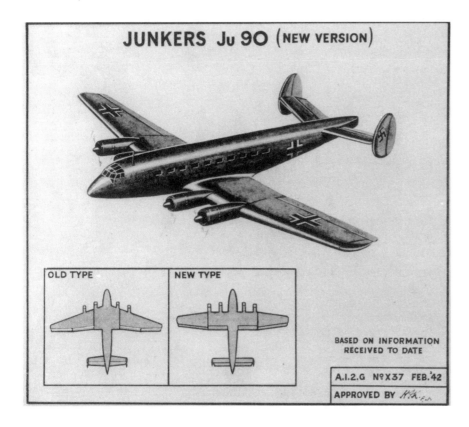

In December 1942, a POW under interrogation disclosed to AI that in his opinion the Ju 290 was merely a Ju 90 with a different wing. This AI2(g) drawing records the difference.

AI Interpretation Report L.161 featured this photograph of two Ju 290s at Berlin Templehof airfield. The picture was taken during a PR operation over the airfield on 19 February 1943. The Ju 290s are easily recognizable by the design of the wing.

Bordeaux and successfully completed a trial flight to within sixteen miles of New York City. At the end of 1944 these plans were overtaken by events, and the Ju 390V1 was laid up at the Dessau factory airfield until destroyed in 1945.

Intelligence History

Authors' note: As information was received about these aircraft, differentiation between the Ju 90 and Ju 290 was not always obvious, which helps to account for the confusion that existed in AI over which aircraft was which.

The Ju 290A-7 long-range maritime reconnaissance bomber could carry three Hs293 guided bombs for offensive antishipping attacks. It was additionally equipped with eight defensive weapons stations, either 13 mm or 20 mm—each operated manually by a member of the eight-to-ten-man crew.

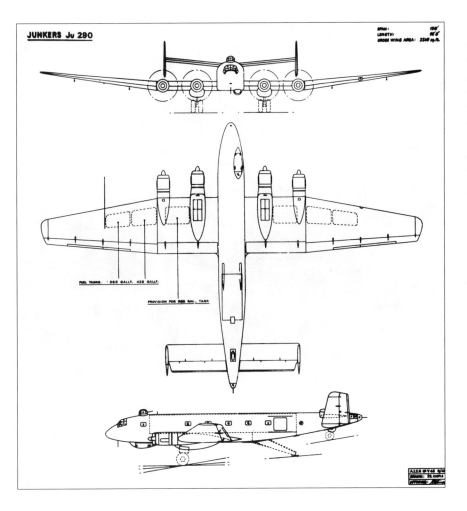

JUNKERS Ju 290

In mid-1943 AI produced this set of Ju 290 drawings illustrating the transport variant of the aircraft. At about the same time as these drawings were issued, AI learned that a special *Staffel* from I/KG 40 was training on the Ju 290 for long-range bomber reconnaissance duties. The unit was to be posted to Russia in an effort to sever communications between European Russia and the rest of the Soviet Union, east of the Ural Mountain range. The defensive armament had been significantly enhanced and included two turrets on top of the fuselage.

16 August 1941. AI discovers that the Junkers Ju 90 is being developed as a long-range bomber, with an endurance of seventeen hours.

30 September 1942. AI learns from Middle East Command that the Ju 290 is operating at night between Eleusis and Tobruk. The aircraft can carry a light Panzer Mark II or 4 × 7.62 cm antitank guns and a platoon of infantry. The Ju 290 is said to have a loading ramp at the rear for loading small tanks.

15 February 1943. A "source" states that the Ju 90B has been upgraded and converted into a military transport. Its new designation is "Ju 290," and it is primarily a paratroop transport.

10 May 1943. When Allied ground units captured Bizerta in Tunisia, they overran the Sidi Ahmed airfield. The Advanced Field Unit, North African Air Force, examined the remains of a Ju 290 on the airfield. The span is measured at 138 feet, and the engines are confirmed to be BMW 801s.

6 June 1943. Col. George McDonald, Assistant Chief of Staff A-2 (Captured Intelligence), North African Air Force, issues Technical Report 132 on the Ju 290 at Bizerta airfield. The wrecked aircraft belonged to I/Transportstaffel

Colonel McDonald's report on the Ju 290 at Bizerta (see entry for 6 June 1943) stated, "The aircraft was found, crashed and damaged on the S.E. boundary of Sidi Ahmed aerodrome. It appears that in landing on the runway the machine had overshot badly, crashing into the railway embankment at the end of the field, with the result that the entire front portion of the fuselage was broken off, and the engines were torn from their mountings." In complete contrast, and illustrating the work of propaganda, this image was issued to the media and designated British Official Photograph BNA.2741(XT). Alluding to the cause of the destruction of the aircraft, the accompanying caption read, "Bizerta aerodrome represented a sorry sight, thanks to the work of Allied bombers. The Germans left many fighter and transport planes which they had been using to reinforce their badly battered armies."

5 and was identified by the radio code "J4+AH." This was only the second Ju 290 to fall into Allied hands, the first being found at Megrine airfield. From the factory number, 154, it was determined that the aircraft was delivered to the unit in only February 1943.

26 September 1943. A POW reveals that the Ju 290 "is reported to be the carrier of the latest new secret weapon about which much is spoken but little known."

10 January 1944. AI are informed the new Ju 390 has a load capacity of 120 infantrymen.

30 April 1944. The British military mission in Moscow sends Report S.52/5 to AI upon examination of a crashed Ju 290. Only fragmentary details were obtained, "as the aircraft is smashed up and many parts are buried in the snow."

9 June 1944. Air attaché Stockholm reports that considerable numbers of Ju 90s and Fw 200s were recently fitted with astrodomes. The "source" saw five of each aircraft type thus equipped, including Admiral Doenitz's personal aircraft.

11 June 1944. AI learns that in January 1944 a Ju 390 was delivered to Fernaufklarungsgruppe 5, based at Monte de Marsan, near Bordeaux. The ten-man crew completed a thirty-two-hour reconnaissance flight to within twenty kilometers of the U.S. coast, just north of New York.

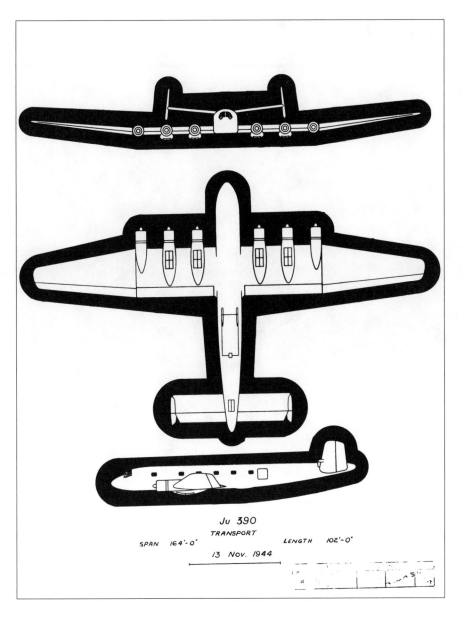

Ju 390
TRANSPORT
SPAN 164'-0"   LENGTH 102'-0"
13 Nov. 1944

In March 1942 the RLM awarded Junkers a development contract for a long-range reconnaissance aircraft, transport, and guided-weapons carrier that, with a 7,452-mile range, could reach the U.S. coast. The Junkers design team in Prague, led by Heinz Kraft, began work on a six-engine variant of the Ju 290. By adding additional fuselage bays and wing sections to the existing Ju 290, they presented the RLM with a simple solution to its requirement. Additionally the RLM also considered developing the Ju 390 as an in-flight tanker for Luftwaffe strategic bombers. In light of its fine flying characteristics, series production was approved. However, it never came to much, as the RLM ordered a halt in May 1944, switching virtually all aircraft production to the emergency fighter program.

12 July 1944. AI learns that the Luftwaffe has been conducting trials on the Ju 90 using four parachutes, fastened to the end of the fuselage, that open on landing and thus reduce the length of runway required.

10 October 1944. AI Report GER.333/44, from a secret "source," declares the tail section of the Ju 290 is hinged and can be lifted hydraulically. The load capacity is given as four 88 mm guns or four jeeps.

12 October 1944. An AI report on the Ju 390 asserts that this six-engine bomber has been in mass production for months.

7 November 1944. Wing Commander Proctor, AI2(g), issues AI Report 2285 on the Ju 390. It estimates that the average speed would be 200–210 mph at twenty-six thousand feet carrying a staggering bomb load of twenty thousand pounds over a distance of about four thousand miles.

Messerschmitt Me 321/323

The vast and ungainly *Gigant* seen in flight. The original Me 321–glider version was supplemented by six Gnome-Rhone 14N engines. In this photograph the outer engine on the starboard wing appears to be stopped.
[AIR 40/127]

War Record

The Me 321 giant glider was originally conceived to be used in the invasions of Great Britain. The *Gigants* were to ferry troops and supplies across the English Channel. After the cancellation of Operation *Seelöwe*, Me 321s entered service with Grossraumlastensegler 321 at Leipheim. The huge gliders were capable of carrying either 120–130 fully equipped troops, twenty-two tons of supplies, or an 88 mm artillery piece. Me 321s were initially towed by Ju 90s and later by the extraordinary He 111Z (twin fuselage version) or a "*troika-schlepp*" of three Bf 110s. The latter variant caused several accidents on take-off that would often kill the crews of all four planes involved.

When French-made Gnome-Rhone 14N engines became available, the Me 323 powered version was developed. While somewhat more practical than the glider variant, it proved highly problematic in service. Its lack of inherent stability kept the two flight engineers constantly adjusting the six throttles to keep the plane level during flight.

The Me 323 entered service in the Mediterranean theater in November 1942. The high toll on Axis shipping necessitated a great airlift of equipment across the Mediterranean to Tunisia to keep Rommel's Panzer Armee Afrika supplied. On 22 April 1943 the Me 323's second great weakness, its slow cruis-

Data File (Me 323D)

DIMENSIONS

Wingspan	180 ft. 5½ in.
Length	92 ft. 4¼ in.
Height	33 ft. 3½ in.
Max. Speed	177 mph
Ceiling	13,100 ft.
Range	684 miles
Engines	6 × 1,140 hp
	Gnome-Rhone 14N
Armament	5 × MG 131

ing speed of 120 mph, was exposed. Seven squadrons of Spitfires and P-40s attacked a formation of twenty-seven fully laden Me 323s being escorted across the Sicilian Straits by Bf 109Gs. No less than twenty-one *Gigants* were shot down, causing a huge loss of men and of nearly three hundred tons of vital fuel.

Despite their great vulnerability, Me 323s continued in service on the Eastern Front with I and II Gruppen of Transportgeschader 5. During some evacuations they carried up to 200 troops. The Wehrmacht's huge transport problems kept the plane in service until they were virtually wiped out.

Intelligence History

17 March 1942. The first report is received of an Me 323 with "Centipede undercarriage" and rails for loading and unloading Mark IV tanks.

11 November 1942. A wrecked aircraft is sighted at Tunis El Aouina airfield fitting the description of the Me 323 "Meresburg glider" (the Allied code name for the Me 323, having been first sighted at Meresberg Aerodrome).

22 November 1942. A German document is captured, a circular dated 16 April 1942. It informs antiaircraft personnel that from 1 May the Me 323 heavy freight gliders will be in use. They are described as having six engines, single rudders, and "rough country" multiwheel undercarriages.

2 December 1942. Aerial reconnaissance photos of Naples Capudichino aerodrome show "2 Meresburg Gliders with 6 engines."

6 December 1942. A POW states "Meresburg Glider" is the Me 323, capable of carrying 140 fully equipped troops. Fully laden the aircraft need two Ju 52s to tow them at take-off; the planes then land as near to the front as possible, unload, take off under their own power to a rear landing ground, are then picked up by towing aircraft and returned to base for the next load. The POW states that men do not like the aircraft, because if they are shot down too much life and equipment is lost.

December 1942. A negative of a photo from a crashed Ju 52 is retrieved off the Kerkennah Islands by an RAF Malta aircraft. Dated 28 November 1942,

The wreckage of an abandoned Me 323 is examined by Allied officers at Tunis El Aouina aerodrome, North Africa. Many German aircraft were discovered at El Aouina in November 1942. The Luftwaffe had placed explosive charges in the aircraft to sabotage them, but this did not prevent AI from learning much useful information on several types. [AIR 40/127]

AI vulnerability and armament diagram of the Me 323 produced in 1944 [AIR 40/5]

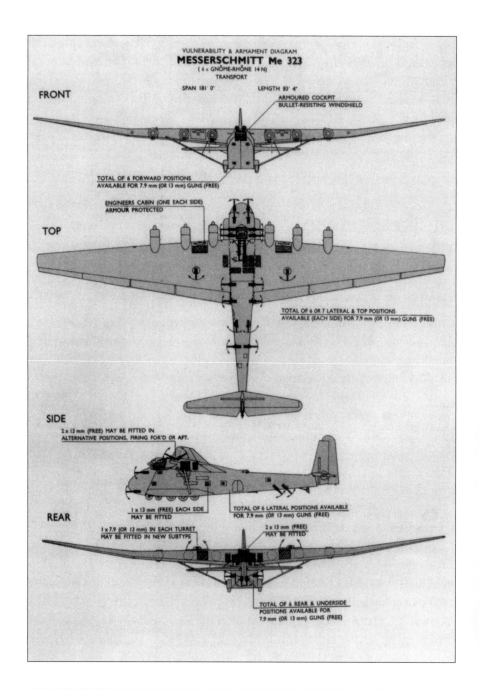

An evocative photograph of two huge Me 323s in the frozen winter of the Eastern Front. The caption in French simply says, "Aircraft of the type 'Giant'" [AIR 40/127]

Troops disembark from the open front doors of an Me 323. Their padded coats and hoods suggest the winter clothing of the Eastern Front. The presence of a horse-drawn sled belies the intended propaganda message of this image—that the Germans possessed a modern transport system for their armies. The German caption reads, "The Me 323 brings an infantry division to the action." [AIR 40/127]

it shows an Me 323 at Capudichino aerodrome. A drawing based on the photo and descriptions is made in January 1943.

14 May 1943. Eleven Me 323s are found abandoned at El Aouina airfield in Tunis. Planes have been destroyed by placing 250 kg bombs beneath them, but enough survives to produce a comprehensive report. Their design suggests an attempt to produce a large transport as cheaply as possible; four rockets can be used to assist takeoff.

4 October 1943. Information from the Gnome-Rhone factory in France indicates that an order has been received for 1,450 14R engines for Me 323s being assembled at Friedrichshafen, Berlin.

26 June 1945. USAAF T1.12 interrogates Willi Messerschmitt. He describes the Me 321 and Me 323 as being of "primitive" construction.

Photograph acquired from occupied France showing construction work on the Me 323's huge "centipede" undercarriage. [AIR 40/127]

Siebel Si 204

An Si 204D-1 of NJG 102, which surrendered at Copenhagen/Karsrtup. [AIR 40/128]

War Record

The Si 204 was used for bombing, gunnery, radar, navigation training, and as a transport capable of taking eight passengers. It was derived from the smaller Fh 104 and first flew in early 1941. Wartime production was exclusively outside Germany, at SNCAC in France and BMM in Czechoslovakia. Both countries continued production after the war.

Data File (Si 204A)

DIMENSIONS

Wingspan	69 ft. 11¾ in.
Length	39 ft. 2½ in.
Height	13 ft. 11½ in.
Max. Speed	226 mph
Ceiling	24,605 ft.
Range	1,119 miles
Engines	2 × 600 hp
	Argus As 411
Armament	none
Crew	2

Glossary

37 mm cannon large caliber cannon armament used for ground attack and bomber destroyers

Abwehr Foreign and counterintelligence department of the German High Command

A/C Military abbreviation for aircraft

ADI(K) Assistant Director of Intelligence (prisoner interrogation) at the Air Ministry

AI1(c) Air Intelligence Liaison with MI6

AI1(e) Air Signals Intelligence (later AI4)

AI1(g) Air Intelligence, Technical (later AI2(g))

AI1(k) Air Intelligence, Prisoner Interrogation (later ADIK)

Air Attaché Embassy official responsible for air force matters

Air Ministry British department of Government responsible for aviation

Aufklaerungs Luftwaffe reconnaissance units or Aufklaerungsgruppe (AufklGr). These units were not needed in such large formations as Geschwader so tended to be organized into smaller ad hoc independent formations; e.g. see "1/ObdL," below

B-17 American bomber aircraft, also called the "Flying Fortress"

B-24 American bomber aircraft, also called the "Liberator"

Balkankreuz Black and white cross markings used on wings and fuselage of Luftwaffe aircraft

Bf (Bayerischeflugzeugwerke) Lit. Bavarian aircraft works, alternative name for the Messerschmitt Company, used as prefix for early Messerschmitt aircraft (up to 110) until replaced by Me in honor of Willi Messerschmitt

Bletchley Park Stately home near Cambridge, England, housed the Government Code and Cipher School, where the German ENIGMA code was deciphered—see GC&CS

Blitz The Luftwaffe night bombing campaign of British cities, 1940–41

Blitzkrieg Lit. lightning war, term for the Germans' fast, motorized campaigns of conquest in Poland, France, the Netherlands, Belgium and the Soviet Union in 1939–41

Borderflieger Warship operated floatplane

Bordermekaniker Flight engineer

Combat Report Reports produced by Allied aircrew of engagements with the enemy

Condor Legion German air units which fought for General Franco's rebel Falangist forces during the Spanish Civil War 1936–1939

DB Daimler Benz, engine manufacturers

Deutsche Lufthansa German national civilian airline

Dive Brakes Flaps fitted to dive bomber aircraft to improve their aerodynamic stability during the bombing run

E/A Military abbreviation for enemy aircraft

ENIGMA Code used by German forces for signals

Erprobungskommando Luftwaffe test unit

Fallschirmjaeger Paratroopers

Fernaufklaerungs Luftwaffe long-range reconnaissance units. 2/(F)123 was second staffel, Fernaufklaerungsgruppe 123

Flak (fliegerabwehrkanonen) Luftwaffe anti-aircraft artillery

Fliegerkorps Luftwaffe air corps; Fl. Korps VIII was the eighth air corps

Flugkapitan Lit. "flight captain," a civilian test pilot in the employ of the RLM

Foreign Office Department of British government responsible for foreign affairs, equivalent of U.S. Department of State

Fritz X Radio-controlled glider bomb

FuG 202 Lichtenstein BC German airborne radar used in night-fighting

GAF Abbreviation for German Air Force, alternative name for Luftwaffe, commonly used by Allies

GC&CS Government Code and Cipher School—see Bletchley Park

Generalfeldmarschall Equivalent of USAAF five star General, RAF Marshal of the Royal Air Force

Geschwader The largest of the Luftwaffe flying formations; equivalent of Allied Group, it had a nominal strength of ninety-four aircraft, comprising three Gruppen and a Stab of four aircraft. Later in the war some bomber Geschwader were given a fourth (and in some rare cases a fifth) Gruppe to enable crews to undergo operational training before they were sent to the frontline units for combat duties. The Geschwader commander was a Major, an Oberstleutnant, or an Oberst. The Geschwader predominantly comprised aircraft for the same role. Therefore they were named accordingly with the relevant prefix attached—e.g. KG 26 was Kampfgeschwader 26, III/KG 26 was the third gruppe of KG 26, while 5/KG 26 was the fifth staffel of KG 26.

Geschwaderkommodore The commander of a Luftwaffe geschwader, see "Geschwader" above

Gestapo (Geheime Staatzpolizei) German Secret Police dedicated to maintaining the Nazi state

Gruppe Three Staffeln and a Stab of three aeroplanes formed a Gruppe, making a pre-war fighting strength total of thirty. With the wartime the addition of a fourth Staffel (each of sixteen planes) and a Stab in some cases a Gruppe had a strength of sixty-seven. Usually one complete Gruppe occupied a single airfield, but, owing to the necessities of wartime it was not unusual for an individual Staffel to be separated from its Gruppe and sent to another base—particularly so in the case of strategic reconnaissance units. The Gruppe was commanded by a Hauptmann or a Major who carried the title of Kommandeur.

Gruppenkommandeur The commander of a Luftwaffe gruppe, see "Gruppe" above

Ha Alternative prefix for Blöhm und Voss aircraft, abbreviation for Hamburg, where the company was based

Hauptmann Equivalent of USAAF Captain, RAF Flight Lieutenant

HS293 Radio-controlled, rocket-propelled glider bomb used against shipping

Jabo (Jagdbomber) Ground attack aircraft

Jagd Luftwaffe fighter unit; Jagdgeschwader (JG), Jagdgruppe, Jagdstaffel

Jagdverband (JV) Fighter unit

Jumo Designation for Junkers aero-engines

K Reports

Kampf Luftwaffe bomber units; Kampfgeschwader (KG), Kampfgruppe

Kette Formation of three aircraft

Kriegsmarine German Navy

Kustenflieger Luftwaffe naval co-operation unit; Kustenfliegergruppe 606 would be abbreviated thus KuFlGr 606

Lehr Luftwaffe tactical development units, the Lehrgeschwader (LG) were formed to test all the various types of new aircraft that the Reich developed under combat operational conditions and to assess and evaluate new tactics

Luftlandes Unit operating with airborne forces; Luftlandesgeschwader

Luftflotte Air fleet typically covering a front, e.g. for most of the war Luftflotte 4 was assigned southern Russia, Luftflotte 5 covered Norway and northern Russia, while Luftflotte 6 was allocated central Russia. These three were the Luftflotten (pl.) serving in Russia

Major Pronounced "my-or" the equivalent of a USAAF Major, RAF Squadron Leader

MG 131 Maschinengewehr, cannon 13 mm caliber

MG 151 Maschinengewehr, cannon 20 mm caliber

MG 81 Maschinengewehr, machine-gun 7.9 mm caliber

MI6 (Military Intelligence Department 6) British department responsible for intelligence and espionage outside the British Empire

Minensuchs Luftwaffe naval mine searching unit; Minensuchsstaffel

MK 108 30 mm cannon

Nachtjagd Luftwaffe night fighter unit; Nachtjagdgeschwader (NJG)

Nachtschlacht Luftwaffe night ground-attack unit; Nachtschlachtgeschwader

Nachtaufklaerungs Luftwaffe night reconnaissance unit

Nahaufklaerung Luftwaffe short-range reconnaissance unit

ObdL Oberbefehlshaber der Luftwaffe, the Commander in Chief of the Luft-waffe, namely Hermann Göring

1/ObdL First staffel, aircraft allocated to Luftwaffe HQ reconnaissance operations. Full designation is first staffel, Aufklaerungsgruppe Ober-befehlshaber der Luftwaffe

Oberfeldwebel Equivalent of USAAF Master Sergeant, RAF Flight Sergeant

Oberleutnant Equivalent of USAAF 1st Lieutenant, RAF Flying Officer

Oberst Equivalent of USAAF Colonel, RAF Group Captain

Oberstleutnant Equivalent of USAAF Lieutenant-Colonel, RAF Wing Commander

Operation Seelowe (Sealion) Planned 1940 German invasion of Britain

OVERLORD Code-name for D-DAY landings

PAK 38 38 mm cannon of Czech origin

Phoney War Term for the period of the war between October 1939 and May 1940 when little fighting occurred

Piratangriff German term for nuisance or harassment intruder raids by one or more aircraft at night against British cities

PIU (Photo Interpretation Unit) Intelligence unit that interpreted aerial reconnaissance photographs, based at RAF Medmenham

PR (Photo Reconnaissance) Aerial photography of enemy positions

PRU (Photo Reconnaissance Unit) Allied photo reconnaissance unit

Pulk-Zerstörer German formation destroyer fighters; twin-engine fighters carrying heavy cannon or rocket armament designed to break up tightly packed formations of Allied bombers

Reichsluftministerium (RLM) The German Air Ministry; department of government responsible for aviation

Rotte Formation of two aircraft

Royal Aircraft Establishment (RAE) Located at Farnborough, Southeast England, airfield where enemy aircraft were tested and examined

Schlachtflugzeug (SG) Luftwaffe close support ground attack aircraft

Schleppflugzeug Luftwaffe glider-towing role; e.g. the Ju 52, although predominantly a transport aircraft, could fulfill this additional role

Schnellkampf Luftwaffe fast bomber unit; Schnellkampfgeschwader

Schrage musik "Jazz music," term for upward firing cannon mounted on Luftwaffe nightfighters

Schwarm Formation of four aircraft

Seeaufklaerungs Luftwaffe naval reconnaissance unit; Seeaufklaerungungskommando

Seenot Luftwaffe air-sea rescue unit; 1/Seenotflugkommando operated in the English Channel to rescue downed Luftwaffe aircrew in the 1940 Battle of Britain

Seetransport Luftwaffe floatplane transport aircraft/unit

Siegfried Line Allied term for the German "West Wall" defensive line near their western border

Sigint Signals Intelligence; information derived from intercepted and decoded enemy signals

SIS Secret Intelligence Service; British intelligence see MI6

Sonderkommando Special command, unit dedicated to specialist task

Staffel Luftwaffe unit equivalent to Allied squadron. The Staffel began the war with a strength of nine aircraft although during the war this figure gradually rose to sixteen. It was the lowest level of flying formation and was usually commanded by an Oberleutnant (senior lieutenant) or a Hauptmann (Captain)

Staffelkapitan The commander of a Luftwaffe staffel, see "Staffel" above

Steinbock German bomber offensive against England that commenced 21 January and fizzled out by May 1944

Sturmgruppe Heavy armored Fw 190s for attacking large bomber formations

Sturzkampf Luftwaffe dive bomber aircraft/unit; "Stu-ka" from **Sturzka**mpfflugzeug or **Sturz-ka**mpfgeschwader

Ta Designation used for late Focke-Wulf aircraft in honor of designer Kurt Tank

Transportation Plan 1944 Allied bomber offensive designed to cripple German transport to aid the Normandy landings

Trager Luftwaffe aircraft carrier–based aeroplanes. The Ju 87T Stuka (T = Trager lit. "carrier") was a modified Ju 87C built to operate from the Graf Zeppelin, the Nazi's first aircraft carrier (which was never completed)

Transport Luftwaffe transport aircraft unit; Transportstaffel and Transportgeschwader

Ultra Allied code name for intelligence acquired from top secret German ENIGMA signals traffic intercepted and deciphered at Bletchley Park

Unternehmen German for Operation, e.g. Unternehmen STEINBOCK

Unteroffizer Equivalent to USAAF Staff Sergeant, RAF Corporal

USSTAF United States Strategic Air Forces

V-1 Flying bomb The V-1 (FZG 76) flying bomb was designated by the Nazis as a retaliation weapon

Volkischer Beobachter Nazi newspaper

War Office British Government department responsible for military matters

Wettererkundungs Luftwaffe weather reconnaissance units

Wehrmacht German armed forces

Y Service The organization for listening to enemy radio communications

Zerstörer Lit. "destroyer" these were twin-engined fighters. These Luftwaffe heavy fighter units, the Zerstorergeschwader (ZG), were considered the elite of the German air force prewar.

Bibliography

Air Ministry Official Publication. *The Rise and Fall of the German Air Force.* London: His Majesty's Stationery Office [HMSO], 1947.

Barker, Lt.-Col. A. J. *Stuka, Ju 87.* London: Bison, 1980.

Boog, Horst. "German Air Intelligence in the Second World War." In *Intelligence and Military Operations,* edited by Michael Handel. London: Frank Cass, 1990.

Butler, Phil. *War Prizes: An Illustrated Survey of German, Italian and Japanese Aircraft Brought to Allied Countries During and After the Second World War.* Leicester, UK.: Midland, 1994.

Cox, Sebastian. "A Comparative Analysis of RAF and Luftwaffe Intelligence in the Battle of Britain, 1940." In *Intelligence and Military Operations,* edited by Michael Handel. London: Frank Cass, 1990.

Cox, Sebastian. "The Sources and Organization of RAF Intelligence and Its Influence on Operations." In *The Conduct of the Air War in the Second World War: An International Comparison,* edited by Horst Boog. Oxford, U.K.: Berg, 1992.

Dressel, Joachim, and Manfred Greihl. *Fighters of the Luftwaffe.* London: Arms and Armour, 1993.

———. *Bombers of the Luftwaffe.* London: Arms and Armour, 1994.

Ethell, Jeffrey, and Alfred Price. *The German Jets in Combat.* London: Jane's, 1979.

Faber, Harold, ed. *Luftwaffe: An Analysis by Former Luftwaffe Generals.* London: Sidgwick and Jackson, 1979.

Futrell, R. F. "U.S. Army Air Forces Intelligence in the Second World War." In *The Conduct of the Air War in the Second World War: An International Comparison,* edited by Horst Boog. Oxford, U.K.: Berg, 1992.

Gunston, Bill, and Tony Wood. *Hitler's Luftwaffe.* London: Salamander Books, 1977.

Herwig, Dieter, and Heinz Rode. *Luftwaffe Secret Projects: Strategic Bombers 1935–1945.* Stuttgart, Ger.: Motorbuch Verlag, 1998. English Language version by Midland Publishing UK.

Hinsley, F. H. *British Intelligence in the Second World War: Its Influence on Strategy and Operations,* volume 1. London: HMSO, 1979.

———. *British Intelligence in the Second World War,* abridged edition. London: HMSO, 1993.

———. *British Intelligence in the Second World War: Its Influence on Strategy and Operations,* Volume 2. London: HMSO, 1984.

———. *British Intelligence in the Second World War: Its Influence on Strategy and Operations,* Volume 3. London: HMSO, 1988.

Hogg, Ian. *German Secret Weapons of the Second World War.* London: Greenhill, 1999.

Hooton, E. R. *Phoenix Triumphant.* London: Arms and Armour, 1994.

———. *Eagle in Flames. The Fall of the Luftwaffe.* London: Arms and Armour, 1997.

Hyland, Gary, and Anton Gill. *Last Talons of the Eagle.* London: Headline Publishing, 1998.

Jane's Fighting Aircraft of World War Two. London: Jane's Studio Editions, 1989.

Jones, R. V. *Most Secret War: British Scientific Intelligence 1939–1945.* London: Hodder and Stoughton, 1978.

———. "Scientific Intelligence of the Royal Air Force in the Second World War." In *The Conduct of the Air War in the Second World War: An International Comparison,* edited by Horst Boog. Oxford, U.K.: Berg, 1992.

Lewin, Ronald. *The Other Ultra.* London: Hutchinson, 1982.

Mondey, David. *Axis Aircraft of World War II.* London: Temple Press, 1984.

Nesbitt, Roy Conyers. *The RAF in Camera,* Volume 2, *1939–1945.* Stroud, U.K.: Sutton and Public Record Office [PRO], 1996.

———. *Eyes of the RAF: A History of Photo-Reconnaissance.* Stroud, U.K.: Sutton, 1996.

Nowarra, Heinz. *Junkers Ju 52: Aircraft and Legend.* Yeovil, U.K.: Haynes Publishing, 1987.

Price, Alfred. *Luftwaffe Handbook.* Shepperton, U.K.: Ian Allan, 1977.

———. *The Last Year of the Luftwaffe.* London: Arms and Armour, 1991.

———. *Luftwaffe in Camera,* Volume 1, *1939–1942.* Stroud, U.K.: Sutton, 1997.

———. *The Luftwaffe Data Book.* London: Greenhill, 1997.

Smith, Bradley. *The Ultra-Magic Deals and the Most Secret Special Relationship, 1940–1946.* Shrewsbury, U.K.: Airlife, 1993.

Smith, J. Richard. *Focke-Wulf: An Aircraft Album.* Shepperton, U.K.: Ian Allan, 1973.

———. *Messerschmitt: An Aircraft Album.* Shepperton, U.K.: Ian Allan, 1971.

Turnill, Reginald, and Arthur Reed. *Farnborough: The Story of RAE.* London: Robert Hale, 1980.

Wark, Wesley. *The Ultimate Enemy.* London: Cornell University Press, 1985.

———. "The Air Defense Gap: British Air Doctrine and Intelligence Warnings in the 1930s." In *The Conduct of the Air War in the Second World War: An International Comparison,* edited by Horst Boog. Oxford, U.K.: Berg, 1992.

West, Nigel. *MI6: British Secret Intelligence Service Operations, 1909–1945.* London: Weidenfeld and Nicolson, 1986.

Williamson, Gordon. *Aces of the Reich.* London: Arms and Armour, 1989.

Index

About the Authors

Christopher Staerck is a writer and editor who focuses on topics of twentieth century military and political history. He is the author of the first five titles in the Public Record Office's acclaimed "Battlefront" series, and has published articles for the *Independent* and *Modern History Review*. He lives near London.

Paul Sinnott worked for several years at the Public Record Office, Britain's national archives. He is the editor of *Messerschmitt Bf 109: Pilot's Notes* and *Focke-Wulf Fw 190: Pilot's Notes,* and he has written for *Aeroplane* magazine. He lives in London.